IN THE HANDS OF GOD

In the Hands of God

HOW EVANGELICAL BELONGING TRANSFORMS MIGRANT EXPERIENCE IN THE UNITED STATES

JOHANNA BARD RICHLIN

PRINCETON UNIVERSITY PRESS

PRINCETON & OXFORD

Published by Princeton University Press
41 William Street, Princeton, New Jersey 08540
99 Banbury Road, Oxford OX2 6JX

press.princeton.edu

All Rights Reserved

Library of Congress Cataloging-in-Publication Data

Names: Richlin, Johanna Bard, author.
Title: In the hands of God : how Evangelical belonging transforms migrant
    experience in the United States / Johanna Bard Richlin.
Description: Princeton, New Jersey : Princeton University Press, [2022] |
    Includes bibliographical references and index.
Identifiers: LCCN 2021059900 (print) | LCCN 2021059901 (ebook) |
    ISBN 9780691194974 (hardback : acid-free paper) | ISBN 9780691194981
    (paperback : acid-free paper) | ISBN 9780691230757 (ebook)
Subjects: LCSH: Church work with immigrants—United States. |
    Evangelicalism—United States. | BISAC: RELIGION / Christian Ministry /
    Evangelism | SOCIAL SCIENCE / Refugees
Classification: LCC BR517 .R53 2022 (print) | LCC BR517 (ebook) |
    DDC 277.307—dc23/eng/20220208
LC record available at https://lccn.loc.gov/2021059900
LC ebook record available at https://lccn.loc.gov/2021059901

British Library Cataloging-in-Publication Data is available

Editorial: Fred Appel & James Collier
Production Editorial: Ali Parrington
Jacket/Cover Design: Pamela L. Schnitter
Production: Lauren Reese
Publicity: Kate Hensley & Charlotte Coyne

Jacket/Cover Credit: Christian congregation in the United States, Jackson, NJ, 2021.
Photo by Pamela Schnitter.

This book has been composed in Arno

10 9 8 7 6 5 4 3 2 1

CONTENTS

ACKNOWLEDGMENTS

IN WRITING THIS BOOK, I relied upon the invaluable insight, counsel, and encouragement of many people. First and foremost, I am deeply indebted to the subjects of this study, the many Brazilian migrants in the Greater Washington, DC, area, who opened their homes and churches to me, trusted me with their stories and experiences, and tolerated my frequent and sometimes awkward incursions into their everyday lives. Not only did these individuals believe in the ultimate merit and utility of this project, but they embraced me with warmth, hospitality, and good humor. I am especially grateful to Neusa, Rubém, Felipe, Frederico, Viviane, Paula, Luana, Diana, Gláucia, Pastor Jeferson, Juliana, Pastor João, and Pastor Márcio (all pseudonyms), who appear often in the pages that follow, and without whom this project would never be possible. Several individuals facilitated introductions to local leaders in the Brazilian migrant community that proved essential to this study. I am particularly grateful to Maxine Margolis, Vivaldo Santos, Bryan McCann, Bernardo Brasil, Ana Lúcia Lico, Lucília Tremura, and Viviane de Costa for supporting this research from its inception.

This book results from the expert mentorship and unflagging commitment of my doctoral supervisor at Stanford, Tanya Luhrmann, who provided expert guidance at every step of this decade-long process. The early graduate seminars I took with Tanya on the Anthropology of Religion and on Trauma and Healing nurtured my interests in the therapeutic efficacy of faith and provided me with theories and literatures to ground my emerging ideas. Tanya's encouraging responses to my very rough ethnographic memos in the first months of fieldwork provided me with reassurance that I was, in fact, "seeing" something significant. Tanya commented on multiple drafts and provided critical suggestions on the book's structure, argumentation, and theoretical grounding. All of these contributions undoubtedly improved the final manuscript. As I progress in my career, I can only hope to emulate her skill, dedication, and care in this pivotal role.

At Stanford, I am indebted to Paulla Ebron and Angela Garcia, crucial mentors and members of my dissertation reading committee, who provided unwavering and enduring support from the very beginning of this project and have shaped my understanding of key themes of this book, including identity, care, affect, relationship, and belonging. I am also thankful for the important feedback I received regarding how this project engages with scholarship in Brazilian and Latin American studies and religious studies from Marília Librandi-Rocha and Kathryn Gin Lum, external members on my dissertation committee. I also benefitted from participating in the Dissertation Writers' Workshop at Stanford, where I received important feedback on early chapter drafts from Liisa Malkki, Maron Greenleaf, Jenna Rice, Yasemin Ipek, Jess Auerbach, Jacob Doherty, and Firat Bozcali. During graduate school, I was fortunate to spend a term at Brown University, where I studied Brazilian history and anthropology under the expert guidance of James Green and Ruben Oliven.

The origins of this book predate my formal training as an anthropologist. At Harvard Divinity School, I benefitted from studying with Michael D. Jackson, whose lectures and seminars provided lasting inspiration. Michael's comprehensive and rich discussions of social suffering, existential anthropology, narrativity, and the tumult of human experience have influenced me greatly. While at HDS, I began to understand the entanglement of religion and public life through courses taken with Peter J. Paris, John L. Jackson, and the late Ronald Thiemann. At Wesleyan University, Khachig Tölölyan introduced me to the field of diasporic studies and first suggested that I pursue graduate work in cultural anthropology to study what it means to "belong." I am profoundly grateful to each of these brilliant professors for their inspiration and enduring confidence in my abilities.

I am indebted to Bill Egginton, the director of the Alexander Grass Humanities Institute at Johns Hopkins University, for the postdoctoral fellowship that enabled me to reshape the dissertation into a book. I am also grateful to the Johns Hopkins Department of Anthropology and the many faculty members and graduate students who welcomed me into their stimulating and congenial intellectual community. I am particularly appreciative of Niloofar Haeri, who served as chair during my time at Johns Hopkins, for inviting me to present my research at the departmental colloquium, and for rich conversations on religious experience, prayer, and interiority. My thanks also to Flávia de Azeredo-Cerqueira, who invited me to present my research at the Portuguese Speakers Series.

I have been extremely fortunate to complete this project while serving on the faculty in the Department of Anthropology at the University of Oregon. I am grateful to my chair, Frances White, for consistently advocating for junior faculty, especially during the Covid-19 pandemic. I am also indebted to my colleagues in the cultural anthropology subfield—Lynn Stephen, Carol Silverman, Lamia Karim, Phil Scher, Maria Fernanda Escallón, and Leah Lowthorp—all of whom have provided critical feedback on my research and have served as mentors and friends at UO. Both in the department and at the wider university, I have had the tremendous good fortune of joining a mutually supportive cohort of anthropologists across subfields. I have especially benefitted from conversations with Scott Blumenthal, Alison Carter, Zachary Dubois, Stephen Dueppen, Kirstin Sterner, Bharat Venkat, Lesley Jo Weaver, and Kristin Yarris. I greatly appreciate their encouragement and collegiality.

Jon Bialecki, James Bielo, Naomi Haynes, Rebecca Lester, and Neely Myers offered exceptionally helpful published commentary on my article, "The Affective Therapeutics of Migrant Faith," which was published as a research forum in *Current Anthropology* 60, no. 3 (2019). While substantially revised and reworked, much of the material from that essay appears in chapters 2 through 4 of this book. The expert commentary I received from these colleagues, as well as anonymous reviewers, proved critical as I revised the book. I am especially indebted to Jon Bialecki, who conceptualized evangelical churches as offering "paths of flight" to migrants within neoliberal constraints, and later suggested thinking through affect as a "heuristic." I also want to thank Brian Fay, my former professor at Wesleyan University who first ignited my interest in moral philosophy, for providing exceptionally constructive feedback on the article. His engaging response provided me with the language to propose a hermeneutics of understanding rather than of suspicion that I employ in the book. Some contextual and ethnographic material from this book appears in a forthcoming chapter, "Immigration Influx: The Remaking of Contemporary Christianity," in the *Rowman and Littlefield Handbook for Contemporary Christianity in the United States*, edited by Mark A. Lamport (2022).

I also want to thank the organizers, members, and discussants of several conference panels at which I presented this work and received helpful feedback, including James Bielo, Thomas Csordas, Matthew Engelke, Yasemin Ipek, Elana Resnick, Cristina Rocha, Ian Whitmarsh, and Hua Miranda Wu. My gratitude also to my colleagues in several writing circles who provided enduring support, companionship, and inspiration, especially my ongoing

Faculty Success Program cohort: Amber Woodburn McNair, Emily Paddon Rhodes, and Natalie Weber.

Several institutions provided generous funding for this project, enabling me to complete training, fieldwork, and writing over several years. At Stanford, the Department of Anthropology provided me with multiple summer research grants to study Portuguese and carry out preliminary fieldwork in Rio de Janeiro, Maceió, New York City, and Washington, DC. The US Department of Education's Foreign Language and Area Studies program generously funded language study in Rio. I was also fortunate to receive a Ric Weiland Graduate Fellowship, which provided two years of dissertation funding at Stanford. At the University of Oregon, funding from the College of Arts and Sciences, including a New Junior Faculty Award to fund participation in the Faculty Success Program, as well as a Vice Provost for Research and Innovation Completion Award from the Oregon Humanities Center, supported critical writing phases of this project.

I am profoundly grateful for the expert editorial guidance of Fred Appel, who supported this project from its inception. His editorial assistant, James Collier, production editor, Ali Parrington, and the entire team at Princeton University Press stewarded this project to completion amid a global pandemic. I also want to thank the anonymous reviewers of the manuscript, whose keen insights strengthened the book. Charles Kim and Isaque Kim provided critical transcription assistance, Bill Nelson masterfully created the book's maps, Nanosh Lucas provided thorough bibliographic assistance, and Kim Hastings expertly copyedited the final manuscript.

In the often lonely and uncertain path of academic research and writing, the companionship of many friends and family has kept me firmly tethered. To Jamie Dobie, Emily Greenhouse, Maron Greenleaf, Deb Meisel, Ali Shames-Dawson, and Emma Teitel, thank you for your enduring levity, presence, and wisdom. To my parents, Pamela and Dean, thank you for your unconditional love and support of my pursuits, even when they take me far away from you. To my siblings and the exceptional families they have created, Eli, Sabrina, Dalia, Calla, Noah, Sara, Luis, and Abigail, and to my wonderful in-laws, Kathy, Greg, Jonah, and Kelly, thank you for your unflagging encouragement.

I dedicate this book to my children, Antonia and Reuben, who have filled my life with exuberance, joy, and affection, and to Gabe, my most trusted and treasured companion.

Introduction

Pilgrims of the Potomac

MIGRANT FAITH IN THE SHADOWS

"YOU WERE ELECTED by God, chosen by God," Rubém, a prominent church elder, insisted as he addressed a small group of Brazilian migrants on a cold winter night in December 2013. Pastor Jeferson and his wife, Juliana, the charismatic couple at the helm of this small Brazilian Pentecostal church outside of Washington, DC, were away traveling. In their absence, Rubém beseeched his co-congregants from the pulpit as peers, friends, *irmãos em Cristo* (brothers and sisters in Christ). In contrast to Pastor Jeferson's commanding bravado, Rubém preached softly, addressing the ten or fifteen people before him as equals and intimates. Rather than speak from the pulpit, he walked amid the pews.

Rubém had known most of the men and women before him for years. He had worked and prayed alongside them. Several of those in attendance were his immediate family, including his wife, Neusa; two sons, Felipe and Frederico; daughters-in-law, Viviane and Luana; and two grandchildren, Daniel and Graça. At fifty-three years old, Rubém's face was weathered and reddened from twelve-hour days working in outdoor construction. Yet, on this evening, he had traded his work clothes for a crisp suit and tie. His hair was neatly combed and parted.

Rubém had arrived in the United States in 1999, hoping to earn enough money to repay the serious financial debt he had accrued in Brazil. Saving money took longer than the six months he had anticipated, however, so he instructed his wife and young sons to join him temporarily in the United States. Unable to obtain visas, Neusa crossed the Mexican border with Felipe and Frederico, who at the time were twelve and nine years old. The couple's eldest child, Vanessa, stayed behind to finish high school in the southern

Brazilian state of Santa Catarina, where she expected her parents and siblings to return within the year. When I met Neusa and Rubém in July 2013, however, fourteen years had elapsed since Rubém's arrival, and the family had yet to return to Brazil. During this time, Neusa and Rubém had lived and worked in the United States as undocumented migrants. They had raised their two sons in Montgomery County, thirty miles outside of Washington, DC. For fourteen years, they had not seen Vanessa.

Continuing his remarks on chosenness that evening, Rubém directed the group's attention to 1 Peter 2:9, reading, "But you are a chosen people, a royal priesthood, a holy nation, God's special possession, that you may declare the praises of Him who called you out of darkness and into His wonderful light."[1] Looking up, his eyes shone. "Maybe you feel small tonight," he continued, "and maybe you think that God has forgotten you. You ask yourself, 'Quem sou? Não sou nada!' (Who am I? I'm nothing!)." But when God elected you, Rubém explained, it was different from being elected by politicians who thought only of power and personal gain. God elected you for eternity. God chose the lowliest for greatness. God spoke to the poorest, the most vulnerable. "God chose *you* specifically for *this church*, and *this place*," Rubém asserted. He concluded his remarks by urging the migrants before him to serve God through their daily work. Cleaning homes, doing laundry, and cutting grass was holy, he insisted, when dedicated to God. In serving God, Rubém promised, each migrant believer ensured spiritual progress and forestalled "becoming stuck" in the United States.

———

In October 2019, the Washington, DC–based think tank the Pew Forum released its findings concerning religion in the United States, entitled "In U.S., Decline of Christianity Continues at Rapid Pace: An Update on America's Changing Religious Landscape." In light of new surveys and political polls, the article reassessed findings from 2007 and 2015 that were based on surveys with 35,000 individuals across all fifty states regarding religious belief, membership, and participation.[2] In keeping with the earlier studies, researchers found that Christianity in the US had declined substantially over the five-year period from 2014 to 2019. While 78.4 percent of Americans identified as Christian in 2007, only 65 percent did so in 2018. Churches of all kinds continued to lose members, though mainline Protestant and Catholic congregations experienced the greatest declines in affiliation (from 51 percent to 43 percent, and from 24 percent to 20 percent, respectively). In contrast, the category of "Religious Nones," those who identified with no religious beliefs, had grown to a population of 30 million. The article painted a stark portrait of Christianity's future in the US. With 40 percent of millennials identifying as unaffiliated, and more than 60 percent attending church only "seldom" or "never," it pointed toward Christianity's growing obsolescence, and the delayed fulfillment of the "secularization thesis" of the nineteenth and twentieth centuries.[3]

The study, however, left out a crucial segment of the population: undocumented migrants like Rubém, his family, and his cobelievers. While one Pew study considered "immigration status" in its demographic categories, it did so only nominally, inquiring into how immigrant cohort, rather than legal status, impacted belief and belonging. It considered three statuses: "immigrant," "first generation," and "second generation," and found that immigrants in general made up a growing proportion of all Christians in the US. Immigrants of all cohorts reported intense feelings of religiosity and commitment, with over 50 percent answering that they had certainty in the existence of God, that they prayed daily, and that religion was "very important" to them. If the study *had* accounted for undocumented migrants,[4] however, whom researchers consider to be overwhelmingly Christian and predominantly Latin American, the transformed "face" of US Christianity would be even more striking.[5]

What the Pew Forum's study also failed to capture was the *kind* of Christianity undocumented migrants increasingly, and fervently, practiced. While most of the undocumented population in the United States comes from Latin America,[6] a historically Catholic region, increasing numbers of Latin American migrants have converted to evangelical Protestant churches while in the United States.[7] Ethnographic and social scientific studies over the last two decades have substantiated this fact. Researchers have documented the explosion of charismatic churches catering to majority undocumented Latin American migrants in general, and Brazilians in particular.[8] The demographic shift in evangelical affiliation between 2007 and 2014 also reflects the growing appeal of evangelical Christianity among Latin Americans in the United States. While white adherents declined from 81 percent to 76 percent of the total population of evangelicals between 2007 and 2014, Latinx- or Latin American–identifying adherents grew from 7 percent to 11 percent.[9] What accounts for the growth of evangelical faith among Latin Americans in the United States, especially migrants without legal status?

As both exceptional and representative, Brazilian migrants constitute a fruitful case in the study of Latin American migration and religion. Studies of evangelical Christianity among Latin Americans have historically focused on the poor, and emphasized material rewards of evangelical belonging like jobs or wealth.[10] My research among Brazilian migrants, a comparatively better-off migrant population, instead highlights the centrality of *affective* motivations for conversion.[11] Brazilians overwhelmingly named loneliness, worry, and "feeling stuck," rather than solely financial difficulty, as among their greatest hardships in the US, feelings they likely share with other Latin American migrants. Like their counterparts, most Brazilians in the US live amid increasing suburban sprawl, remain undocumented, occupy low-wage jobs in construction and domestic work, and come from Catholic contexts.[12] While underscoring the affective dimension of migration, this study also offers to reveal a portrait of migrant distress common across nationalities.

In the Hands of God examines the relationship between evangelical Christianity, migration, and affective experience in the United States through an in-depth ethnographic study of Brazilians living in Greater Washington, DC. Drawing on extensive fieldwork, this book considers the explosive rise of evangelical Christianity among migrants in the United States, and particularly for those from Latin America. While the fact of increasing evangelical religiosity among Latin American populations in the United States has been well documented, few studies have examined how their evangelical identity and practice shapes, and is shaped by, the migrant experience itself. *In the Hands of God* addresses this fundamental question: why do individuals become more devoutly evangelical as migrants in the United States, and how does this new identity shape both self-understanding and daily experience? How did Rubém's invocation of age-old tropes of divine election and chosenness emerge from, and then transform, his own migrant experience in the United States?[13] And, how did evangelical belonging relieve the pervasive feeling of "stuckness" that he and so many other migrants I met repeatedly described?

My findings underscore how churches transformed what migrants *feel*. Affective experience, I argue, is key to understanding migrants' turn toward intense religiosity, and their resulting evangelical commitment and evangelical-inspired activity. I show how conditions of migrant experience in the United States imprinted migrants' bodies and minds with specific forms of affective distress. These conditions included family separation, geographic isolation, legal precariousness, workplace vulnerability, and deep uncertainty about the future in both the United States and Brazil. Such conditions, and the feelings they inspired, triggered novel religious yearnings among the migrants I met. Migrant evangelical churches, I learned, deliberately articulated, managed, and reinterpreted negative feelings of distress into positive religious devotion. In doing so, these churches effectively relieved migrant distress.

I ground this broader argument in four main claims, substantiated throughout the book's five ethnographic chapters (chapters 2 through 6). First, I contend that migration itself configured a specific set of maladies marked by loneliness, depression, and the feeling of "being stuck," which triggered migrants' religious yearnings. These affective experiences, what I call an affective imprint of migrant distress, made migrants particularly receptive to evangelical forms of religiosity, divinity, and community. Regardless of religious affiliation, over 51 percent of migrant respondents in my survey study ($n = 49$) answered that they had sought out God more intensely in the US than in Brazil. Forty-five percent answered that they had more frequent encounters with the Holy Spirit and felt God's presence more regularly. Seventy-eight formal interviews and innumerable informal conversations corroborated these findings, suggesting that migrants experienced an intensification of religious experience and commitment postmigration. Second, when compared to other religious groups serving Brazilian migrants, such as the Catholic Church or Spiritist centers, evangelical churches remained the most adept at addressing, managing, and assuaging migrant distress through what I call affective therapeutics—the deliberate attempt to "heal" migrants' psychological and bodily suffering by converting generalized affective distress into positive religious devotion.

Third, I assert that evangelical belonging not only made migrants feel better and more hopeful, but also motivated them to pragmatically pursue goods that would significantly improve their lives—what I call the goods of migration, including green cards, driver's licenses, better housing, and jobs. From the experience of feeling healed and partnered with God, migrant believers engaged in newly confident and hopeful activity in the secular realm. Fourth, I suggest that migrant experience in the United States leads to the broader evangelization of religious experience among US migrants more generally. Despite explicit critiques of evangelical Christianity among nonevangelical migrants, Catholic and Spiritist migrants revealed significant similarities in religious orientations, including intense intimacy with God and cobelievers, and increased susceptibility to spiritual phenomena. These findings point to a striking convergence of religious experience postmigration.

Methodology

This project results from extensive fieldwork conducted between 2013 and 2014 among several communities of Brazilian migrants in Greater Washington, DC. Brazilians increasingly moved to the DC region in the 1980s after the collapse of Brazil's "economic miracle" and in pursuit of employment and education.[14] Estimates for the number of Brazilians in the region range from 10,000 to 60,000 owing to the difficulty in counting a majority undocumented population.[15]

While I set out to understand the growth of evangelical religiosity among migrants, I soon realized that an accurate accounting of this phenomenon depended on sustained comparison with nonevangelical religious groups. Toward this end, my main congregational field sites included three evangelical churches (Adventist, Baptist, Pentecostal), two Catholic parishes, and two Spiritist centers located in the suburbs of Washington, DC, selected for their prominence in the local Brazilian migrant community and because they represent Brazilian migrant religious life throughout the United States. While Washington, DC, attracts Brazilian migrants from every region of Brazil, and from all socioeconomic classes, most of the migrants I met were undocumented, and worked in the domestic services, construction, landscaping, or the restaurant industry. My study reflects the demographic profile of Brazilian migrants in the United States more generally, which scholars estimate to be 70 percent undocumented, as well as the broader profile of undocumented migrants in the United States from Latin America. As such, I am confident that my sample is representative not only of Brazilian migrants throughout the United States but also of affective experience and religious yearnings among undocumented migrants across nationalities.

I formally interviewed 55 women and 23 men and analyzed survey results from 35 women and 14 men (see appendix for further demographic information). I recruited interviewees and survey respondents across my primary field sites as well as through the Brazilian consulate; an email listserv catering to Brazilian women migrants; local Brazilian academics; and word of mouth. The self-authored survey consisted of thirty-eight multiple choice questions and three open-ended questions regarding individuals' religious identities, migratory histories, and spiritual experiences. I distributed paper copies within field sites and sent electronic copies through the email listserv between November 2013 and June 2014. Of the 150 surveys I distributed, I received 49 completed surveys back. Although women were overrepresented in my study owing to the conservative gender dynamics of evangelical communities, and my greater access to women's activities and meetings, my findings among men reveal a parallel portrait of distress and the reshaping of religious yearnings.

I participated in the many religious and social activities that comprised church life across traditions, including institutional events like multiweekly worship services, prayer circles, book groups, and Bible studies, as well as community gatherings like baby showers and holiday celebrations. In addition to recording and transcribing seventy-eight interviews and collecting forty-nine surveys, I amassed a textual archive from relevant English- and Portuguese-language newspaper articles, study guides, consular brochures, and social media postings. While my primary focus remained the ordinary Brazilian migrants I met, I also interviewed diplomats at the Brazilian consulate and attended the consulate's open meetings, including those sponsored by its "Citizens' Council" (Conselho de Cidadãos). In addition to the women's listserv, these affiliations resulted in several interviews with highly credentialed, white-collar, and documented Brazilians that offer a counterpoint to my study of an otherwise largely undocumented population. These interviews revealed a strong correlation between document status, geographic location, and religious affiliation, whereby better-off segments of the Brazilian migrant population tended to assert Catholic or Spiritist identities. I analyze this comparative data in chapters 5 and 6.

Theoretical Frameworks

Affect and Emotion

In the Hands of God investigates migration and evangelical experience through the deliberately expansive heuristic of affect. In doing so, the book considers how migrant experience feels, how it patterns the body and mind with specific residues, and how those common sensations "bind" certain people together.[16] As I document in the following chapters, migrants invoked specific psychic experiences and bodily sensations in their description of migrant life, including loneliness, worry, despair, chronic pain, insomnia, weight gain, and "being stuck." These feelings newly oriented migrants toward evangelical faith and belonging, thus configuring a specific form of self-perception and sociality.

This project interrogates contemporary "structures of feeling"[17] by analyzing the origins and tracing the outcomes of migrant affects. I follow critical theorists who consider private feeling to be enmeshed in political, historical, and social currents, rather than an outcome of personal hardwiring or development.[18] The category of affect thus reveals growing loneliness, depression, and anxiety to be public symptoms of a contemporary world defined by individualization, profit maximization, and socioeconomic bifurcation—what many scholars refer to as neoliberalism.[19]

Importantly, several scholars have explored "stuckness" as a distinctly neoliberal structure of feeling. The culture of busyness, workaholism, and self-scrutiny derived from advanced capitalism breeds an anxiety-ridden "impasse"[20] defined by "depression in the form of thwarted ambition."[21] In the twenty-first century, the promise of capitalism and the free market has largely proven hollow for large swaths of humanity. Instead of experiencing growth, opportunity, prosperity, and mobility, more people find themselves stalled or spiraling downward with no safety net below. The dashing of hopes and devastation of expectations configures the sensation of "stuckness," and related dimensions of "boredom" and "precariousness," in relation to vividly imagined yet unobtainable futures.[22]

Like other scholars, I found that migrants remained acutely susceptible to such "melancholic" paralysis.[23] During fieldwork, migrants repeatedly voiced their frustrations, anxieties, and disappointments through the language of being stuck. They found their expectations of mobility, prosperity, and inclusion in the American "dream" to be repeatedly frustrated. Without legal documents, they could not travel freely, reunite with their families, or plan for the future. They were confined to low-paying jobs that were often demeaning, dangerous, and unpredictable. And yet, they had not saved enough money to secure their livelihoods and warrant their return to Brazil.

Throughout the book, I document how the feeling of stuckness and its components of anxiety, loneliness, and despair drove migrants toward evangelical belonging. The experience of isolation and marginalization engendered the craving for intimacy and power, which migrants increasingly found in evangelical churches. As new converts, migrants learned to depend wholly upon a personal God and Christian brotherhood, and to identify God's presence in both their internal and external environments. This novel epistemological disposition transformed individuals' interpretation of migrant experience in the United States. Rather than feeling immobile, doubtful, and rejected, migrant believers asserted confidence, optimism, and belonging. As revealed in Rubém's sermon on divine election, migrants refuted their marginality and redeemed their dignity by insisting that God had specifically chosen them to live in the United States.

In my approach to affect, I invoke the "phenomenological" tradition, seeing affect not as "autonomous" from emotion, but rather as including both unconscious and conscious feeling states. In contrast to the restrictive definition of affect as "preconscious" or "prediscursive," which makes the naming of affect overly burdensome, the broader definition suggests that feeling, knowing, and being remain deeply entangled and mutually constitutive.[24] As such, it becomes possible to describe the feelings people report, and investigate their likely causes and outcomes. It also becomes possible to see how institutions, like migrant religious communities, target such affect for "healing."

Discussions of affect need not be overly abstract or technical, as critics charge.[25] Rather, the promise of affect lies in its expansive reach. In the stuff of human feelings (whether called "affect", "qualia," "emotion," or "sensation") lie traces of individual and collective experience, including what marginalization feels like and what new orientations, behaviors, and subjectivities such feelings provoke. For the migrants in this study, exclusion in the United States felt like loneliness, despair, immobility, and worry. It also manifested as chronic pain, insomnia, and weight fluctuation. These experiences, in turn, triggered the desire for divine intimacy, cosmological certainty, and personal power.

My invocation of affect in this sense positions my work at the intersection of two traditions often seen to be at odds with each other: the anthropology of emotion and affect theory. While often criticized for essentializing cultures as "integrated wholes," and imposing Western psychological categories abroad, the anthropology of emotion inspired generations of anthropologists to take the feelings of their research subjects seriously and to investigate emotion as key human data.[26] While the anthropological study of emotion has given way to studies of embodiment, cognition, personhood, and subjectivity, the inquiry into feeling in the broadest sense remains robust.[27] The second tradition, affect theory, which arises from feminist and queer studies, grapples with the underlying socioeconomic and political realities that impact public and private feeling. In this tradition, scholars approach affect as bodily and psychic "traces" of much larger social structures and histories. Adopting this approach, I analyze migrant distress in the context of the broader "public feelings" of the twenty-first century.[28]

Migrant Faith and Interiority

Studies of migration often highlight socioeconomic factors in determining migrant behavior. They consider migrant religion primarily as it impacts other spheres of life, such as family, employment, health, or politics.[29] While key to understanding broad trends, these studies necessarily overlook or minimize the deeply personal accounts migrants give of their faith. This book places such narratives at the center of its analysis, arguing that migrant faith and migrant experience remain entangled and mutually constitutive. By inquiring into how migrant experience shapes religious longing, this book contributes to interdisciplinary studies of migrant affective experience and helps to complement predominantly quantitative and psychological studies with intimate human-centered portraits.[30] In addition to documenting how migrants experience, understand, and narrate their distress, I document the robust ways in which migrants respond to their suffering. While large-scale studies may track the frequency with which migrants utilize medical, mental health, legal, and advocacy services, they fail to make visible the alternative paths migrants pursue to alleviate distress, such as religious faith, practice, and community.

This study contributes to ethnographic scholarship that emphasizes how migrants constructively draw upon faith to reconfigure identity and community postmigration. Studies of migrants from various national contexts and religious groups converge on a conclusion that my findings support: religion becomes a crucial psychological, material, and social resource for migrants.[31] Like the Brazilian evangelicals I met, Mexican migrants utilized evangelical institutions, practices, networks, and narratives to decide when, where, and if to migrate;[32] Korean migrants drew upon Buddhism to bolster their self-esteem;[33] Taiwanese migrants invoked Christian and Buddhist lessons to assert new gender identities and understandings of family;[34] and African, Caribbean, and Korean migrants invoked theological terms to make sense of their journeys.[35] These findings resonate deeply with the ethnographic material presented in this book, pointing to the broader therapeutic significance of migrant faith.

While these studies have documented the beneficial effect of religious belonging among US migrants, however, they often do so as part of an explicit inquiry into migrant "incorporation" or "assimilation." To what extent, these studies primarily ask, does religion either enable or inhibit adaptation to the new cultural milieu? Several scholars, for instance, have emphasized that religious belonging across denomination enables migrants to become "more American."[36] Similar concerns animate literature on migration in the European context, but scholars have drawn inverse conclusions, highlighting religion—in this case, Islam—as a "barrier" to inclusion.[37] My account brackets these classic concerns. I shift attention away from questions aimed at measuring inclusion in the national polity and instead emphasize felt experience.

This approach is informed by scholarship on existential anthropology and social suffering.[38] Considering suffering to be both unavoidable and central to human experience, scholars document how people pursue "what really matters"[39] in the midst of distress, uncertainty, and suffering. Furthermore, scholars consider how human collectivity, and the many institutions involved in life together, disproportionately distributes suffering. I consider migrant distress to be akin to other forms of social suffering, defined as "the devastating injuries that social force can inflict on human experience."[40] I examine the kinds of distress migrants endure in the United States as members of a marginalized underclass, and view their turn toward evangelical Christianity as a strategy by which to assert "what really matters" in the context of exclusion. As such, this book contributes to an "anthropology of the good," the study of how "people come to believe that they can successfully create a good beyond what is presently given in their lives."[41] While living in the United States without documents entails a great deal of suffering, it also provokes individual and collective attempts at transcending and transforming distress.

Contemporary Christianity: Against Suspicion and Toward Understanding

Until the early twenty-first century, the study of Christianity was marginal to the discipline of anthropology. Scholars have documented exhaustively how and why Christianity made anthropologists uncomfortable and the consequences of such intellectual as well as personal discomfort.[42] Christians, as an anthropological subject, were both too "familiar" and too "strange," ultimately embodying what Susan Harding calls the "repugnant cultural other" to be intellectually discounted and personally shunned.[43] As a result, generations of anthropologists approached Christianity as "epiphenomenal" when they encountered it in the field, largely in postcolonial contexts, and relegated it to the margins of their study. Rather than concern themselves with the significance of Christian faith, worship, or cosmology per se, anthropologists instead trained their eye on what appeared to be the more rigorous, urgent, and intellectually approved inquiry—the political and socioeconomic origins and outcomes of Christian belonging.[44]

Anthropology's entrenched discomfort with Christianity indexed twentieth-century social theorists' suspicion toward religion more generally. Embedded in disciplines meant to scientifically document and reveal the workings of human society, social theorists worked to "disenchant" religion. This approach aimed to prove that nothing eluded scientific inquiry. Even that which purported to be about invisible and supernatural experience could be captured by reason. Accordingly, the most well-known social theorists of the twentieth century considered religion "to 'really' be something other than what it purports to be."[45] And, more often than not, what it was really "about" amounted to something calculated, utilitarian, and nefarious. For Durkheim, religion produced collective cohesion; for Weber, economic advancement; for Marx, false consciousness; and for Freud, psychological delusion.[46] Taken together, these discipline-defining efforts institutionalized a deep and lasting hermeneutics of suspicion in the social scientific study of religion.

Anthropologists of religion largely followed suit, privileging sociological function of religious practice above the personal feelings of believers. In this vein, prominent scholars in the field portrayed religion to be a practical tool to manage the life cycle,[47] a "symbolic system" that stored deep cultural meaning[48] and separated "order" from "chaos,"[49] and as a collection of historicized "performances"[50] that configured normative subjectivity.[51] Given these entrenched norms, anthropologists who train their gaze at religious interiority—how faith feels to the individual believer, how divine encounter impacts subjectivity, how religious practice is significant in its own right—have had to defend their apparent inattention to power and politics. From the position of suspicion, believers' declarations of faith, healing, and commitment signify delusion, coercion, denial, or apathy. Whether willful or naïve, the hermeneutics of suspicion insists that first-person religious accounts should never be trusted.

What would it mean, then, to instead adopt a *hermeneutics of understanding* toward the faithful, a deliberate effort to take seriously the beliefs and self-narrations of believers *on their own terms*? Would such a position amount to the whitewashing of power, as so many scholars have assumed? Or is it possible to accept the testimony of believers *and* attend to the power structures within which such testimonies are enmeshed? Through investigating the affective lives and religious beliefs of migrants in the United States, this book strives to suspend suspicion without becoming blind or uncritical. It considers religious belief, practice, community, sense of the divine, and testimony to emerge from migrants' encounters with social suffering at the hands of US law and society.

Adopting a hermeneutics of understanding toward migrant faith does not entail representing evangelical Christianity as a "cure-all" for structural inequality, injustice, and marginalization. It does not mean ignoring the hierarchies, exclusions, and inequities endemic to many evangelical institutions that, as other scholars have documented, often exacerbate distress.[52] Rather, the position of understanding entails accepting migrants' prevailing assertions of feeling "healed." It brackets the question of "sincerity" altogether and instead trusts the speaker to be the best interpreter of their own experience of social suffering. Such an approach recognizes healing, and its absence, to have occurred wherever migrants themselves identify it. A hermeneutics of understanding reveals the deep entanglement between power and religion, but rather than from a position of dismissal or ridicule, from engagement. Why do people believe? What does believing do for them, and how does it change their lives?

———

In the following chapters, I advance two goals. First, I offer an ethnographically informed portrait of migrant life in the contemporary United States. While I attend to forms of distress that all migrants arguably face and have faced for centuries, I am especially concerned with the precariousness undocumented migrants experience. By inquiring into the bodily and psychic manifestation of such precariousness, I aim to enrich current debates about migration in the United States, underscoring that being a migrant alters how one feels.

Second, I demonstrate that such feelings carry important consequences. In the context of insecurity and loneliness, migrant distress gives rise to novel religious yearnings. From loneliness, isolation, and feeling stuck, migrants come to desire a personal God, an intimate community, and a comprehensive cosmology. Within this context, evangelical Christianity's massive growth and outsized popularity among migrants becomes newly intelligible. Not only does migrant distress lead to a distinctly evangelical religious orientation among migrants, but evangelical churches deliberately and effectively target migrant interiority for healing.

1

Stories of Exceptionalism

BRAZILIANS AS A SPECIAL CASE IN THE STUDY OF MIGRATION AND RELIGION

ON MY FIRST OFFICIAL DAY of fieldwork, I traveled to the Brazilian consulate in downtown Washington, DC, to meet with Nelson, a diplomat. I had first met Nelson the previous autumn at DC's Brazil Day, a festival celebrating Brazilian food, culture, and commerce, sponsored by the consulate and local Brazilian organizations. Introduced by Leo, my former Portuguese instructor who was his friend, Nelson immediately offered his assistance, inviting me to interview him at the consulate when I returned the following year. Tall, bearded, and in his midforties, Nelson struck me as courteous yet duty bound. Despite his casual attire, it was clear that he was there in his professional capacity, speaking to visitors as a serious representative of Brazil. My later interactions with Nelson, including our formal interview a year later, confirmed this impression. He spoke to me as an emissary of Brazil's government, and the viewpoints he expressed sounded like polished talking points.

The Brazilian consulate is located near Judiciary Square on the corner of Fifteenth and L Streets, a few blocks from the Farragut North metro stop. Sitting on an expansive corner lot, the large gray building was offset by the brightness of the green and yellow Brazilian flag. I entered the door on L Street along with a bustling crowd of people in jeans, shorts, and t-shirts taking tickets and waiting in line with young children to speak with consular workers behind plated glass. For a Wednesday morning, it seemed incredibly busy. Quickly realizing I was in the wrong place, and that a ticket was probably not what I needed to meet with a diplomat, I left and circled the building a few more times, before finally spotting an unmarked entrance on Fifteenth Street for "visitors." Attended by two security guards in an immaculate lobby, it seemed more promising. On the fourth floor, the elevator opened to an expansive and smiling portrait of then-president Dilma Rousseff. Nelson, this time wearing a suit and tie, greeted me at the door to his office and sat down behind a large desk piled high with papers.

Over the next hour, Nelson spoke about the growing preponderance of "new immigrants" (*imigrantes novos*) from Brazil in the jurisdiction he represented, versus what he called the "traditional immigrants" (*imigrantes tradicionais*) of the past.[1] Over 50 percent of Brazilians, he explained, now came to the United States as students, professors, researchers, and scientists, while what he called traditional immigrants, whom he described as "unskilled" laborers in pursuit of fast money, had left the United States en masse after the financial crisis in 2008. At the time of our conversation in June 2013, the Brazilian economy was continuing to expand, and Dilma Rousseff's presidency had not yet imploded in the wake of "Operation Car Wash."[2] Experts still touted Brazil as among the major world economies and celebrated its simultaneous economic growth, poverty reduction, and climate protection, all of which have since been reversed under President Jair Bolsonaro. At the time, the international consensus projected Brazil to continue to grow, alongside the other so-called BRIC countries (Brazil, Russia, India, and China), and to compete with US dominance in world markets.[3]

Given this context, it is unsurprising that Nelson exuded unadulterated pride in his country's elevated international standing, and furthermore, related current and future trends in Brazilian migration to the shifting relationship between the United States and Brazil. According to his telling, Brazil continued to grow while the United States, and its partners the world over, had suffered a severe economic blow following the 2008 housing crisis (referred to as *a crise* by Nelson and other Brazilians I met). In the aftermath of the *crise*, the United States could no longer offer migrants what it had promised from its inception: economic opportunity and class mobility for determined and industrious newcomers. Brazil, on the other hand, promised untold possibilities. Recognizing this tectonic shift and geopolitical realignment, Brazilian "traditional migrants," Nelson explained, had increasingly made the decision to return to their *terra natal*:

Many of these traditional migrants returned to Brazil . . . these people were without jobs, these people were working in construction, they were waiters, in domestic jobs, and they became unemployed. At the same time, the economy of Brazil was growing, growing, growing. Many people had stories like this, "Ah. Here I don't have work. And my cousin's neighbor is opening an ice cream store and I'm going to work with him."

Nelson explained that this "traditional" migrant flow, made up of construction workers, waiters, au pairs, and housecleaners, motivated by economic necessity, was replaced by "new" migrants motivated by professional ambition.

Such new migrants, according to this telling, did not intend to stay permanently in the United States. Rather, they came to better themselves through educational and professional advancement, and then to return to Brazil in order "to contribute to their nation." Nelson described to me this cadre of elite migrants-turned-nation-builders: "You have a lot of [Brazilian migrants] with higher education, that have office jobs, work in universities, are here legally, are here in the exchange programs." Guided by short-term professional and educational goals, Nelson emphasized, new Brazilian migrants remained "law-abiding." They respected rules and rarely got into legal trouble. Those who did were few in number, and, according to Nelson, maintained a tenuous claim on Brazilian identity. To illustrate his point, he told me the story of a recent arrest:

> The only person I have here in the jurisdiction who was arrested for serious crimes, she is Brazilian. But she was adopted when she was young, brought here by an American, and here the American, a horrible story . . . sexually abused her and someone found out, and he was imprisoned, and she went into "the system." There she became involved in gangs, and doesn't even speak Portuguese, and doesn't even remember Brazil (*nem fala português, nem lembra do Brasil*). She is Brazilian . . . *so to speak* [spoken in English for emphasis].

The only "criminal" Brazilian migrant Nelson could conjure, he implied, was one whose Brazilian-ness was in doubt.

Nelson's account struck me as persuasive. His narrative framed my early expectations of what I might encounter in my study of migrant religious experience. But it also seriously shook my confidence, making me doubt the relevance of what I had imagined to be a carefully planned project. Informed by extensive secondary literature and prior research trips to study Brazilian evangelicalism in both Brazil (Maceió and Rio de Janeiro) and the US (New York and Washington, DC), I expected my research to illuminate the entanglement of religious and migratory experience, and to reveal how evangelical churches capitalized on this entanglement. Furthermore, I presumed that Brazilians were an ideal migrant population to study given their status as economic and religious "exceptions" among Latin Americans more generally, reasons for which are outlined further below.

Nelson's narrative appeared to deny the very foundation of my study by offering an updated exceptional framework to the one I had woven into my proposal. He asserted that the demographic I had proposed to study, whom he called traditional migrants, and those most likely to belong to evangelical churches, had left in droves after 2008. While he acknowledged that these migrants had been *somewhat* exceptional owing to their comparatively better-off socioeconomic resources and law-abiding nature, the new Brazilian migrants he described remained *exceedingly* exceptional. Scientifically minded, cosmopolitan, and primarily concerned with Brazilian nation-building, this group, Nelson suggested, was, at best, minimally engaged with religion. Against this narrative, my determination to study evangelical Christianity among primarily undocumented, low-wage migrant workers, appeared both ill-informed and foolhardy.

Throughout fieldwork, I learned that Nelson's telling was, in part, accurate. I met and interviewed many professional, highly educated, and well-off Brazilians, precisely the new migrants Nelson described as the current majority of Brazilians entering the US. During conversations with these individuals, they too repeated the same "exceptional" narrative regarding the composition of Brazilian migrants in both DC and the US more generally. They implicitly questioned the legitimacy of my study, taking issue with my emphasis on evangelical experience among their compatriots. Academics, scientists, and doctors pointed to the highly educated and professional profile of their local community and emphasized that the Brazilians they knew in the US studiously avoided Brazilian evangelical churches and instead participated somewhat casually in Catholicism, Spiritism, or progressive American churches. A Brazilian academic who had recently moved to the region, and was Catholic, for instance, reported that she had met only highly educated and well-off Brazilians since moving to the region. She doubted whether any undocumented Brazilians at all lived in Washington, DC. Amid such conversations, it was easy to doubt the central premise of my study that had long been substantiated in existing scholarship: that evangelical growth among Latin American migrants in the United States remained robust and expanding.[4]

When I interviewed Brazilian migrants living in Montgomery County, a suburban district about thirty miles north of the Brazilian consulate, a very different profile emerged. The Brazilian migrants I met did not tout prestigious credentials, nor list nation-building and career advancement among their motivations for moving to the United States. Instead, migrants most often named financial necessity as spurring their migration. And, they reflected on the profound toll such migration had exacted on their bodies and minds. In formal and informal conversations, migrants highlighted the lasting imprint of protracted isolation and exploitation in their lives on the margins of US society. Migrants recounted bouts of anxiety, depression, weight fluctuation, sleeplessness, chronic pain, and, for some, suicidal thoughts.

The story of exceptionalism that Nelson related, and that several elite Brazilians echoed, simply did not convey the full range of migrant experience I encountered. The first half of this chapter considers multiple stories of Brazilian exceptionalism. Brazilians have long asserted their own exceptional nature in terms of their history, geography, demographics, culture, and religion. Scholars of Brazil and Brazilian migration have adopted this same framework to describe Brazil's distinctiveness when compared to Latin America as a whole. In placing Nelson's comments in this tradition, it is possible to better understand his insistence that "new," highly educated, and nation-building migrants now outnumber "traditional" migrants. Such comments reflect deeply embedded national tropes. Furthermore, they reveal the heterogeneous and segregated nature of Brazilian migrant experience in Greater Washington, DC, which often mirrors entrenched class divisions in Brazil itself.

Importantly, these considerations also frame my own narrative of Brazilian exceptionalism, one that modifies rigid claims of difference, distinctiveness, and superiority. Instead, I suggest that Brazilian migrants constitute an especially productive case in the study of migration and religion because of what makes them *both* representative and exceptional among Latin American migrants to the United States.

Brazilians in the United States: Exceptional or Representative?

Historical Roots of Brazilian Exceptionalism

Exceptionalism came to define Brazilian national consciousness in the nineteenth century, when intellectuals explicitly forged their nation's identity in contrast to América Latina or América Hispánica. Brazilian writers and politicians emphasized their nation's distinct political, cultural, and demographic attributes, and codified these positions in isolationist policies that resisted regional cooperation. Highlighting the particularity of their Portuguese inheritance, and Brazil's revered role in the Portuguese Empire, intellectuals vociferously refuted claims of common "Latin" descent.[5] Instead, they asserted kinship with the United States and Europe, citing Brazil's expansive territory, diverse population, and political stability.[6] As Spanish-speaking republics resisted American political and economic incursions, Brazil instituted a formal policy of *americanização,* making close relations with the United States central to its foreign policy.[7] Later, when intellectuals rejected *americanização,* they still insisted upon their nation's irrevocable separateness, writing that Brazil was "a continent unto itself" such that "neither the physical nor moral [space of] Brazil can form a system with any other nation."[8]

The assertion of Brazil's exceptionalism framed subsequent efforts by President Getúlio Vargas to build a coherent and distinctive "national culture" during his regime, the Estado Novo (1937–1945).[9] To compete on the international stage, Vargas brought several popular cultural forms under state control, asserting them as national assets, rather than as diverse regional or local genres. Soccer became the national pastime, and Carnival a national pageant, both cultivated by generous state funding and promotion. In doing so, the state explicitly championed Afro-Brazilian identity, and by extension multiculturalism, as distinctive and exceptional national assets.[10] Such national efforts broadly disseminated the myth of "racial democracy,"[11] a central tenet of contemporary claims of Brazilian exceptionalism.[12] These efforts to define Brazil and its people as distinctive and superior have continued to shape national discourse, including how scholars, and Brazilians themselves, regard migrants.

Brazilian Migration to the United States

Although Brazilians began to enter the United States in 1965 under the expanded US Immigration Act, Brazilian migration did not become widespread until the mid-1980s. With the collapse of the military-backed economic miracle of the 1970s, migration to North America and Europe exponentially increased as middle-class, educated, and mostly southern Brazilians fled rampant underemployment, unemployment, and hyperinflation in Brazil.[13] As several scholars have noted, this period marked the first time in Brazil's history that the country experienced out-migration that outpaced in-migration.[14] While difficult to assess owing to Brazil's more fluid classification of race as compared to the United States' enduring model of hypodescent, scholars have suggested that most Brazilian migrants in the US self-identify as "white."[15] Initially, the majority of migrants were single men who hoped to accrue fast money in the United States and then return to their families in Brazil. Brazilians moved to traditional migrant hubs, like New York City, Newark, and Chicago, or to places with established Portuguese-speaking communities, like Boston, Framingham, Martha's Vineyard, and Providence.[16]

Between 2000 and 2008, the Brazilian migrant population in the US continued to grow steadily, with equal numbers of men and women arriving. With the presence of dense Brazilian communities in many major US cities, migrants took advantage of ready-made pathways to employment, housing, and social support. Migrants increasingly married, had children, invested in property, owned businesses, and established churches, making return to Brazil less certain. Furthermore, they migrated to new locations where they faced less labor competition and greater entrepreneurial opportunities. Since the early 2000s, Brazilian migrants have established communities in the so-called new destinations of the American South and West, attracting recent ethnographic attention in places such as Atlanta, New Orleans, Miami, San Francisco, and Washington, DC.[17]

While the 2008 financial crisis[18] paired with Brazil's economic boom motivated rampant return migration among Brazilians after 2008, as Nelson suggested during our interview in 2013, migration to the United States grew anew beginning in 2014. The 2017 American Community Survey (ACS) reported a 33 percent increase in Brazilian migration between 2010 and 2017.[19] The country's economic sluggishness and political instability most certainly motivated increased migration. While the ACS estimated that only 280,000 Brazilians lived in the United States as of 2011, and 450,000 as of 2017, the Brazilian Ministry of Foreign Affairs conjectured that 1.4 million Brazilians resided in the US.[20]

Brazilian Migrants as Economic and Religious Exceptions

Scholars extend stories of exceptionalism to examinations of Brazilian migrants when compared to other Latin American populations. Similar to the arguments for regional exceptionalism, such narratives rely on the distinctiveness of Brazilian migrants' Lusophone ties, and more significantly, on their relative socioeconomic and educational advantages.[21] Nelson's discourse at the consulate, discussed at the outset of this chapter, rehearsed many of the themes found in this literature: Brazilian migrants remain exceptional when compared to other Latin American migrants because they arrive with better socioeconomic resources, more clearly defined plans to return home, and intentions to contribute to Brazilian nation-building efforts.

Scholars underscore that Brazilian migrants largely come from the Brazilian middle class. Rather than migrate because of violence, civil war, or political instability, as do regional counterparts from Guatemala, Ecuador, and El Salvador, Brazilian migrants generally migrate in search of better economic opportunities.[22] A large proportion of Brazilian migrants enter the United States via airplane using legitimate tourist or educational visas, rather than through dangerous and illicit border crossings.[23] Brazilian migrants engage in "return" and "yo-yo" migration at much higher rates than other Latin American migrants, leading scholars to designate them "sojourners" rather than "settlers,"[24] a distinction that many Brazilian migrants I met reiterated. They bristled at my questions about their experience as "migrants," a term that conjured constant mobility, open-ended dislocation, and marginalized status. Instead, the individuals I met jokingly retorted, "Migrante, não! Sou turista!" (Migrant, no way! I'm a tourist!). Unlike migrants from countries destabilized by civil war and drug-trafficking, Brazilian migrants could and did return home.

In addition to constituting economic exceptions, Brazilian migrants constitute religious exceptions in their own and scholars' estimation due to Brazil's presumed religiosity. Historians and anthropologists have long defined Brazil to be uniquely Christian, and more broadly, uniquely religious. Scholars have variously called Brazil the "largest Catholic" and "largest evangelical" nation in the world because of the sheer number of self-identified believers of both denominations.[25] These assertions stem from the central role Jesuit missions played in the development of Brazil as a Portuguese colony in the sixteenth century,[26] as well as the prominence of Christianity in contemporary politics.[27] They also emerge from Brazil's growing influence on global Christianity, including evangelical Christianity and the Catholic Charismatic Renewal (CCR).

In addition to hosting one of the largest populations of evangelicals in the world, Brazil influences global Christianity by disseminating Brazilian missionaries and their home-grown church networks throughout the Americas, Europe, Africa, and Asia.[28] Brazilian evangelical Christianity, especially its most visible forms, including Pentecostalism and Neo-Pentecostalism, now rival American evangelical Christianity as a global religious phenomenon.[29]

Besides circulating pastors and planting satellite congregations, Brazilian evangelical churches widely produce and disseminate gospel music, study guides, seminary trainings, and radio and television content throughout the Brazilian diaspora. While the Igreja Universal do Reino de Deus (IURD; Universal Church of the Kingdom of God) remains the most well-known of these media-savvy megachurch influencers,[30] it now operates alongside multiple evangelical actors engaged in transnational activity.

Although it is not the explicit focus of my study, I noted ample evidence of the impact and reach of these Brazilian transnational church networks in my field site and the project of "reverse mission" they performed.[31] They saturated the homes and churches of the migrant believers I knew. Migrants incessantly listened to Brazilian gospel music in their homes and cars, and sang these hymns with gusto each week. Each of the evangelical churches I studied, described in the following section, utilized study materials and Bibles produced in Brazil. Clergy and adherents often invoked well-known Brazilian pastors and missionaries, and circulated YouTube clips of especially moving sermons. Church services frequently featured guest preachers from Brazil, who translated the vastness of the transnational Brazilian evangelical circuit into intimate and deeply personal connections.

In addition to Brazilians' exceptional Christian inheritance, scholars tout Brazil's singular syncretic traditions, including the melding of Christian, Indigenous, and Afro-Brazilian cosmologies. Long repressed by the government, the syncretic traditions of Umbanda, Candomblé, and Spiritism now permeate the national culture, and have been cultivated as lucrative tourist attractions. The new-age healing guru John of God attracts thousands of international visitors each year, as do ayahuasca spiritual retreats.[32] Along with soccer, bossa nova, and Carnival, Brazil markets itself, and is recognized globally, as a land of remarkable faith and healing.

The Brazilian migrants I met were acutely aware of this spiritual bounty, and frequently cited its potential benefits and pitfalls. In explaining their decision to attend Brazilian rather than American churches, they emphasized the latter as "cold" and "impersonal," and the former as "alive" and "renewed." Migrants further noted that it was difficult to feel the presence of God without the national religious forms that moved them: prayers, gospels, study guides, and musical arrangements produced in Brazil, in their native Brazilian Portuguese, and according to their own cultural logic. And yet, migrants also warned against Brazilian charlatanism and corruption. They mentioned the growing fame of Brazilian religious leaders, and often spoke of the many impostors who exploited faith for wealth. "If you want to make money in Brazil," Brazilian migrants pronounced sardonically, "either play soccer or become a pastor."

The Limits of Exceptionalism

While such stories of economic and religious exceptionalism promote Brazilian migrants as singular, such an analysis overlooks the significant commonalities Brazilian migrants share with other Latin American migrants. In Greater Washington, DC, four circumstances that more broadly impacted Latin American migrants across the United States shaped Brazilian migrant life and helped configure their turn toward evangelical Christianity. These included (1) suburban sprawl, (2) undocumented status, (3) low-wage work, and (4) Catholic predominance in country of origin.

First, like other new immigrant gateways such as Atlanta, Dallas, and Miami, the Washington, DC, region witnessed the rapid increase of foreign-born populations as well as massive suburban sprawl in the postwar period.[33] The population of foreign-born residents in the region increased tenfold between 1970 and 2016. By 2016, the US Census Bureau found that 1.3 million foreign residents—15 percent of the total population—lived in Greater DC, making it among the largest concentrations of foreign-born residents in the United States, and outranking traditional American migrant hubs such as Boston, and other new destinations like Dallas.[34] As living costs of the city center soared during this same time, new migrants increasingly moved to the suburbs, where they lived in dispersed apartment complexes rather than the "ethnic enclaves" of the twentieth century.[35] This geographic dispersal contributed to common feelings of isolation and loneliness among the migrants I knew.

Second, 70 percent of Brazilians in the United States remained undocumented. Like most Latin American migrants, Brazilian migrants experienced family separation, uncertainty, and work exploitation as a result of this status. Third, and often related to their status, migrants worked in construction and the service economy in Greater Washington, DC. Women generally worked in the domestic services, while men most often worked in restaurants, construction, and landscaping. These two sectors, heavily reliant on undocumented migrant workers, expanded in the wake of President Roosevelt's New Deal to support the growth of foundations, think tanks, universities, and international organizations.[36] As I discuss in chapter 2, the kinds of work migrants performed triggered specific affective conditions, including loneliness and feeling "stuck."

Fourth, Brazilian migrants, like their Guatemalan, Mexican, and Salvadoran counterparts, originated from an overwhelmingly Catholic country. Despite significant incursions from evangelical Christianity and Afro-Brazilian syncretic traditions, Catholicism has remained the culturally dominant religion in Brazil and across Latin America.[37] In 2010, almost two-thirds of the Brazilian population, about 123 million people, identified as Catholic. While this reflected a 9 percent decrease from 2000, and a 27 percent decrease from 1970, such numbers reveal the embeddedness of Catholicism in Brazil, as in Latin America as a whole. Forty percent of the world's Catholics reside in Latin America, and 69 percent of the population still identify as Catholic.[38] Many of the migrants I met described Catholicism not as a "religion" but rather as a *cultura*, defining it as a broader way of life. For those who considered themselves to be either nominally or devoutly Catholic, Catholic feast days and life-cycle events undergirded Brazilian sociality, as they did across Latin America. It is notable, therefore, that among Brazilian and Latin American migrants in the United States evangelical Christianity predominates.

These four attributes of contemporary migrant life suggest that Brazilian migrant experience, rather than being wholly exceptional, represents important features of Latin American migrant experience more generally. Across nationality, Latin American migrant experience in the United States is characterized by geographic sprawl, undocumented status, and low-wage work. Significantly, it is also marked by the disruption of Catholic faith and sociality, and the emergence of evangelical forms in its place.

Rather than being either exceptional or representative, Brazilian migrants are both, thus constituting a special case in the study of migration and religion in the United States. Existing scholarship on evangelicalism as a "religion of the poor" would expect this "exceptional" population—rooted in the Brazilian middle class and with comparatively better educational and socioeconomic resources—to resist conversion.[39] Yet, as migrants in the United States, Brazilians, like their Latin American counterparts with fewer socioeconomic advantages, found evangelical Christianity deeply compelling. Brazilians I met often reported that they had repudiated evangelical Christianity while in Brazil, dismissing pastors and churches as corrupt, exploitative, and insincere. As migrants in the United States, however, they came to organize their life around such churches. Migrants who had converted to evangelical Christianity in Brazil described their premigration faith as tepid or insincere. As migrants, they insisted, they became "really" *cristão* (Christian). How did migration provoke this change of heart?

This study offers a critical perspective on how migrant experience itself encourages evangelical belonging. The daily experience Brazilians faced, including low-wage work, geographic isolation, and societal marginalization, confronts migrants across nationalities in the United States. As a result, such migrants likely experience forms of distress similar to those I documented among Brazilians, including loneliness, despair, anxiety, and feeling stuck. By tracing the emergence of novel or intensified religious yearnings among Brazilians, and how evangelical churches uniquely satisfied such feelings, this book provides a window into the reshaping of Christianity in the United States.

The Field

Brazilians in Greater Washington, DC

While the most recent American Community Survey estimated that fewer than 11,000 Brazilians lived in Greater Washington, DC, the Brazilian consulate estimated a regional population twice as large, and more than quadruple in the wider DC jurisdiction, which includes populations in Maryland, Virginia, West Virginia, Kentucky, and Delaware.[40] Commenting on the vast discrepancy between these estimates, Nelson, the Brazilian diplomat with whom I spoke, explained why counting Brazilian migrants was both difficult and imprecise. First, official surveys grouped Brazilians together with Latinx and Latin American populations, designations Brazilians often rejected given their claims of exceptionalism discussed above. By filling in "Other," they remained invisible as a distinct migrant population. Second, most Brazilian migrants in the US remained undocumented, and frequently did not participate in official surveys out of fear of apprehension. Third, Brazilians did not cluster in specific neighborhoods. Instead, Nelson explained, they frequently intermarried, lived apart from other Brazilians, and rejected the term "migrant" altogether. Fourth, the US Census's definition of "resident" remained ambiguous. Because many Brazilians planned to eventually return to Brazil, they viewed themselves as long-term "tourists" rather than "residents."

Most Brazilians I met migrated to the region after 2000, reflecting DC's status as a new migrant destination. Of the 48 Brazilians who responded to the survey question regarding year of arrival, 28 (58 percent) had arrived in the area after 2000, and 9 (19 percent) after 2005. Out of 76 interviewees, 52 (68 percent) arrived after 2000, and 20 (26 percent) after 2005. These numbers reflect findings regarding Brazilian migrant populations throughout the US, where 2 of every 3 migrants arrived after the year 2000.[41] While many Brazilians arrived in Greater Washington, DC, others settled in the region after living in US cities with larger populations of Brazilians, including Danbury, Connecticut, and Boston, Massachusetts. When I inquired into this trend, one interviewee expressed what I had learned from historians and demographers. Since 2000, he explained, the DC area was known to have greater opportunities for migrant work, particularly in construction. Earlier destinations like Boston and New York had become oversaturated with migrant laborers.

Most Brazilians I met came from the southern and southeastern Brazilian states of Santa Catarina, Minas Gerais, and São Paulo.[42] In keeping with the demographic profile of this region, most migrants in my study self-identified as racially white and of European descent. All migrants named economic, educational, or employment goals as motivating their migration. Migrants planned to accrue money over a short period of time and then return to Brazil. Migrants regularly invested money in Brazil, building homes and businesses, and supporting loved ones. As such, migration constituted an important household strategy. In the year 2018, migrants in the US sent home $2.9 billion in remittances to Brazil.[43]

I spent most time with Brazilian migrants who lived in the "inner suburbs" of metropolitan DC, and more specifically, Montgomery County, Maryland. Broad, multilane highways and suburban shopping plazas marked the area, with residential communities fanning out from congested thoroughfares. I spent many hours writing up field notes and conducting interviews in parking lots or chains like Starbucks, Panera Bread, and Barnes and Noble. Of the three evangelical, two Catholic, and two Spiritist groups I attended regularly, six were located in the inner suburbs. In this region, several Brazilian bakeries, restaurants, salons, and churches revealed a dense and visible Brazilian presence alongside other robust migrant communities.

Yet, I also conducted interviews with many Brazilians who lived in Northern Virginia, and several who lived in Baltimore. While most Brazilians I spent time with in Montgomery County worked in domestic service and construction, others who lived in downtown DC and across Northern Virginia had advanced degrees and worked in high-prestige and high-wage jobs. I conducted most interviews in small, anonymous apartment complexes near highways and amid suburban sprawl, but several took place in luxury

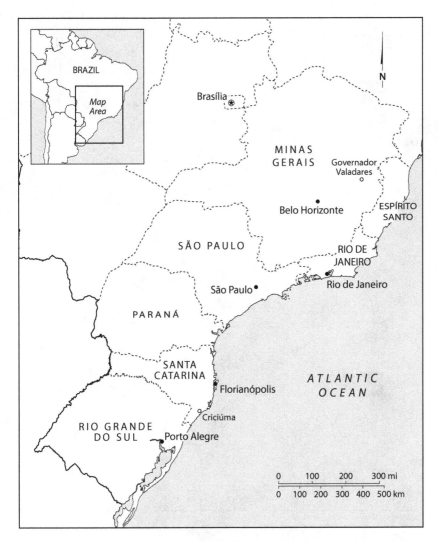

FIGURE 1.1. Southern Brazil

condominiums in downtown DC or in large homes in some of the wealthiest zip codes in the United States, such as Chevy Chase, Kensington, and Bethesda, Maryland. Although I spent the greatest time among migrants Nelson would identify as "traditional" according to his typology, I also came to appreciate the significant presence of migrants he deemed "new," who were well-positioned across universities, think tanks, and intergovernmental agencies.

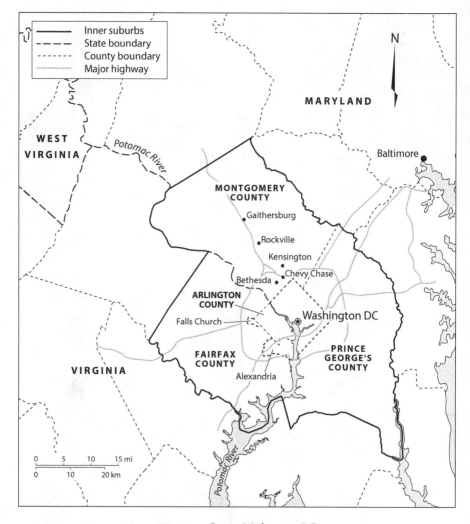

FIGURE 1.2. Greater Washington, DC

Such geographic divisions mirrored disparities in socioeconomic status, migration status, education, and profession among Brazilians I met. While Brazilians with legal status, education, and professional jobs lived in wealthier neighborhoods in Northern Virginia and downtown DC, those without legal status lived farther from the city center, in Montgomery County. Widely divergent state policies targeting undocumented migrants encouraged this pattern. Just as Maryland passed progressive legislation in 2009 that enabled undocumented migrants to secure driver's licenses, counties in Virginia formalized punitive legal measures aimed at apprehension and deportation.[44]

Religious Considerations

Most Brazilian migrants living in the United States identify as evangelical Christian (*crente, cristão, evangélico*), Catholic (*católico*), or Spiritist (*kardecista, espiritista*), reflecting the predominant religious affiliations of Brazil. Recent studies have documented the predominance of evangelical churches among Brazilian migrant populations, indicating the greater proportion of Brazilian evangelicals relative to the Brazilian population in the United States than in Brazil (65 percent versus 42 percent).[45]

I conducted research in three evangelical congregations: Pentecostal, Baptist, and Seventh-day Adventist (SDA).[46] These three denominations represented the most visible Brazilian evangelical movements both in the region and in the United States more generally. Brazilian Adventists date their origins in the region to the 1970s. The SDA presence in Greater Washington, DC, was particularly significant due to the wider international SDA organization's impressive world headquarters location in nearby Potomac, Maryland. Many SDA theologians from Brazil and around the world traveled through Greater Washington, DC, for employment and speaking tours during my research period. Furthermore, several Brazilian Adventist migrants moved to the region owing to ties to Adventist churches, schools, and universities. The Brazilian Baptist movement emerged in the 1980s, and the Brazilian Pentecostal movement in the early 2000s.

Given the frequency and intimacy of their meetings, I spent the greatest amount of time with members and clergy of the Pentecostal congregation. My findings, while predominantly based on research with this one congregation, were corroborated by interviews and observations conducted among Adventists and Baptists. Throughout the book, I illustrate my findings with data and interviews drawn from all three congregations, gesturing toward the significance of general "evangelical experience" among migrants, rather than specific denominational engagement.

At the time of study, each of these congregations was affiliated with larger transnational organizations that maintained churches throughout the mid-Atlantic region, the United States, Brazil, and beyond. These important facts, and the literatures to which they speak, remain largely beyond the scope of this study.[47] Denominational allegiance remained fairly unimportant to most congregants with whom I spoke. While clergy members, church workers, and members with generational ties asserted the centrality of theological differences between denominations, and often warned me about competing churches, most migrant believers seemed uninterested in what they considered to be rigid, manmade church doctrine. Believers frequently dismissed denominationalism, saying emphatically, "Deus é Deus!" (God is God!), and self-identifying simply as "Christian" (*cristão*).

Congregants of each of these three churches exhibited beliefs and practices that scholars consider to be emblematic of evangelical religiosity. These markers included (1) being "born again" through intimate or embodied experience of Jesus; (2) a near literal understanding of the Bible; and (3) a commitment to evangelize.[48] Most importantly, Brazilian believers, like other groups of US evangelicals, sought out intimate and bodily knowledge of God unlike nonevangelical Christians. Brazilian evangelicals across congregations shared a devotion to prayer, testimony, and discernment as the practices par excellence of evangelical faith, as well as a commitment to intimate church fellowship marked by frequent social involvement. I consider these markers of migrant faith in chapter 3.

While the term "evangelical" defines a wide spectrum of belief and practice in the United States, the term encompasses an even broader population of Christians in Brazil. Due to its long history as a majority Catholic nation, the term *evangélico*, or more colloquially *crente*, refers to *all* Protestants in Brazil, in contrast to the term *católico*.

My invocation of a more generalized category of "lived" evangelical religiosity among migrants, detached from denomination or theology, remains consistent not only with studies of religious flexibility and syncretism among Brazilians, but also with evidence of the weakening of denominations in both the United States and Brazil. Scholars of religion charge that denominations in the United States remain "on the cusp of extinction"[49] while nondenominational and independent evangelical and charismatic movements surge, leading to the "Californization" of US Christianity.[50] Scholars also note the withering of denominations in Brazil, where Pentecostal and charismatic Christianity have influenced all religious groups, including traditional Protestant denominations, such as the Presbyterian and Methodist churches, and even the Catholic Church. Each of these groups maintains a growing "renewalist" wing in Brazil and Latin America that incorporates Pentecostal and charismatic styles of worship, including music and faith healing.[51]

Congregants and clergy across these three religious groups did, however, underscore key theological and stylistic distinctions when comparing their beliefs and practices to the other groups in my study. First, Pentecostals emphasized the centrality of speaking in tongues, and baptism by the Holy

Spirit, which made their worship style deeply emotive, vocal, and easily identifiable. Stylistically, Baptists and Adventists worshipped in a much quieter and more self-contained manner, and, theologically, they rejected baptism by the Holy Spirit. Despite these differences, however, individual congregants reported spiritual experiences outside of church akin to what I heard from Pentecostals, including dreams, prophecies, and God's hand in their daily life.

Second, while each group formally maintained restrictive behavioral codes, the Pentecostal and Adventist congregations adhered to these rules most stringently. The Pentecostal and Adventist congregations prohibited the use of alcohol, tobacco, and drugs, while the Baptist congregation preached moderation but ultimately empowered individuals to decide for themselves. Similarly, the Pentecostal and Adventist congregations institutionalized gender norms in formal dress codes, whereas the Baptist church embraced casual attire. Even in the more formal groups, however, congregants often told me that Brazilian churches had dramatically loosened these rules for migrants in the United States, thereby explaining the wide array of clothing worn by visitors and members alike. Each church professed conservative views in regard to marriage, sexuality, gender roles, and abortion.

In general, the SDA theological principles remained the most distinct. Adventists hold that the Old Testament covenant between Moses and God remains binding, thus differentiating them from mainline Christians who consider the New Testament to supplant Moses's teachings. As such, Adventists keep the Sabbath on Saturday, and encourage vegetarianism as a means of adhering to the dietary restrictions contained in the book of Leviticus. Furthermore, Adventists articulate a concrete mapping of Heaven through the "Heavenly Sanctuary," and consider the writings of their modern-day prophet, Ellen G. White, to be divinely inspired. Given the unorthodoxy of these espoused beliefs, many evangelical Christians firmly exclude the SDA Church and its members from Christianity, often demeaning the group as a "cult" or "sect." Adventists cite these very same practices, however, as evidence of their biblical literalism. In their estimation, Adventists remain the only group to accurately and consistently uphold all of God's commandments.

For the main purposes of this study, however, such theological distinctions remained largely unimportant. Like Pentecostal and Baptist believers, Adventist migrants reported an intensification of their religious identity in the United States and found faith to be essential to daily life. The resources migrants found through faith and church belonging remained identical across denominations, including tools for emotional uplift and empowerment, dense social connections, and a sense of meaning and purpose. For these reasons, I treat the specific theological divergences and genealogies of each movement briefly in the endnotes.[52]

At the time of my research, three Catholic dioceses served the Washington, DC, metropolitan region: Arlington (Northern Virginia), Washington, DC (the District and southern Maryland), and Richmond (the remainder of Virginia). I conducted research in the Arlington and Washington, DC, dioceses, where two Catholic parishes regularly offered Mass in Portuguese and maintained an explicit focus on migrant populations. In the Diocese of Arlington, Mass occurred exclusively for Brazilians once a month at a local parish. The Catholic Church organized these Masses, as well as Masses in Spanish and other languages, according to its expansive Multicultural Ministry, initiated in 2005 with the motto, "Unity in Diversity." In the Diocese of Washington, DC, the local parish I attended provided weekly Portuguese Mass for all Portuguese speakers, including Brazilian, Portuguese, Cape Verdean, Angolan, and Mozambican adherents.[53]

Through these institutional settings, I met practicing Brazilian Catholics who gathered regularly for prayer, community, and service. I attended several prayer meetings of ten to fifteen Brazilians, Cape Verdeans, and Portuguese throughout my research. Many of the Brazilian Catholics I met through this group were as devout and committed to their faith as the evangelicals with whom I spent time. Like their *crente* counterparts, Brazilian Catholics traveled to neighboring cities to hear popular priests' homilies and aspired to grow their local Brazilian Catholic community. At the end of my research, one group was in the midst of organizing a *retiro* (retreat) with a popular Brazilian Catholic Charismatic Renewal (CCR) priest, attracting registration from a few hundred Brazilians in the region.

Yet, such popular events among Brazilian Catholics remained rare. Brazilians often felt alienated by the Catholic Church in the United States. Several Catholics and former Catholics told me that the church's services and events remained excessively formal. This institutional "coldness" led many Brazilian Catholics to distance themselves from the church, practice at home, or seek religious comfort elsewhere, such as at evangelical churches and Spiritist centers. In chapter 5, I discuss the Catholic Church's approach to Brazilian and Latin American migrants, identifying the absence of an individualistic, affect-centered approach to migrants' distress as an important reason for the institution's relative failure to attract greater adherence among this traditionally Catholic group.

During early stages of fieldwork, I learned about Spiritism only incidentally.[54] Many migrants who first told me they were Catholic gradually revealed alternative faith practices and affiliations. While attending Spiritist centers and conferring with mediums privately, they refrained from publicly revealing their identities for fear of judgment or misunderstanding. As many scholars note, overlapping and flexible religious identities among Brazilians render numeric estimations difficult and problematic.[55] As I encountered the robustness of the movement among Brazilians in Greater Washington, DC, however, I recognized the need to include these centers and their practitioners within my study.

Because of the movement's explicitly egalitarian structure, no single regulative Spiritist organization exists. Instead, centers that promote the spiritual teachings of Allan Kardec, the nineteenth-century French philosopher and medium, call themselves "Spiritist." These organizations generally teach Kardec's five canonical books, *The Spiritist Codification*, and remain loosely affiliated with national and international Spiritist organizations, such as the International Spiritist Council, the United States Spiritist Federation, and the US Spiritist Medical Association.

Unlike Catholics and evangelicals, Spiritists reject the label "religion" altogether. Instead, they consider their movement to offer a holistic "way of life," integrating three essential strands of human experience: philosophy, religion, and science. Like Brazilian Catholics and evangelicals, however, Brazilian Spiritists asserted faith as fundamental to their migrant experience in the United States.

Although I interviewed Spiritists from several organizations and attended regionwide Spiritist events, I visited two centers regularly. These centers represented the oldest Spiritist groups in the region. Brazilian professionals established one group in 1992 after Divaldo Franco, the most prominent Spiritist leader and medium in Brazil, visited Johns Hopkins University. Brazilian students studying at area universities organized a second group in the early 2000s. These two groups represented an important ideological division in the movement. One organization, which I call the Center of Healing and Peace, offered programming exclusively in English, explicitly aiming to attract English speakers and facilitate migrant assimilation, whereas the other group, which I refer to as the Washington Kardecistas, conducted its affairs exclusively in Portuguese, embracing and promoting Brazilian culture.[56]

Among the Washington Kardecistas, leaders suggested that the majority of migrant members were documented and had traveled to the United States for professional or educational opportunities. Yet, within the Center of Healing and Peace, leaders estimated that over 50 percent of Brazilian Spiritists in the region remained undocumented. While it was beyond the scope of this research to produce a comprehensive demographic portrait of Spiritists in the region, anecdotally, I found that most Spiritists I met held positions at area universities and international organizations, had attained US citizenship through employment or marriage, and had no plans to return to Brazil.[57] Like the evangelical groups, these organizations offered multiple events per week for members. Activities included weekly lectures on Spiritism's main tenets, as espoused by Allan Kardec and other important Brazilian mediums, mediumship training, energetic healing, and spiritual counseling.

Migrant Experience and Pragmatic Faith

Brazilian evangelical churches in the United States and abroad have received significant scholarly attention owing to their growing visibility and relationship to homegrown Brazilian denominations. Researchers have evaluated the impact of these institutions on the well-being of Brazilian migrants, particularly when compared to the Catholic Church, and have evaluated the ability of evangelical churches to mobilize migrants in pursuit of collective goods and community betterment.[58]

In the context of thin infrastructural support for Brazilian migrants, scholars suggest that evangelical churches provide essential resources within a community that remains internally "disunited,"[59] frequently invisible due to its "exceptional" status,[60] and predominantly undocumented.[61] Scholars have outlined several meaningful benefits that evangelical belonging confers on migrants, including intimate sociality, gathering space outside of the home, and emotional catharsis through group prayer.[62] While evangelicalism grows in popularity among migrants, Catholicism, these scholarly accounts document, is in steady decline.[63]

While my research corroborates and builds upon these important insights, it also shifts the locus of attention from the concrete benefits migrants derived from evangelical belonging to the mutually constitutive nature of migrant and evangelical experience. Migrants do of course make use of religious belonging as a pragmatic strategy to secure scarce resources in diaspora, examples of which abound in the ethnographic material that follows: a woman who left the Catholic Church because a priest charged her money for her son's baptism; a man who joined a Pentecostal church because he needed to find work; a woman who left an Adventist congregation because of gossip; another, because no one would teach her to drive.

While migrants I spoke with expressed the relative ease with which they made friends and found employment in evangelical churches, they also revealed how evangelical churches met their deeply personal psychic and bodily needs. Through evangelical faith, practice, and community, migrants learned to interpret and work on their emotions according to specific theological principles related to God and righteousness. As a result, migrants newly understood their bodies and minds as "healed," and their lives in the United States as dramatically improved. Highlighting pragmatism, and how migrants make use of religion, produces an incomplete and flattened portrait of migrant experience, subjectivity, and belief. Pragmatic orientations toward religion that fail to take interiority seriously risk minimizing the subjective and affective significance of belief, and in doing so, miss how religion can lead to pragmatic benefit. It is necessary to examine how it feels for an individual to believe, and how such feelings then mobilize individuals and communities to act within and beyond the church.

Taking belief seriously and placing this second set of concerns at the very center of analysis, this study approaches religious experience as fundamental, and inextricably tied, to the migration experience itself. I consider how being a migrant shaped religious longing, and how evangelical membership in turn shaped the identity, self-understanding, and behaviors of Brazilian migrants in the United States. Such an account neither precludes nor denies pragmatic relationships to religious belonging and belief. Rather, evangelical belonging among migrants, and the affective transformation it triggers, facilitated increased pragmatic action. And, such pragmatic action emerged from evangelical beliefs and orientations. Evangelical faith practices like prayer (*oração*), discernment (*discernimento*), and testimony (*testemunho*) enabled Brazilians to reinterpret their often demeaning and exploitative experiences. By learning to put themselves fully in the hands of God (*nas mãos de Deus*), Brazilian migrants radically altered the way they perceived, and therefore coped with, migrant distress.

2

Stuck and Alone

THE AFFECTIVE IMPRINT OF
MIGRANT DISTRESS

There are only winners and losers now. Dream meets nightmare in the flick of an eye. . . . Anxiety ranges without object. But so does the sense of potential.

There are bodies out of place. There are plenty of people in free fall. There are people whose American dreaming is literally a dreaming cut off from any actual potential. But that doesn't stop it—far from it.

—KATHLEEN STEWART[1]

I MET NEUSA in July 2013, when I visited her Pentecostal congregation in suburban Maryland for the first time. Having found the congregation's listing on a flyer at a local Brazilian bakery, I emailed and called the pastor to arrange a meeting. With no response, I decided to introduce myself in person and request permission to conduct research. I arrived at 7:30 p.m., thirty minutes prior to the start of services. The small brick church was located off a four-lane thoroughfare in Montgomery County. A placard out front listed the multiple migrant congregations that rented space from the African Methodist Episcopal church, including Brazilian, Korean, and Spanish-speaking Latin American congregations.

When I walked into the chapel, I found three women quietly chatting while a toddler played at their feet. Neusa, a small woman in her midfifties with straight black hair pulled into a tight ponytail, welcomed me enthusiastically. After introducing me to her granddaughter and two daughters-in-law, and then learning of my research intentions, she declared herself to be my *igreja mãe* (church mother) for the duration of my study. The pastor was traveling, she explained, but would soon return. During the service led by a visiting pastor, Neusa positioned herself beside me in the pews, shared her Bible, and gently prodded me to participate. At the conclusion, she accompanied me to the door, hugged me tightly, and to my great surprise, pressed a delicate white tapestry with green embroidery into my palms. "Here," she said. "Um presente para você" (A gift for you).

After several months spending time together at church, I asked to interview Neusa and her husband, Rubém, at their home. They lived in Appletree Condominiums, a sprawling apartment complex about a mile from the church. I soon learned that many Brazilian migrants lived there. The management company accepted tax ID numbers from applicants in lieu of social security numbers on rental applications, making their units particularly attractive to undocumented migrants. The large, gray, cinderblock complex lay at a major intersection with gas stations, fast food restaurants, and strip malls to either side.

After wending my way through the parking lot, I turned onto Cherry Lane and parked in front of Building 500 around 6 p.m. During my second pass through the hallway, I spied the number 9 faintly etched into the metal door knocker. Neusa opened the door, hair wet and skin freshly scrubbed, and welcomed me with a warm smile and embrace. The apartment was brightly lit and smelled of the *pão de queijo* she had prepared. Glass tables and plush leather furniture sat on pristine, wall-to-wall white carpeting. Photos of Neusa's children and grandchildren hung on the walls, alongside decorative flourishes, reading in English, "Believe," "Faith," "Love," and "Family."

Neusa escorted me to the couch and instructed me to wait for her while she finished preparing the evening meal. Rubém and their nephew, Adriano, soon arrived from work, removing their work boots and setting aside their construction hats as they entered the freshly cleaned apartment. Rubém nodded, greeted his wife, and said he would return after showering. Adriano, eighteen, swapped work boots for soccer cleats and ran to meet friends at a nearby field. Neusa's younger son, Frederico, suddenly appeared from the upstairs apartment, where he lived with his wife and toddler, to rifle through his mother's refrigerator. Just as suddenly as he came, he gave his mother a kiss on her head and returned upstairs with a plate piled high with cake, cheese, and cold cuts. After the burst of activity, Neusa sat down next to me and invited me to ask her questions about her life.

———

Throughout my fieldwork, Neusa opened her home and encouraged me to learn as much as I could about her life and faith. As a result, I got to know Neusa, Rubém, and their sons, Felipe and Frederico, particularly well. I saw them several times per week at church and at Neusa's home, where she frequently invited me to visit and help her to practice English. While some migrants I met never fully trusted me, nor my notebook or recorder, Neusa stated during our first conversation that she "had nothing to fear." She shared her experiences over coffee and cake that first autumn evening and several more that followed, and encouraged her family members and friends to do the same. She introduced me to her pastor, his wife, and prominent church members, and recommended congregants for me to interview. She distributed my surveys to her husband, two sons, daughters-in-law, and niece, and nagged them until they had completed them. Neusa's characteristic generosity, friendship, and warmth anchored me in the congregation.

Her openness also allowed me to better comprehend the contours of Brazilian migrant experience. I recognized echoes of her family's stories and sentiments in the many migrant narratives I heard: family separation, loneliness, disrupted expectations, culture shock, workplace vulnerability, generalized fear, uncertainty about the future, ambivalence about return to Brazil. This chapter examines these defining conditions of migrant life in the United States through Neusa and her family's experiences as well as those of many of their peers. Such conditions induced particular bodily and psychic maladies—what I call the affective imprint of migrant distress.

It is important to note at the outset of this chapter on migrant suffering, however, that migrant life was not exclusively marked by distress. Rather, I witnessed countless examples of migrants overcoming the social fracture, physical pain, and psychic disturbance that their status engendered through various forms of robust sociality and intimacy with others. Many migrants I met had satisfying partnerships, relationships with children, and multiple close friendships, all mitigating the forms of distress I outline below. As the above vignette demonstrates, migrant life was often defined by stark contradictions. Like the concrete complexes in which they often lived, migrants like Neusa found themselves hidden from view and shunted into the unwanted corners of society. Migrant work, geography, and living undocumented carried significant consequences. And yet, migrants also lived warm and vibrant lives within these confines. Often, it was evangelical belonging, community, and faith that enabled such spaces of connection, despite the extreme distress migrants encountered.

Of the 49 migrants who responded to the self-authored survey I distributed regarding migration experience and religious belief (see the appendix), 23 (47 percent) noted a dramatic increase in their feelings of loneliness (*solidão*) once in the United States. Twenty-two (45 percent) answered that they felt anxious (*ansioso*) more frequently since arriving in the United States, and 17 (35 percent) described themselves as more frequently depressed (*deprimido*). Furthermore, 11 (22 percent) explicitly ranked "depression (*depressão*), loneliness (*solidão*), and isolation (*ficar isolado*)" among the most difficult aspects of living in the United States. Given the cultural stigma among Brazilians attached to acknowledging emotional distress publicly, these numbers of self-reported psychic suffering remain significant.[2] More substantial than these survey findings, however, were the numerous informal conversations and recorded interviews I gathered that demonstrated Brazilian migrants' intimacy with loneliness, anxiety, depression, and generalized psychic distress.

The chapter is divided into three parts. First, I discuss features of migrant experience that likely impacted individuals regardless of national origin, including migrant work, family separation, suburban sprawl, and culture shock. Through this discussion, I hope to draw out the ways that migrant life in the United States, especially for the undocumented, exacts a bodily and psychic toll across ethnicity, race, and gender. As such, my research among Brazilians serves as a case study of a more general phenomenon among US migrants.[3] Second, I explore the features of Brazilian migrant experience that make Brazilian migrants especially susceptible to distress. Here, I return to the theme of Brazilian exceptionalism to consider the unique linguistic and cultural isolation Brazilians faced as Portuguese speakers of mixed racial and ethnic identity, their incessant deliberation over return to Brazil, and Brazilians' vocalized mutual distrust. Finally, I describe how the conditions of migrant experience became imprinted on the bodies and psyches of the individuals I met, leaving them with a common complex of maladies, what I theorize as an affective imprint of migrant distress.

Daily Distress

In 1998, Rubém left Criciúma, Santa Catarina, a southern Brazilian state, for Somerville, Massachusetts. Crippled by severe debt, and unable to keep up with payments on his miner's salary, he left his wife and three young children to *juntar dinheiro*—make fast cash. He was forty years old. His brother-in-law, who already lived in Boston, promised he would make money rapidly on booming construction sites and soon return to his family. His brother had lived in Virginia for almost a decade and encouraged him to try his luck. Rubém expected to stay in the United States for no more than six months.

After arriving, however, he found it much more difficult to save, and the anticipated six-month separation ballooned into over two years of familial fracture. Rubém bounced from room to room, experiencing exploitation by relatives and strangers alike. His brother-in-law underpaid him for work and overcharged him for rent. He worked long hours in all seasons, with little time for leisure. His relationships were marked by fear, mistrust, and competition. He ate meagerly and slept little. For the first time in his adult life, he felt deep loneliness and despair.

With the distance, financial strain, and emotional burden of separation, Rubém and his wife, Neusa, struggled to connect. They were on the brink of divorce when, as a last attempt to save their relationship and keep their family intact, Neusa took her two sons, Felipe, then twelve, and Frederico, then nine, to Mexico in 2000. She left Vanessa, her eldest child, in Brazil with her parents to finish high school. Like her husband, Neusa anticipated a brief stay in the United States, and envisioned a rapid return to her first-born child in Brazil. From Mexico, Neusa arranged for a coyote to bring her and her sons across the border with other migrants, including another Brazilian mother and daughter from their hometown. The two Brazilian women, both trying to reunite with husbands in the United States, jointly protected their children during the harrowing crossing. They were eventually apprehended by border police, detained for twenty-four hours, and subsequently freed when Rubém's brother, a US citizen, arranged for them to be released on bail, with deportation hearing orders in hand.

Neusa and Rubém lived with Rubém's brother in Virginia for several months until they moved into their own apartment in Montgomery County, Maryland. After cleaning homes with another Brazilian woman, serving as her "helper," Neusa soon started her own business, often cleaning eight homes in a single day. Fourteen years later, she had never missed a day of work. Rubém continued to work in construction, and at one point owned his own business, managing fifteen employees and multiple work sites. After the US financial crisis in 2008, however, many of his employees returned to Brazil, and work became scarce. He gave up his company and worked for other contractors. Over time, Rubém paid off his debt, and he and Neusa accrued savings, which they invested back in Brazil. Over the course of their decade and a half in the

United States, they built three homes—one of them on the coast of Santa Catarina, the location of their eagerly anticipated retirement. They also funded their eldest child Vanessa's pharmaceutical education and helped her open her own pharmacy. Owing to their undocumented status, they had not seen their daughter in fourteen years.

Family Separation

The Brazilian Portuguese word *saudades* connotes yearning, nostalgia, and the pain of absence. More than the common English translation "to miss," the phrase *ter saudades* (to have yearning/pain of absence) or *estar com saudades* (to be with yearning/pain of absence) carries existential weight, particularly when used in reference to long absent loved ones. For most migrants I knew, the experience of living in the United States brought with it deep and lasting knowledge of this state. Young migrants left behind parents, siblings, nieces, and nephews whom they now saw only virtually. Older migrants left behind children and aging parents, the former growing into adulthood without them, the latter facing aging and death in their absence. Still others had lived with family members in the United States for years or decades, until someone decided to leave and could not return, or others were deported on minor violations. Prolonged and indefinite separation from loved ones contributed to migrants' acute feelings of loneliness and overall distress.

While documented migrants enjoyed the relative freedom of visiting significant others in Brazil once or twice a year, and hosted visitors in the United States, the undocumented migrants I knew contended with the semipermanence and impending threat of absence. According to a 2013 Pew Forum report, an estimated 9 million people live in "mixed-status" families in the United States, where some members had obtained work permits, green cards, amnesty, or citizenship while others remained undocumented.[4] Between 2008 and 2015, 2 million migrants had been deported, more than during any other executive administration. Sixty-seven percent of these deportees were stopped on minor traffic violations or were picked up for attempting to reunite with family members in the United States.[5] Immigration and Customs Enforcement (ICE) arrests and deportations continued with heightened fervency and expanded autonomy under the Trump administration, resulting in increased numbers of arrests and removals each year, and a greater percentage of arrests leading to deportation. Between 2017 and 2019, ICE deported nearly 750,000 migrants.[6] In the context of the ongoing Covid-19 pandemic, and the invocation of Title 42, the "public health law," by both the Trump and Biden administrations, deportations have continued at an unprecedented pace, with 1 million deportations in 2021 alone.[7]

The promise of comprehensive immigration reform, which would curb family separation, remained elusory for most migrants I met. While a few had found temporary relief through programs like President Obama's 2012 Deferred Action for Childhood Arrivals (DACA), many others hoped for broader amnesty measures. Toward the end of my fieldwork in 2014, President Obama issued an executive order to expand DACA to adults over thirty-one, pledging temporary relief to parents of US citizens through Deferred Action for Parents of Americans (DAPA). Furthermore, a progressive immigration bill (S. 744) had passed in the Senate, outlining a potential "pathway" to citizenship for 5 million undocumented migrants. Politicians promised to reunite families and bring individuals "out of the shadows."

After I completed fieldwork, however, each of these proposals stalled in political quagmire during the remainder of President Obama's tenure. The House of Representatives struck down S. 744, and twenty-five states, led by Texas, argued the unconstitutionality of Obama's executive orders.[8] With the election of President Trump in 2016, and the hard-right turn of national immigration policy, each of these progressive measures was denounced and then overturned. It remains to be seen whether comprehensive immigration reform, including a pathway to citizenship for undocumented migrants, will be passed under the Biden administration. While the Biden administration introduced the most expansive immigration reform proposed in decades, encapsulated in the US Citizenship Act of 2021, the plan faces widespread opposition in a deeply polarized nation.[9]

———

As we sat alone at her kitchen table on a cold winter evening, Neusa's profound grief about Vanessa's absence remained palpable and wrenching. I had come to help her practice English, but she seemed distracted and fatigued. Rubém was away in South Carolina for a construction job, and Neusa was alone for the night after having cleaned eight houses in a single day. Instead of reviewing English exercises, she offered me some coffee and cake and told me about her daughter, who was a few years older than me.

After she and Rubém had realized it would take longer to save enough money to pay off their debts, accrue savings, and invest in property in Brazil, they decided to bring Vanessa to the United States. When she arrived at the airport in Washington, DC, and tried to enter the country on an Italian passport, she was immediately deported. Neusa later learned that Vanessa had momentarily glimpsed her awaiting parents through the security glass. Neusa and Rubém did not see Vanessa but soon learned that she was turned back after being within feet of them for the first time in several years. Of this moment, Neusa recalled, "I cried as if I had lost a child."

Following her failed attempt at entry, Vanessa invested in her future in Santa Catarina, Brazil, with the help of her parents' remittances. She opened a pharmacy, married, and had a daughter. At the time of our conversation, it had been fourteen years since Neusa, Rubém, and their two sons had seen Vanessa. None of them had met Vanessa's husband or daughter in person, but interacted with them through frequent messages, video calls, and photographs. Neusa spoke to her daughter every day and told me about her as if she was intimately present in her daily life.

While she had remained stoic during previous conversations concerning the painful details of her life—including her infant son's near death, her treacherous crossing of the Mexican border and subsequent detainment with her two young children—on this particular evening, I found her rawness exposed. She looked up at me with a pained expression and asked, "How can a mother miss half her daughter's life? Can you imagine? What would you do not seeing your mother for fourteen years?"

During our conversations in the spring and summer of 2014, Neusa explained that it was time for her and Rubém to return to Brazil to be with their daughter. Their sons, having practically grown up in the United States and having no desire to return to a country they barely knew, would stay. Neusa's eldest son, Felipe, had received deferred action status according to DACA. He had obtained a renewable work permit, allowing him to stay lawfully in the United States for up to two years at a time. Frederico, Neusa's youngest child, was unable to obtain this status, having already received a deportation letter to which he never responded. Neither son, however, would be able to travel lawfully to Brazil. And, once Neusa and Rubém left the United States, they would not be allowed to reenter. As she explained this impossible situation to me, and the certain separation from her children and grandchildren she faced, she cried and shook her head, saying only, "It's very, very difficult."

———

Many mothers related similar stories of unanticipated, and potentially unending, separations from their children. Lúcia, a devout Catholic, revealed that her middle son had moved to Brazil to attend college, after spending most of his childhood in the United States. Lúcia explained that she and her husband simply could not afford American universities, especially when they would have to pay out-of-state tuition. Yet, when her son returned to Brazil, he discovered that he was behind in coursework and struggled with Portuguese. Unable to qualify for Brazilian universities, he worked in manual labor while living with relatives. He soon became desperate to return to the United States. When he went to apply for a visa, he learned, along with his family, that his rights to travel to the United States had been revoked, because he had lived in the country without documents for several years. Since he had already left the country, he no longer qualified for deferred action under DACA. At the time of our conversation, Lúcia and her husband had recently obtained green cards through his employer, making travel to Brazil possible for themselves and their eldest son. Yet, their middle son remained undocumented and therefore unable to travel without the risk of apprehension. Lúcia exclaimed that she would never have encouraged her son to pursue university education in Brazil had she anticipated family separation as an enduring consequence.

While separation from one's children remained excruciating, mothers retained the confidence that they would, one day, be reunited with their sons and daughters again. Time was on their side. Yet, for adult children who had migrated to the United States in their twenties, thirties, or forties, the reality of illness and aging among parents left in Brazil became more pressing as the years passed. One of the greatest fears migrants expressed, and one of the greatest tragedies many had already endured, was the death of a parent while they were abroad. In an instant, death made an indefinite separation permanent.

Gláucia, a devout woman in her early thirties whom I had met at the Pentecostal church, lost her mother three years prior to our interview. In 2002, her entire family had migrated from Santa Catarina to pursue better work opportunities. Two years later, her mother returned to Brazil with Gláucia's two younger brothers, having separated from Gláucia's father. Gláucia's father soon decided to return to Brazil as well. Having forged her independence in the United States, Gláucia decided to remain on her own. In Brazil, she had suffered two assaults and never felt safe at home or on the streets. In the United States, she enjoyed walking at night and living on her own. She never anticipated, however, that her mother would suddenly fall ill, and that living far away in the United States, she would never have the opportunity to see her again.

For those with aging parents, remaining in the United States often provoked intense guilt. Many Brazilians had lived with their parents into adulthood and felt a deep obligation to care for them in old age. This duty came into direct conflict with migrants' personal desires—whether to stay for a time and ultimately return, or perhaps to settle in the United States indefinitely. Despite the challenges of living undocumented, Luiz explained that he felt more at home in the United States than in Brazil. Yet, he agonized about returning to Brazil, especially as his great aunt, the woman who had raised him, reached advanced age. Luiz had not seen her since leaving Brazil almost ten years ago. She was now an octogenarian with failing health, and he feared that he would never see her again. But, he was not yet prepared to give up his life in the United States.

Helplessness in the face of death became one of the many ways that migrants experienced the sensation of being stuck. Unable to work, travel, or pursue education freely, men and women also found themselves barred from the normal activities associated with loss. They could not travel to be with dying or sick loved ones, or grieve with siblings and parents, without jeopardizing their entire future and making a lasting decision prematurely. When Angela, whom I met at the Baptist church, found out that her twenty-eight-year-old younger sister had suddenly died from diabetic shock, she could not do what every fiber in her body urged her to do. Rather than book the next flight to Brazil to grieve with her mother and older sister, she resolved to stay in the United States, where she would face this devastation alone. Her salary earned from cleaning American homes had become indispensable to her mother's and sister's livelihoods in the poor community outside of Brasília where they lived, and so, she felt duty bound to stay.

Domestic Work

Without a car and living in the basement of her employer's house for seven years, Beatriz, a live-in domestic worker for a Brazilian family, shared that she felt like a prisoner. I soon learned that Beatriz's experience remained common, especially among migrant women, who noted the particular burden of spending ten-hour days confined to their employer's home as *empregadas domésticas* (domestic workers), cleaning, cooking, and babysitting. Most Brazilian women I met worked in homes throughout the DC metropolitan area. Some women, like Beatriz, had moved to the United States already employed as *domésticas* by Brazilian diplomats or employees of international organizations. Other women, like Neusa, had come with their own families or by themselves, and became "helpers" to friends and relatives before starting their own businesses. And, many others had come to the United States as au pairs, working as nannies in exchange for room, board, and an educational stipend. Despite varied trajectories, most *empregadas domésticas* expressed some level of exhaustion, loneliness, vulnerability, and exploitation due to their work.[10]

Fifty-eight years old at the time of our meeting, Beatriz came to the United States *por necessidade* in 2007 after losing her sewing shop in Salvador da Bahia and separating from her husband. She had no way to support her adult, yet struggling children, and so accepted a position with a Brazilian diplomatic family in Washington, DC. Beatriz told me that she did not leave the house for nonwork activities for the first four months she lived in the United States, and even thirteen years later, she left the house only once per week, on Sundays, when her friend would bring her to church. Despite working seven days per week, she received no paid vacation, sick days, or medical benefits.

Yet, Beatriz was emphatic that her situation was much better than many other *domésticas* she knew. As proof, she enumerated to me her employers' small kindnesses: stocking the refrigerator with foods she liked, inviting her to their son's graduation, driving her to appointments. Unlike many others, Beatriz had a work permit and was able to periodically visit Brazil. Beatriz explained, "I have liberty . . . the liberty to offer a coffee, to give you a juice. I have the liberty to open the refrigerator and eat what I want. I have this liberty." Yet, these words did not mask her awareness of what such meager "liberties" revealed—the dramatic shrinking of her daily existence. If it depended on her, she explained, she would have left long ago. Like most other migrants I met, however, she had not yet saved enough money to secure her family's livelihood in Brazil, so she stayed.

When we met in her small basement room, I couldn't help but feel Beatriz's confinement viscerally. The spacious brick row home above impressively displayed treasures from frequent trips abroad, while Beatriz slept on a pullout couch across from a large television and the washer-dryer. She filled her days with watching Brazilian programming while doing her employers' laundry and cooking their family meals. She cared for the home and the children while her employers were off *passeando* (traveling for leisure), and yet, had not seen her own children for many years. It became clear to me that her life and her time were not her own. When Beatriz's employer returned to the house with her teenage son late in the afternoon, she dropped off an enormous bag of laundry for Beatriz to wash, and left instructions for dinner in thirty minutes, a not-so-subtle encouragement that I be on my way.

Beatriz's identification of such basic activities as eating what one likes, and coming and going as one pleases, as "liberties" indicates the frequently exploitative and suffocating nature of the domestic services industry. In the United States and throughout the world, in-home services increasingly depend on the largely invisible and cheap labor of women migrants.[11] In this hidden "care economy," migrants fill the most intimate spaces in society, yet do so for little financial compensation or societal recognition.

Angela, a live-in *doméstica* in her early thirties, told me a *tragédia* was unfolding in the home where she had worked for the past three years, which she described as "the worst three years of my life." Angela's employer berated her constantly, only to turn around the next day, ask for forgiveness, and give her small presents. Once, the woman and her husband held Angela's passport and wages hostage because she refused to travel with them to Brazil for fear of forfeiting her temporary work permit. Another woman noted that her employers routinely laughed at her expense, savagely mimicking her accented English. Others revealed that employers and clients expected them to perform tasks far outside of their job descriptions. Refusing such requests meant risking losing one's job, or worse, one's precarious perch in the United States.

During our weekly English lessons, Neusa, my *igreja mãe*, often asked me to help her communicate with clients who sent her lengthy text messages in English. Usually, I helped her clear up minor misunderstandings about dates or times, but once, she shared an angry and demeaning outburst. Her client fumed, "I'm very disappointed in you, Neusa, because I already pay you so much money. Because of you, I missed my appointment." The woman was enraged, Neusa explained, because she had refused to babysit the woman's young son during an impromptu medical appointment. As I translated the message for her, Neusa bristled. "I'm not a babysitter!" she cried. "I run my own business!"

Scholarship has documented the psychological ramifications of migrant domestic labor and the intensive "emotional work" entailed in navigating such fraught, asymmetrical, yet intimate power relations.[12] Of migrant women in Lombardy, Italy, Andrea Muehlebach writes, "The immigrant, locked into a relationship that is invisible to the outside, hidden from public view, can hardly escape the claustrophobia of care."[13] In her writings on migrant domestic workers in Germany, Encarnación Rodríguez notes the relationship between the physical and political erasure of migrants from view, concluding, "The physical, societal and political invisibility linked to care and domestic work is a function of the character and the location of the work, as it is done in privacy and isolation."[14] The intense emotional work of caring for others combined with the spatial confinement described above produces concrete consequences. Migrant women like Beatriz, Angela, and Neusa, and so many others I met, found themselves shrinking, becoming invisible, and eventually "ghost-like."[15]

The Shock of the Cold

Brazilian migrants remarked that in contrast to the vibrancy, enmeshment, and warmth (*calor*) they associated with Brazilian social life, US culture prized busyness, work, and self-sufficiency. Those who came *por necessidade* like Neusa, Rubém, and Beatriz pragmatically reflected on the grave sacrifice they had made, and continued to make, to live in the United States. To pay off debts, support family members, survive as single parents, or simply begin anew, they had left the "warmth" of Brazilian street life, camaraderie, and festivity, in exchange for the "cold" security, monetary gain, and predictability of the United States. In this trade, migrants assumed what they considered to be deeply solitary existences. Most men and women I spoke with explained that they had little time or means to socialize. I learned that most migrants, regardless of employment and gender, experienced a similar dampening of self and withdrawal from social relationship associated with traditional domestic work.

Anderson, a single man in his early forties, shook his head in disgust as he shared with me his final judgment of life in the United States: "Aqui, ninguém depende em ninguém" (Here, no one depends on anyone). He struggled to get through each day on his own without any assistance, noting that because he had no wife or family nearby, he cooked and cleaned for himself. In Brazil, he had lived with his parents, and within walking distance to siblings, aunts and uncles, cousins, and friends. In Montgomery County, Maryland, he shared a small apartment with another unmarried middle-aged man and spent most of his time working in construction. I asked if they chatted at work. He shook his head "no," and muttered, "É trabalho" (It's work).

After hearing his palpable disdain for life in the United States, I wondered why Anderson had decided to come to the United States, and to stay for so long. "Por necessidade," he answered—financial necessity. Like Neusa's husband, Rubém, he had migrated from a rural community in Santa Catarina, where he found little opportunity for financial security. So, he followed the many other migrants from his region who had journeyed to the United States to save money. One year had turned into nine, and now he was stuck in a similar holding pattern. Should he risk returning home? Would he earn enough money?

Anderson's roommate, Luiz, another Brazilian migrant in his early forties, expressed similar concerns. Despite enjoying easier work as a masseur, he too remained frustrated with his prolonged solitude. When conversing before church services one Sunday, we chatted about travel, and about the many places he wanted to visit, like California, Florida, and Arizona. He arched his eyebrows resignedly, saying that unlike most migrants he knew, he had the time and even disposable income to travel, but no one would accompany him. His friends earmarked every penny they earned for an eventual return to Brazil and feared being apprehended by ICE if they traveled by plane. Brazilian migrants kept their heads down, Luiz told me, always saving and always working.

Felipe, Neusa's eldest son and an aspiring pastor, delivered a moving sermon one Thursday evening concerning the ceaselessness of migrant work. Felipe gave voice to migrants' pervasive sensation of being stuck. He began by reading Mark 8:22–25, describing Jesus's miraculous healing of a blind man by spitting in his eyes and laying hands on him. Felipe preached that many in the church currently lived as blind men, counting their steps to work, counting their steps home again, counting their money, without looking up to see the world around them. Felipe animated his sermon by embodying the grotesquely stooped and wandering blind man, groping in the dark, without lifting his head or opening his eyes.

Gabriela, a Spiritist in her late twenties, who had lived in the United States for nearly a decade, longingly recounted street scenes with friends and family getting together nightly in open-air restaurants and cafés after work. She noted that when in Brazil she was never really alone. Here, Gabriela observed, people worked all day and then wearily retreated to suburban neighborhoods and subdivisions separated by highways and sprawling shopping plazas. At the time of our interview, Gabriela was expecting her first child and lived with her American husband in a remote suburb far from the few close friends she had made in Baltimore. She expressed strong aversion to the farm where she currently lived, and the foreignness of her husband's American family. Conveying her acute unease, she remarked:

> The problem is that I *hate* this place. I need *people*. Brazilians, I think we are very [used to] touching and hugging and seeing each other, and my family

is very . . . it's huge. We are this bunch of women that gets together on Sundays, and on Sundays, you go to a market and you have a *pastel* [Brazilian pastry] and that's the best thing that can happen on Sundays. I miss that a lot. And his family, it's together too, but they're so formal. Because they [are] rich, and [so] they have [a set] time to eat, they have [a set] time to do things. You have to call, you cannot say certain things, or do certain things.

When Gabriela married a year earlier, none of her family or friends from Brazil attended because they could not secure tourist visas. When I asked her how she had felt during her wedding, she responded immediately and unequivocally, "I was very upset that day. I was very upset. Because there was nobody. There was no family. *None* of my family."

Many migrants described social life in the United States and the shock of winter weather by invoking the same word with great emphasis: *frio* (cold). Brazil was *hot* and the United States was *cold*. Migrants repeatedly told me that in Brazil, people befriended strangers reflexively, even at bus stops, and then immediately invited them to intimate family gatherings. When visiting someone for the first time, I was always greeted with "Fica à vontade!" (You're welcome! Make yourself at home!), and casually invited to stay for dinner, and then late into the night. A meeting set for 5 p.m. would have no reliable end time, but rather would carry on until I abruptly announced my departure. I never became accustomed to this practice, plotting my exit when I became tired or apprehensive about the late drive home. Yet, in my awareness of time and fatigue of social interaction, my "American-ness" was all too evident.

In the United States, Brazilians found that it was much more difficult to make friends or truly trust others. If you knocked on a stranger's door, people responded with suspicion. If you tried to chat with someone on the street, strangers turned their backs and averted their eyes. Because of this perception of US frigidity, evangelical pastors subtly lowered their parishioners' expectations for US-based proselytizing. During a sermon, an Adventist pastor commented on his strained relationship with his American neighbors. Would he knock on their door randomly to evangelize, as he would do in Brazil? Of course not! Here in the United States, he instructed, you must evangelize through personal relationships. He underlined this message by telling horror stories about his hostile neighbors: they had accused him of animal neglect and sent the police to his home twice; they had returned his smiles and greetings with overt disdain; they had left him aggressive notes over petty things like parking. Here, he implied, Americans prized privacy over sociality, work over leisure, and decorum over friendship.

Because of the cultural obsession with work and money, Brazilian migrants charged that the United States lacked *o calor humano*—human warmth. "In America, everything becomes about money, even those things that should *never* be about money," Marina, a Spiritist, warned. When I pressed her further, she asked me to turn off the recorder and continued, her face flushed with emotion. An unmarried woman in her late thirties, she had recently decided to adopt a child. When she called US adoption agencies, the first questions she encountered concerned money and employment. She learned that she would have to endure three months of "observation" before qualifying as a suitable parent. As she recalled this experience, she conveyed profound upset, humiliation, and revulsion. When she later called an agency in Brazil, she reported immediately feeling at home. The Brazilian woman on the other end of the line, she told me, spoke about the child in need, never once introducing the subject of money. When considering whether or not she would stay in the United States to raise her future son or daughter, Marina worried that any child she raised in the United States would be corrupted by money, materialism, and a lack of human concern.

Liminality, Isolation, and Mutual Distrust

On my first visit to Neusa's apartment, she took out her iPhone and proudly scrolled through several photographs of her and her husband's beachfront home in Brazil—a large, modern, white-washed structure two blocks from the ocean in Santa Catarina. The new construction, their eventual retirement home, glistened in the sun. Next time I traveled to Brazil, she insisted, I would have to come and stay with her there. Given the whir of rush-hour traffic from her small basement apartment of Building 500 at Appletree Condominiums, the discrepancy between her current and longed-for circumstances remained stark. Perhaps sensing my confusion, she reassured me with a gentle pat on my knee and a broad smile, "We'll go back this year. It's almost finished!"

———

In evaluating all they had left behind in Brazil, and considering the "human warmth" of Brazil in contrast to the "coldness" of the United States, many migrants frequently considered return, telling me during interviews or in casual conversations with friends that they planned to leave next year, or the following year, or perhaps sooner. When I encountered the prevalence of this explicit planning, it seemed as if the entire population of Brazilian migrants might suddenly disappear within eighteen months. And yet, by the end of my research period, only two Brazilians I met had actually left, and many more had arrived. When I followed up with others to inquire about the plans they had detailed earlier, they pushed their estimated departures off by another year or two, or they cited newfound hopes of obtaining legal documents in the United States—or intensified fears about circumstances in Brazil.

The prevalence of talk of return underscored to me the precariousness Brazilian migrants felt. Always reflecting on when and if to permanently leave the United States for Brazil, few migrants truly viewed themselves *as* immigrants, placing themselves in a liminal category of neither here nor there. When I initially described my research as a study of religion among Brazilian "immigrants," individuals often rejected such a label with playful sarcasm, joking, "Não sou imigrante não. Sou turista!" (I'm not an immigrant at all. I'm a tourist!). Yet, most Brazilians I spoke with had lived in the United States for almost a decade or more. The uncertain nature of their status in the United States, and the very real possibility of return they maintained, added to many Brazilian migrants' acute experience of distress. The United States did not feel like home to most of the migrants I met, but when they reflected on returning to Brazil, many worried that there, too, would strike them as foreign.

Homeless

Unlike many groups of Latin American migrants in the United States, particularly those in the Greater DC region, Brazilians maintained the very real possibility of return. While migrants from El Salvador and Guatemala fled from civil war and acute violence throughout the 1980s, thus relinquishing any hope of return, Brazilian migrants pursued short-term wealth accumulation, often planning to return to Brazil within a few years at most.[16] For this reason, ethnographers who have studied Brazilians in the United States have often referred to this population as "sojourners" rather than "settlers."[17] In keeping with this finding, most migrants I met asserted their intention to return to Brazil within six months to a year of arrival. Yet, they had stayed. Migrants found partners, raised families, supported their Brazilian kin in both countries with US dollars. With every passing year, their lives became more embedded in the United States, making an actual return more challenging and consequential.

Brazilians living in the US wagered whether they and their families would be better off in Brazil or the United States.[18] In such deliberations, migrants weighed the importance of economic and physical security, associated with the United States, against improved quality of life and emotional well-being, associated with Brazil. Should they trade relative safety and certain income in the United States for renewed belonging and human warmth in Brazil? Neither the United States nor Brazil represented an unadulterated "home," embodying what Fran Markowitz defines as a "safe, divinely-sanctioned and life-giving place," for Brazilian migrants. Rather, both countries incorporated elements of "home" and the "antihome"—an "alien, satanic and life-threatening space."[19] Caught between the unsavory realities of home and antihome in both Brazil and the United States, Brazilian migrants again sensed the acuteness of their paralysis, of being stuck.

One migrant articulated this daily deliberation in response to my survey question asking if he considered his experience in the United States to be mostly positive or negative. He wrote:

> It's like a grand avenue running in two directions (*gran avenida de dois sentidos*). It has a good side and a terrible side. We have to weigh things to see what weighs more, or rather, where it is most worthwhile (*vale a pena*) to live in every aspect, not just one. Today it is better for me here in the United States.

Another migrant gave voice to the specific considerations she, and many others like her, evaluated when deciding whether to stay in the United States or return to Brazil:

> In terms of the quality of life, it's positive, because the United States has much better infrastructure than Brazil. The houses are better, the cars are better and less expensive, the roads, the schools, education. But when you arrive here and you don't know anyone, you don't speak the language correctly, and the worst, you don't have a work permit, and you have to subject yourself to more inferior work than you did in Brazil, it's very negative.

The constant deliberation was symptomatic of, and contributed to, migrants' overwhelming feeling of being stuck. Not only were migrants constrained by employment, geography, language, and separation from loved ones, but they also found themselves prisoners of economic booms and busts and ever-shifting political horizons in two countries.

Talk of Return

While the Brazilian population in Greater Washington, DC, climbed throughout the early 2000s, experts and migrants alike witnessed a dramatic exodus in 2008 when the US economy collapsed, and Brazil's economy skyrocketed. Men who worked in the construction industry suddenly found themselves without work during the American *crise* and newly dependent on their women partners or relatives for stability. While no one at the Brazilian consulate in Washington, DC, knew the exact number of Brazilians who left in or after 2008, the staff emphasized that the population decline had been sudden and dramatic. With the slowing of the Brazilian economy after 2008, and the recovery of the US economy, the flight of Brazilians from the United States ebbed, and more Brazilians arrived. The massive flight of migrants after the *crise*, and their subsequent reentry into Brazilian society, became a key concern for Brazilian migrants who remained in the United States.

In considering return, migrants frequently spoke about increasing violence and economic sluggishness in Brazil. Migrants' reflections on these subjects approximated what Teresa Caldeira describes as the "talk of crime" in her study of violence and insecurity in São Paulo.[20] She describes such talk as "contagious" and considers how obsessive everyday ruminations on insecurity reinforced residents' "feelings of danger, insecurity and turmoil."[21] By endlessly circulating stories of insecurity in Brazil, both personal and financial, migrants amplified these feelings in one another, and thereby encouraged one another to *ficar*, to stay put. Migrants told each other daily about carjackings, drug-trafficking, kidnappings, robberies, and murders, as well as failed businesses, low wages, unemployment, and exorbitant prices.

Every time documented church members traveled to Brazil, or whenever visiting family members returned, clergy prayed to keep them safe from violence and crime. When Juliana, the Pentecostal pastor's wife, anticipated her own travel, she prayed over her suitcases, asking God to deliver them untouched to her destination. Other migrants commented that they would love to visit Brazil multiple times a year but could no longer live there. They had already become accustomed to life in the United States where "things functioned" (*coisas funcionam*) and laws were enforced.

Luana, Neusa's twenty-three-year-old daughter-in-law, was apprehensive about visiting Brazil for the first time in eight years. Brought to Brazil by her parents at age three, she had subsequently received legal status under her father's employer-sponsored green card, and then his eventual citizenship. Her freedom to travel was rare among Brazilian migrants in Montgomery County, and especially so among her husband's family. Luana's itinerary included a trip to the interior state of Minas Gerais to visit with her family, as well as to the city of Criciúma in Santa Catarina, where she would meet Vanessa, her sister-in-law, in person for the first time.

After hearing stories of increased crime in Belo Horizonte, the capital of her home state, Luana feared traveling there alone with her three-year-old daughter, Graça. As she prepared to go, other women shared stern warnings: "Don't wear big jewelry or makeup," "Leave your purse at home," "Wear jeans and flip-flops," "Don't tell anyone you live in America." When I spoke to Luana upon her return, she told me that after a few days, she had been ready to return to her home in Maryland. Everything was dirtier than she remembered, she explained, and she missed the comforts of American life. Overhearing our conversation, Juliana, the pastor's wife, joked, "Isn't it a miracle when *anyone* returns from Brazil unscathed?"

Migrants also circulated stories of migrant returnees who faced economic precariousness upon reentering Brazil. Neusa told me about her sister who had returned in 2008, thinking she would find work and enjoy newfound leisure time with her family. Instead, her sister continued to *lutar* (struggle). Too many Brazilians, people frequently commented, had left the United States, imagining days spent on beaches with friends and grandchildren, only to find that they did not have enough money, that there was little work, that violence was rising, and that the economy was slowing. All returnees, I heard from migrants, eventually arrived at *arrependimento*. Regret.

Despite such vocal fears, most migrants I interviewed and surveyed still planned to return to Brazil. Sixty-four percent of survey respondents answered that they intended to return to Brazil at some point in the future.[22] These plans structured daily habits among the migrants I knew: individuals spent frugally, maximized their earnings by working nights and weekends, and invested in a postmigrant life in Brazil. Like Neusa and Rubém, many migrants built beachside homes in their rural hometowns, bought businesses for their children, and sent comparatively inexpensive electronics to friends and relatives at home.[23] The talk of return revealed migrants' anxiety at being stuck between two countries, planning for a life in Brazil yet never quite certain when to forgo the predictability of the United States, or what might meet them upon their return.

Institutions catering to Brazilian migrants heavily contributed to and reflected the talk of return, including the Brazilian consulate in Washington, DC, and migrant newspapers. The consulate, for example, hosted an event meant to address the challenges returnees faced reentering Brazil. During this meeting, consular employees asserted that the number of Brazilians living outside of Brazil had fallen by 20 percent between 2011 and 2013, dropping from 3.1 million to 2.5 million.[24] Most of these returnees came from the United States. In discussing the challenges facing returnees, those in attendance remarked on the vulnerability of migrants who returned without work, resources, or concrete plans. The objective of the meeting was ostensibly to determine how to better prepare Brazilian migrants who planned to return.

The panel made clear that they were not concerned about elite Brazilians who returned to certain employment and security. Rather, they targeted their efforts on undocumented migrants, whom they portrayed as failing to acquire "concrete skills" and "education" while abroad. Members of the council lamented that after spending their years in the United States working in manual labor, most migrants had failed to accrue English-language proficiency that they could leverage back home. Nelson, the deputy to the consul general, summarized this sweeping evaluation. Such migrants returned to Brazil, he concluded, "completamente vulneráveis" (completely vulnerable). It was unsurprising, then, he noted, that so many migrants came to regret their decision to return.

Pastor João, an eminent Adventist leader, explained that in his decades-long work with Brazilian migrants, he had learned that most returnees came to regret their decision. When they thought of return, he asserted, they imagined warm reunions with friends and loved ones, and immersing themselves in their own language and culture. Yet, their business ventures often failed, and they learned how difficult it was to maintain the same quality of life in Brazil that they had enjoyed in the United States, including, for instance, greater purchasing power with lower wages and a higher degree of safety and security. After a year or less, Pastor João asserted, returnees frequently wanted to return to the United States. Having previously overstayed tourist visas, however, migrants could no longer obtain legal travel documents. If they wanted to return, they would have to falsify papers or cross the Mexican border. Pastor João shook his head and quietly muttered, "I'm so tired of getting these kinds of calls."

AcheiUSA, a popular Brazilian migrant newspaper published in Florida and circulated throughout Brazilian migrant communities in the United States, also reflected this preoccupation with returnee regret. In 2013, the publication ran a three-part series considering the plight of migrants from Governador Valadares, one of the central Brazilian hubs of out-migration to the United States. In the first article, the newspaper interviewed Sueli Siqueira, a prominent Brazilian sociologist of migration. In evaluating the personal and collective costs of migration, Siqueira emphasized return migrants' inability to adapt to Brazil. The ambivalence they felt in the United States, and their years-long desire to return to the familiarity of friends, family, and culture, culminated in grave disappointment. They confronted continued frustration, disillusionment, and anomie, except this time back home in Brazil. Siqueira commented:

> [The return immigrant] arrives here with back problems, panic syndrome, etc. The culture of emigration is perverse, because there is a high valuation of the exterior, and a devaluation of the interior. [The returnees] find every-thing very dirty, everything hot, they find the leaves on the ground here dirty, and those of the exterior a natural beauty. This is the culture of emigration: even their trash is more beautiful than ours, and even their poor are more beautiful than ours here. And then, when [the immigrant] returns, five, ten, or fifteen years later, he wants to return to the place and the time of when he left. And the worst of all is that many times he returns without speaking English, and without any qualifications for the job market. He perceives that everything changed, his wife, children, family, city. There are people who cannot adapt. It's called a crisis of not feeling like one belongs anywhere.[25]

Such widely publicized fears concerning returnee experience contributed to migrant anxiety and overwhelming liminality. As they faced unending work, and long-term separation from family members, they commonly dreamed of return to Brazil. In such moments, however, migrants reminded each other of the deep regret, *arrependimento*, they would likely face upon return.

What Community?

After introducing my research and explaining my intention to learn about the lives of Brazilians in the region, I often began conversations by asking migrants if they believed that a Brazilian "community" *(comunidade)* existed in Greater

Washington, DC. I used this word cautiously, learning from previous ethnographic studies of Brazilians living in Boston and New York City that Brazilians
in the United States remained notoriously "disunited." Ethnographers in multiple studies had documented the ways in which Brazilians themselves rejected
the idea of community, and often expressed ambivalence toward other Brazilians in the United States.[26] Upon asking this question, I found a similar trend.
Migrants rejected the idea of solidarity or community, and cited competition,
suspicion, and socioeconomic class as factors that created fragmentation
among Brazilians. I learned that migrants' perceptions of disunity and mutual
distrust among Brazilians exacerbated their felt isolation.

Maria, who had lived in the United States for over fourteen years, reflected
on the absence of Brazilian solidarity. She noted, "No one has anything in
common. Everyone is completely divided." Like many migrants with whom I
spoke, she expressed her sense of the relative disunity of the Brazilian
population by reference to the much larger, comparatively more organized
Latinx population in the region. Many Brazilians expressed envy of the
apparent solidarity and organization of Spanish-speaking migrants, whom
they viewed as politically active and engaged, with their own institutions,
advocacy groups, and community leaders.

Brazilian migrants often shared stories of exploitation at the hands of
relatives and friends after arriving in the United States. Neusa and her eldest
son, Felipe, told me about their mistreatment by Rubém's brother in Virginia.
Without documents, English fluency, or money, they lived with him and
worked for little money. The man scared them so thoroughly regarding the
police and possible deportation that they rarely left the house. Grácia, a devout
Catholic I met in Baltimore, had come to the United States at the insistence
of her uncle, who had promised to help launch her art career. Instead, when
she arrived, he demanded that she compensate him for her travel costs by
cleaning his home indefinitely. Anderson moved to Maryland with the promise
of exceedingly high wages in his cousin's construction company. When he
arrived, his cousin paid him a fraction of what he had promised and charged
him rent to stay at his home. Stories like these abound in my notes. Because
of such frequent mistreatment at the hands of their compatriots, migrants
often preferred to work for American or Latinx employers.

During lunch one Sunday afternoon, Débora and her friend Miriene,
middle-aged women who worked as *domésticas*, compared their experiences
with their respective Brazilian and American employers. Débora asserted that
her Brazilian employers treated her "como uma escrava" (like a slave). They
made fun of her English, laughed when she made grammatical mistakes in

Portuguese, and refused to compensate her for sick time or vacation. They paid her $9 per hour to cook, clean, and care for their young daughter from 6 a.m. until 6 p.m. During our lunch, as it began to snow heavily outside and the radio announced school closures, Débora sighed. Despite the treacherous conditions, she would still be expected to arrive at her employer's house at 6 a.m. Miriene, in contrast, loved the American family for whom she worked and with whom she lived. They paid for her health insurance, provided her with $5,000 to buy a new car, and treated her like "a member of their family." Extrapolating from their individual experiences, Miriene asserted that, as a rule, she stayed away from Brazilians in the United States because they often "hated other Brazilians."

Débora's and Miriene's reflections concerning their employers revealed another root cause of division among Brazilians: the socioeconomic divide between highly educated, white-collar, and documented migrants and those arriving without documents and with few educational, financial, or social resources. Those migrants who moved to the United States in pursuit of higher education or prestigious work opportunities often had limited social interaction or contact with undocumented migrants living in Montgomery County. The Brazilian diplomats, bankers, and academics I interviewed generally lived in large homes in the wealthier suburbs surrounding Washington, DC, such as Alexandria and Arlington in Virginia, or Bethesda, Kensington, and Chevy Chase in Maryland. They spoke English fluently, had advanced degrees from prestigious Brazilian and US universities, held green cards or US citizenship, had often married American citizens, and viewed themselves to be largely assimilated to US society. Some of these individuals seemed generally unaware of the large population of undocumented Brazilian migrants living in Montgomery County, despite employing these very same individuals as domestic workers, manicurists, hair stylists, or landscapers.

Perhaps most representative of this massive disconnect between socioeconomic classes were the sporadic events organized by the Brazilian consulate in Washington, DC, explicitly meant to address migrant needs and offer assistance, such as the event geared toward return migrants described above. While most meetings were open to the public, they were announced only a few days in advance, and were held at 5 p.m. on a weekday in downtown Washington, DC, making it logistically impossible for most Brazilian migrants to attend. The usual attendees were five members of the Conselho de Cidadãos (Citizens' Council), exclusively made up of well-off, documented, and professional Brazilians. Aside from these representatives, the consul general, his staff, and I were in attendance. The much larger community of undocumented

Brazilians in Montgomery County remained absent, and often without knowledge of the events' happenings.

During another meeting in December 2013, one of the council members addressed this glaring absence. Pastor Márcio, a prominent Baptist leader, had invited one of his congregants, Jorge, to speak to the experiences of undocumented migrants like him. While everyone else in attendance wore casual attire, Jorge sported a black pin-striped suit and thick gold watch, calling attention to his difference. He had a serious demeanor as he was introduced to the small group of diplomats, researchers, and entrepreneurs. He addressed the consul general, his staff, and the members of the council deferentially, thanking them for allowing him to attend. He then shared an account of his life in the United States.

Jorge had lived for twelve years in Montgomery County, where he had opened a cleaning business and supported his wife and three children. While paying taxes yearly, and obeying the law scrupulously, he asserted, he "struggled for everything." To rent an apartment, buy a home, pay college tuition, or access health insurance, undocumented migrants faced exorbitant fees, he noted. The consul general suddenly interrupted Jorge, suggesting in a calm but pedantic tone that such higher fees were unavoidable, for they protected companies from the higher risks they assumed by dealing with undocumented migrants. The consul general continued in no uncertain terms, sharply cutting off Jorge's testimony. The consulate simply would not be able to help with "these kinds of issues."

Confronted with such open dismissal, Jorge momentarily lost his composure. He boldly challenged the consul general, raising his voice and asking pointedly, "*Who* represents the vast majority of the Brazilian population? *I do!*" In return for his impassioned statement, Pastor Márcio proposed adding Jorge to the council, to "better represent" the needs of undocumented migrants. Jorge accepted this small gesture. Yet, at the next meeting I attended, he was conspicuously absent, and business proceeded as usual.

The Affective Imprint of Migrant Distress

The accounts of diffuse and generalized distress I heard from migrants struck me as similar to critical theorists' employment of the term *affect* to describe profound but elusive feeling states. The term *affect*, theorists have asserted, describes raw feeling, a kind of "intensity,"[27] "trace," and "force"[28] that impresses itself on the body and mind, instead of culturally intelligible and fully formed emotions, like anger, joy, or sadness. These scholarly understandings of affect assert that living in the world becomes "inscribed on our nervous system and in our flesh before it appears on our consciousness."[29]

Diffuse feelings like loneliness, depression, and anxiety, therefore, cannot be understood solely as individual pathologies or feelings, but rather as the affective imprint of specific structural arrangements, such as neoliberalism, the retreat of social welfare, and entrenched inequality. While these affective experiences approximate widespread "public feelings"[30] that scholars have long identified as endemic to, and proliferating in, neoliberal societies, the intensity and frequency of such affects remain particularly acute for migrants, who endure greater precariousness and have fewer avenues for relief.[31] Migrant experience in the United States, marked by family separation, workplace exploitation, American "coldness," the talk of return, and mutual distrust, literally impressed itself on the bodies and minds of the individuals I met, leaving them with feelings of depression, worry, loneliness, and an overwhelming sense of being stuck.

There is growing evidence to support this finding in interdisciplinary studies of mental health risks among migrants. One study found, for instance, that Mexican migrants in the United States faced an elevated risk for anxiety and depression when compared to their nonmigrant family members who remained in Mexico.[32] In a national study, the Centers for Disease Control and Prevention (CDC) found that migrant youth were much more likely "to feel sad or hopeless (36.3 percent), to seriously consider suicide (15.9 percent), and to attempt suicide (10.9 percent)" than their white and Black American peers. The report further concluded that 7 percent of 281 respondents met diagnostic criteria for depression, while 29 percent of respondents met criteria for anxiety—higher incidences than found among the general population.[33] A study of migrant youth outlined the pervasive "virus of fear and mistrust" migrants experienced in the context of increased deportations from the US, where 2 million people were deported between 2008 and 2016. Such fears, the report concludes, restrict the ordinary movements of migrants, and lead to "internalized self-monitoring." The effects of such internalization are magnified, the report argues, due to undocumented migrants' limited ability to access physical or mental health care.[34] Below, I summarize the key markers of what I came to understand as this affective imprint of migrant distress.

Bodily Betrayal

In recounting their lives in the United States, most migrants reflected on the onset or intensification of bodily suffering soon after arrival. In the first months and years away from Brazil, individuals experienced fluctuations in weight, disordered eating, insomnia, fatigue, chronic pain, and illness. For some migrants, such symptoms resurfaced and intensified in the United States after abating in Brazil. For others, bodily distress emerged for the first time due to the physical and emotional toll of migrant life.

Beatriz recalled that she lost forty-five pounds in the first two months of work as a live-in *doméstica* for Brazilian diplomats. It wasn't that her employers mistreated her, she insisted; rather, she felt so strange and out of place that eating in their presence literally caused her shame. She explained:

> For the first month I was here, I basically didn't eat . . . when I arrived, [my employer] told me, "Only make a little food so that the children don't get fat." So after I put the food I made on the table, there wasn't anything left for me to eat. I would drink water when I was hungry, for a whole month.

Then, Beatriz fell ill with a severe urinary tract infection, confining her to bed for fifteen days, where she became further diminished. The seriousness of her condition, however, improved relations with her employer. The woman's sister was a doctor and announced to the household, "No. She has to eat the moment she's hungry."

Another migrant, Laura, remarked on the troubling resurgence of bulimia after she migrated. Having recovered from the disease under the supervision of a psychiatrist in Brazil, she found herself in its grips once again upon arrival in the United States. She vomited so much that she began to spew blood, stoking her mother's fears of irrevocable bodily harm. Other migrants I met remarked on rapid weight gain in the United States, where they spent more time in cars and buses, ate heavier and saltier food, and exercised little. Cleiton, a recent arrival from Brazil, often carried a bottle of water with him to social engagements, pronouncing that he was on a "water fast." He had gained fifteen pounds in the six months since his arrival.

In addition to dietary problems and weight fluctuations, migrants bore the bodily consequences of the kind of labor they performed. Men appeared leathery, sunned, hardened, and aged due to constant weather exposure on construction sites. When I sat with Neusa and Rubém one evening at their home, she gingerly touched his cheeks and worried aloud about his battered skin. He playfully deflected her hand, insisting the redness was from the wind and would soon disappear. It was November, and he had been working most of the day inside. Much better, he assured his wife and me, than working outside in the summer heat. Besides sunburn and frostbite, Rubém hated the long drives all over DC, Maryland, and Virginia to get to job sites. As a young man, he said, he could tolerate the demanding physical work and long hours. But at the age of fifty-three, he felt utterly exhausted. The almost twenty years of migrant labor showed on his face. Sitting across from him, I had assumed he was in his midsixties. His hair was completely white, and his eyes squinted under a creased, furrowed brow.

In addition to fatigue, chronic pain, and sunburn, men like Rubém risked work-site injuries to every part of their bodies. Mateo, a painter in his fifties from Minas Gerais, became emotional as he recounted a horrific workplace injury that had happened almost a decade earlier. While painting the second-floor walls of a large home in Potomac, Maryland, Mateo fell off his ladder, mangling his foot. When the owner of the home saw the splashed paint on the home's stone floors, he became enraged, instructing Mateo to clean up the paint immediately. As he choked back tears, Mateo recalled:

> It still upsets me to talk about this. I remember that I felt the foot swelling, and as I descended the ladder, I couldn't steady it (*não firmava direito*). I took off my boot, and saw it there, swelling. But, then I went to work until lunch.

His boss soon arrived and surveyed the situation. He didn't speak to Mateo, who sat alone in excruciating pain. Instead, he spoke quietly to another Brazilian worker, saying, "Take him to the hospital, but don't tell anyone that he works for me." Overhearing this exchange, Mateo felt a new wound open. "I felt like a dog," he recalled. Despite having no health insurance and receiving no financial assistance from his company, Mateo went to the hospital. Although he was supposed to stay off the foot for one month, he couldn't subsist without work. Soon he went back to the same company in a cast, working a few hours a day through excruciating pain to pay his medical bills and cover his rent.

Despair and Feeling Stuck

While many migrants reported bodily pain and injury, others recalled more generalized feelings of depression and anxiety. They could not get out of bed in the morning; their chests, heads, and stomachs hurt under the burden of worry, loneliness, and doubt; they became listless, hopeless, and at times suicidal. Ultimately, such pain and suffering drove many to seek relief from psychological, medical, and spiritual services. Some migrants experimented with antidepressants, sleep aids, and antianxiety medication with varying degrees of relief.

Paula came to Maryland with her younger brother, Nico, when she was twenty-three years old to reunite with their mother, Maria. Divorced and desperate to provide for her teenage children, Maria had migrated to the United States five years earlier. The pain of being separated for years had been excruciating. Despite their joy at being reunited, however, Paula and Nico found life in the United States to be unbearable.

After only a few years, Nico returned to Brazil, unwilling to endure the grueling and unending demands of all-season construction work. Paula decided to stay but struggled. The high school degree she had earned in Brazil would not transfer to the US educational system, and she had dropped out of her program in cosmetology in Brazil to migrate. As she navigated American life without documents and little English, Paula found her opportunities drastically limited. She arranged part-time work as a manicurist but paid the lion's share of her wages to her boss.

Recounting this time, Paula explained that she increasingly found it difficult to get out of bed in the morning, and felt depressed, fatigued, and apathetic for the first time in her life. Experiencing what she described as a great emptiness (*vazio*), Paula told me that she searched for ways to "fill herself up" (*preencher-se*). She drank, used drugs, and threw parties. During the midnight hours, she surrounded herself with *amigos da festa* (party friends) and moved in a dream-like haze. But when she awoke in the morning, she again succumbed to the crushing weight of feeling utterly alone. Paula detailed this cycle:

> You drink and do drugs, and then what happens? The next day, you are stressed out, depressed, alone, you don't have a single friend, because your money ran out having spent it on everything, the drinks ran out, your happiness ran out, and you wake up without happiness, depressed, and sad with the urge to simply cry. . . . This emptiness, this sadness consumed me from deep in my soul.

Paula became so distraught that her mother admitted her to a hospital where she was treated for depression. She was prescribed antidepressants and sleep aids. When her suffering did not cease following medical treatment and release, Paula decided "to put a final punctuation mark on [her] life," resolving to die by suicide. Recalling this moment, she explained, "When I had been [in the United States] for one year, I went crazy (*fiquei doida*). Depression. I thought to myself, if I take a mountain of sleeping pills, I'll go to sleep and never wake up." Paula's description of apathy, depression, suffering, and brushes with death reverberated throughout many migrant narratives.

Daniela, a twenty-nine-year-old woman who funded her education by cleaning cars, repeated the same phrase, switching from Portuguese to English, several times in our conversation: "I feel *stuck*. I don't want to be stuck anymore." Daniela went to school full-time and then worked nights. She returned home at 9 p.m. and then studied until 3 a.m. She sacrificed sleep, friendship, and sanity, and yet remained unsure of the benefit. All around her, she witnessed Brazilian migrants stuck in the same jobs they had vowed to quit after saving enough money. The problem was, she realized, they *never* saved enough. Even migrants who had received their green cards, like her boyfriend's parents, failed to move on from thankless, low-paying manual labor. She shook her head and repeated another familiar phrase, "It's just not worth it" (Não vale a pena).

Alícia, a woman in her midthirties, reported a week-long hospitalization for psychological distress in her first years in the United States. She had worked as an au pair for two difficult families and ultimately left, eking out a precarious existence without documents or employment. In Brazil, she explained, she had a very easy life as the daughter of a prominent car executive. She had traveled to England to study English and attended university in São Paulo. Yet, "in this country," she told me, "I began to suffer." Recounting her worst episodes of distress, Alícia vividly described her panic attacks, night terrors, anxiety, and depression. She recalled, "I didn't have money, I suffered, no one helped me. I suffered a very intense depression, I became skinny, I lost a lot of weight, I was debilitated physically. The panic was very strong. And one day, I went to the doctor, and he said to me, 'Look, if you don't take care of yourself, you're going to die.'"

Anxiety and Becoming Bitter

Along with bodily distress, depression and feeling stuck, many migrants reported that their lives in the US had generated debilitating worry. Extended work hours, long commutes, financial pressure from family in both Brazil and the United States, separation from loved ones, and the tenuousness of living undocumented contributed to overwhelm and dread. The discrepancy between what they had expected in the United States, or others had expected them to achieve, and the reality of their daily, persistent struggles provoked feelings of resentment, regret, and bitterness.

During my conversation with Mirtes and her partner, Leandro, whom I had met at a Catholic prayer group, Mirtes revealed that she had recently been prescribed antianxiety medication. Apart from supporting multiple family members in Brazil, kin she described to me as very poor, she also worried about providing adequately for her nine-year-old son, José. She wanted to shield him from the kind of manual labor she and other undocumented migrants performed, so she pushed him to excel academically. Although Mirtes currently lived with Leandro, she had separated from José's father soon after her son was born, raising him for most of his life on her own.

The loneliness Mirtes felt exacerbated her anxiety. Cleaning homes for a living, Mirtes spent ten-hour days on her own, relying on her blue-tooth earpiece to remain socially connected to friends in both Brazil and the United States. Without this device, she said, she would go crazy, spending all day alone and silent. She joked darkly that she was so reliant on this electronic appendage that Leandro and José often had to remind her to remove it before showering. Once, when she forgot, she even shampooed her hair with the earpiece on. While she recounted this story with levity, it punctuated the absence of opportunities for social contact in her life and in the lives of many migrants like her. Mirtes noted that her anxiety, though nascent in Brazil, had intensified dramatically in the United States. Her doctors had recently prescribed anti-anxiety medication, which had contributed the added stress of unwanted weight gain, sixty pounds in the last year. Now, her doctor wanted to prescribe additional medication for ADHD, which she refused.

Mirtes also told me that she often felt lied to and manipulated by relatives she supported in Brazil. With anger flushing her cheeks, she explained that her own mother had fabricated a cancer diagnosis to compel her daughter to send additional funds. She shouldered a "double responsibility" (*responsabilidade dupla*) to keep her family afloat in both Brazil and the United States. Yet, her family was blind to her sacrifice, and assumed that everyone in the United States was rich. After relenting to her mother's request, and sending additional money, Mirtes discovered photos of her nieces and nephews sporting expensive clothing at an upscale Brazilian barbecue. As she detailed this perceived betrayal, she struggled to remain composed. She told me that the greatest thing she had lost when moving to the United States was closeness with her family. When I asked if she ever considered returning to Brazil, Mirtes explained that return was no longer thinkable. She could never face her mother or siblings again after feeling so used.

For each of the migrants described above, the conditions of life in the United States left a visible mark on their bodies and minds, an affective imprint of distress. Often confined in homes as domestic workers, or on the streets as manual laborers, migrants endured the specific maladies described above: weight fluctuations, eating disorders, sleep disruption, workplace injuries, despair, depression, anxiety, loneliness, and oftentimes, bitterness. Migrants like Beatriz, Paula, Alícia, and Mirtes often sought treatment from physicians, taking antidepressants and antianxiety medication, or even admitted themselves to hospitals for prolonged treatment. Yet, such treatment failed to allay the smarting wounds of migrant life.

The Turn Toward God

I took the pills, and God did not permit me to die. I was in agony, but my brain worked, my mind worked, and I was there. God permitted these things in my life so that I could carry this message and today testify that I was truly proof that God transforms, God liberates, and God is love.

—PAULA, 32, PENTECOSTAL

Four years after her suicide attempt, having fully committed to her Pentecostal faith and congregation, Paula was by her own estimation, and the estimation of her friends and loved ones, thriving as a *mulher de Deus* (woman of God). She had given up drinking, drugs, smoking, parties, and her *amigos da festa* (partying friends). She no longer wore jeans, highlighted her hair, or bared her legs or shoulders in public. She attended church multiple times per week and volunteered in various ministries. She had married a young man from church, also a Brazilian migrant, and they had just welcomed their first child after suffering two miscarriages. Now the image of righteousness and triumph, Paula offered her testimony frequently, encouraging other migrants to remain faithful despite their own struggles.

At the conclusion of an intimate Saturday prayer meeting toward the end of my fieldwork, I witnessed the powerful admiration Paula's story elicited from other women. When Juliana, the pastor's wife, invited each woman to offer testimony, Neide, a middle-aged woman who had recently begun to attend church, ventured to speak publicly for the first time. She looked at Paula and exclaimed at the beauty of her life. Paula had truly become a *mulher de Deus*, Neide commented, and she prayed fervently that her own niece who struggled with the same "demons" of Paula's past (alcohol, drugs, depression, suicidal thoughts) would similarly find liberation through God's salvation. She marveled at Paula's beautiful daughter and faithful husband, exclaiming how Paula radiated happiness and righteousness. Wiping away tears, Paula reminded the group how much she had struggled, and how much she had needed liberation.[35]

In the sections above, I describe the context in which Brazilians experienced profound psychic and bodily distress as migrants in the United States. Family separation, exploitative work, and American coldness contributed to overwhelming feelings of loneliness, depression, anxiety, and "being stuck" among Brazilians. While such experiences likely afflict many migrants, especially those without documents, I suggest that the talk of return, community fragmentation, and mutual distrust due to socioeconomic stratification exacerbated such maladies among Brazilians, culminating in a recognizable and pervasive imprint of migrant distress.

I learned that this imprint, marked by bodily suffering, generalized depression, profound anxiety, and deep loneliness, corresponded with renewed, intensified, or novel religious seeking. Migrants reported feeling more desiring of, and dependent on, an ever-present, personal, and wholly in-control conception of God, as well as a dependable community of like-minded believers while in the United States. Regardless of religious affiliation or migration status, 51 percent of migrant respondents answered that they sought out God more intensely in the United States than in Brazil. Further-more, 45 percent responded that they had more frequent encounters with the Holy Spirit and felt God's presence more regularly in the United States than in Brazil. Formal interviews and informal conversations corroborated these findings. In the face of mounting emotional and physical suffering, migrants like Neusa, Rubém, Beatriz, Paula, Alícia, and Mirtes found medical help to be inaccessible or insufficient. Instead, they sought out comfort and healing from local Brazilian churches, through intimate relationships with their cobelievers, clergy, and God.

In the following two chapters, I argue that migrant evangelical churches were particularly effective at articulating and relieving the specific affective maladies that characterized migrant distress. These churches, more so than Catholic and Spiritist congregations, aimed to directly transform the interior landscapes of adherents. Through prayer, book clubs, sermons, and Bible studies, clergy and church workers taught adherents strategies to assuage their loneliness, anxiety, and depression, defuse their anger, cope with their *saudades*, redirect their love, and become unstuck.

3

Church as Hospital and God as Consoler

THE AFFECTIVE THERAPEUTICS OF MIGRANT EVANGELICAL CHURCHES

Freedom to be happy involves, at least for some, the moral and emotional labor of becoming unstuck.

—SARA AHMED[1]

THIRTY MINUTES BEFORE services began, I found myself on bent knees, forehead pressed against interlaced hands, joining the other migrant *crentes* in the posture of faith. For a solid half hour, Pastor Jeferson and his wife, Juliana, paced the aisles, encouraging communion with God by offering their own spoken prayers. While their voices echoed throughout the room, I heard the softer, yet equally insistent, voices of the women to my left and right, and the men to the front and back. Periodic rumbles and shouts punctuated the collective whispers as individuals delved deeper into prayer, alternatively thanking and beseeching God for His activity in their daily lives.[2] On Sunday evenings, attendance for group prayer (*oração*) before worship services in this small Pentecostal congregation was robust—perhaps twenty or thirty people.

Juliana clenched her fists to her heart, and closed her eyes tightly, while she cried out to God, Jesus, and the Holy Spirit to attend to the needs of the congregants. She asked God to relieve believers from insecurity in a foreign land. She prayed that God liberate the *irmãos* from the police, and help them secure social security cards, driver's licenses, and green cards. Along with these

69

mundane but pressing requests, she urged God to cast away the evil spirits of divorce, separation, and familial discord. While walking up and down the aisles, Juliana paused frequently to raise her hands above those on bent knee or place them on the tops of congregants' heads. As she passed by, eyebrows knit together, and lips quickened, unleashing ever-more fervent prayer peppered with "Glória!" and "Aleluia!"

As her voice increased in volume and urgency on this Sunday evening, Juliana arrived at her ultimate and recurrent prayer. With mounting intensity, she called out, "Help us God, and free us in the name of Jesus from the evil spirits of depression (*depressão*), anxiety (*ansiedade*), and loneliness (*solidão*)!" She prayed that the Holy Spirit fill the deep emptiness that plagued so many migrants in the United States and forced them down paths of pain, suffering, and sin.

———

Entreating God to eradicate multiple forms of emotional distress among migrants became a familiar trope in Juliana's and her husband's prayers, as well as in the book clubs, prayer vigils, and Bible studies they led in their small congregation. These concerns also reverberated in the other evangelical churches and religious centers I attended. Not only did migrant evangelical churches name the specific forms of distress migrants encountered, but they outlined a spiritual strategy by which to combat them.

I began to understand this strategy as a deliberate affective therapeutics within migrant evangelical churches after repeatedly encountering two phrases: *a igreja é um hospital* (the church is a hospital) and *O Deus é meu Consolador* (God is my Consoler). These phrases, I learned, loosely corresponded to evangelical adherents' and clergy members' twin objectives of migrant healing—the first rooted in social embrace, the second in personal transformation.

Church as hospital contended that the role of the church was to embody a community of care and treat the wounds of all who entered it. Regardless of malady, believers and clergy asserted that churches ought to restore people to physical, psychological, and spiritual "wholeness" by facilitating communion with God in the context of intimate Christian community. Articulating an explicit orientation toward healing, adherents explained that the church should liken itself to a hospital rather than to a tribunal (*corte de justiça*). Migrants aimed to suspend judgment of others and deliberately practice love. The church, Pastor Jeferson preached, should be a laboratory proving the healing potential of frequent expressions of love, care, and attention.

In keeping with the vision of church as a place of communal care and healing, churches represented God as *Consolador*, consoler and companion, rather than disciplinarian and judge. The personal, evangelical God adherents sought out and discovered in evangelical churches remained distinct from the remote, authoritarian divinity of the traditional Latin American Catholic Church.[3] Instead of largely aloof, transcendent, and stern, this God was physically felt, immanent, and warm. Embodied intimacy with this evangelical God, marked by the sensorial experience of being in this consoling divinity's presence, brought about relief from suffering as well as personal transformation, the second objective of affective therapeutics.

On Facebook, churchgoers frequently circulated slogans articulating evangelical churches' mandate to help and heal congregants (see figs. 3.1 and 3.2). They criticized congregations and adherents they perceived as judgmental, exclusive, and vitriolic—those that made certain categories of people feel unwelcome, such as single mothers, LGBTQ-identifying individuals, divorcées and divorcés, and those with histories of substance abuse. The ideal church, Brazilian evangelicals asserted, should welcome all people, and embrace them as sufferers in need of God's healing.[4]

When criticizing their own church, migrants also employed the phrase *a igreja é como hospital* (the church is like a hospital) as a way to highlight what they perceived to be their congregation's flaws. Paula, whom I introduced in the previous chapter as an exemplary *mulher de Deus* (woman of God), asked during Sunday school why her church failed to help the needy with funds collected through tithes and offerings.[5] After all, she asserted, the church should be a hospital for all who needed it, regardless of religious affiliation. When she raised this concern at Sunday school, Juliana responded decisively, "We are an immigrant church! Our congregants clean homes for a living! In an entire year, they contribute what an American doctor can give to his church in one week. We are immigrants in this country simply trying to survive!" While Juliana's defensive response ended the public conversation, Paula later shared with me her deep disappointment in Juliana's reply. If they did not help others heal, she asked, how could they make good on the promise to be a hospital for the spiritually sick?

Despite congregants' perception that the church often failed to embody the ideal hospital, the metaphor remained central to the espoused mission and identity of the church. From the pulpit, Pastor Jeferson stated that each person

FIGURE 3.1. The church needs to be more of a
hospital and less of a tribunal. (Facebook flyer,
circulated in 2013, accessed March 30, 2015)

FIGURE 3.2. The church is a hospital for sinners, not a
museum for saints.—Abigail Van Buren. Until Jesus comes!
(Adventist Church Facebook posting, accessed March 30,
2015, fb.com/IgrejaAdventistadoSetimoDia)

in attendance, including himself, had endured hardship, suffering, and wound-
ing prior to turning to God. Because of each believer's personal experience
with "illness" and eventual "healing," the church must reach out to everyone,
including those currently immersed in "prostitution, drugs, and crime."

During my formal interview with Pastor Jeferson at his home, he articulated
how the church ought to embody a hospital even for those who had committed

"sins." He insisted, "We condemn acts, never people." The church opened its arms to LGBTQ-identifying individuals, even while vociferously promoting heteronormativity and condemning same-sex relations. This helped to explain the surprising frequency with which I met Brazilian migrant *crentes* who self-identified, or were identified by others, as gay or lesbian. Pastor Jeferson went on to explain that his congregation treated migrant suffering by alleviating "loneliness" (*solidão*), "depression" (*depressão*), and "being isolated" (*sendo isolado*). In enabling migrants to draw close to God in the context of social intimacy with other migrant believers, he proclaimed the church's transformative mission: "to bring people to live a better life."

Frequent personal encounter with this consoling divinity remained central to healing and a key component of the therapeutics I witnessed in evangelical congregations. Believers strived for embodied intimacy with God through daily private and group practice, and the achievement of such intimacy promised relief. Migrants' survey responses pointed to this understanding of God as Consoler. To the question "When you pray, how do you see God?" believers identified God as friend, comforter, protector, and guide, rather than judge. Responses included "I imagine God seated here on my bed, and I am kneeling at his feet. Sometimes I even imagine him stroking my hair (*afagando meus cabelos*) and saying, 'It's okay!'"; "[I see God] as someone powerful and saintly, as my Helper and Father"; "[I see God] as a magnificent being that with the power of words can create planets and stars, but also as a father and friend ready and willing to help me"; "[I see God] as my friend (*amigo*), guide (*guia*), my protector (*protetor*)."[6] As hospital, the church provided the physical and social context for healing. As *Consolador*, God, and the frequent embodied experience of God, constituted the therapeutic cure.

Apart from these slogans, how did churches make these metaphors, and the healing they promised, real for believers? What strategies and discourses transformed church into hospital and God into *Consolador*? This chapter outlines the affective therapeutics I encountered in three Brazilian evangelical churches across Greater Washington, DC. Composed of teachings regarding correct emotional dispositions, interpretations of interiority, and orientations toward God, evangelical affective therapeutics taught migrants how to cope with, justify, and transform migrant-related distress into productive religious devotion. Evangelical churches' clear articulation and effective management of migrant distress help shed light on what compels migrants to increasingly turn to evangelical religiosity in the United States.

While churches failed to remove the legal and socioeconomic sources of congregants' suffering, they succeeded in teaching migrants to reinterpret their hardships through the eyes of God and fellow believers. Portraying the external world as permeated by temptation, disappointment, and distraction, these churches worked to reorient migrants to a new locus of promising activity and potential agency: their internal affective lives. Through shifting the terrain of action from one's external to internal landscape, evangelical churches asserted each believer's individual responsibility for their own affective experience.

While the distress migrants experienced largely stemmed from entrenched social and political structures, they learned in church that return to health depended on daily behaviors, decisions, and practices that were wholly within their control. Church actors, including pastors, their wives, and senior church officials (*obreiros*), presented feelings, moods, and dispositions as personal decisions dependent on one's enacted and felt commitment to God.[7] Church officials rarely, if ever, discussed the injustice and hypocrisy embedded in the US immigration system, economy, or foreign policy, each of which directly influenced the forms of distress migrants experienced. Rather, they framed feeling as stemming from an individual's relationship with God and engagement with Christian fellowship. As such, migrant affective experience could be transformed by teaching believers to feel close to God and to one another. Migrant evangelical churches, and the social imagination of God and forms of community they promoted, uniquely worked to alleviate migrant distress. Below, I explore the constitutive discourses and desired outcomes of such affective therapeutics, including the feeling states churches aimed to eradicate and instill in migrant believers.

In my invocation of *affect*, I follow Ann Cvetkovich's broad description of the term as "force, intensity or the capacity to move or be moved."[8] Importantly, I adopt the most expansive definition of *affect*, including conscious and unconscious feeling states, impressions, and sensations across the body and mind. My use of *therapeutics* emerges from both colloquial definitions and critical studies of subjectivity. In the first sense, *therapeutics* signifies methods to alleviate suffering. In the second sense, it elicits understandings of the self as constructed through specific "technologies" of power,[9] whereby "experts of the soul" guide patients to reconfigure their interiority.[10]

In bringing these two concepts together, I consider the affective therapeutics of migrant evangelical churches to be a distinct form of scrutinizing, working-on, and ultimately reshaping the interior lifeworlds of adherents. As such, clergy members and church workers positioned themselves as experts of the soul. In doing so, such churches addressed those who felt "burdened by selfhood" in the United States, and aimed to "restore" to them the "status of a choosing individual," complete with "unity and personal purpose."[11] Churches strived to convert the negative imprint of migrant affective experience (loneliness, anxiety, depression, being stuck) into positive religious dispositions, articulated as happiness, faith, peace, and gratitude. I trace this conversion from negative affective distress to positive religious devotion.

First, I explore the central rhetorical pairing of affective therapeutics, *amor e dor* (love and pain), suggesting how it articulates a theology of personal responsibility. Equating love with divine intimacy, and pain with divine rejection, evangelical churches placed the burden of health and healing on migrants themselves. Then, I describe three key discursive tactics that churches employed to instill personal responsibility in migrants: "the happiness of believers," "be God's vessel," and "siblings in Christ" (*irmãos em Cristo*).

Reverberations of an American Tradition

Before examining the distinct healing tactics of contemporary migrant churches, it is important to note that what I witnessed and what I term affective therapeutics remains deeply embedded in the American evangelical tradition. Rather than being wholly unique, migrant churches espoused and repurposed a theological message that emerged in the very roots of popular evangelical Christianity in the United States, beginning in the Second Great Revival of the nineteenth century. Three strands of the message that crystallized during this period reverberated in the rhetoric I encountered in twenty-first-century migrant evangelical churches: (1) an emphasis on personal conversion rather than social uplift; (2) the centrality of free will and an understanding of divine communion as choice; (3) the belief that Christian devotion depends upon believers' feelings more than thoughts.[12]

Evangelical Christianity, in its current form, emerged from a period of historical, economic, and cultural foment. In the mid-nineteenth century, Americans faced an uncertain economic, political, and cultural horizon due to the impending Civil War, rapid industrialization, urbanization, and an influx of European migrants. Prior to 1865, Protestantism in the United States, as practiced in denominations such as Methodism, Presbyterianism, and Baptism, centered on obeying God's command. Following 1865, however, independent preachers increasingly called attention to the transformative power of the Holy Spirit, which, conceived of as God's presence, promised to overwhelm human will and restore purity to the sinner. In places like Kentucky,

Tennessee, and upstate New York, all geographically and culturally removed from the upwardly mobile centers of capital, revival Christianity rejected elitism, intellectualism, and the theological rigidity of Calvinism, and instead emphasized "religious ecstasy," public conversion, and a "disdain for authority and tradition."[13]

In the teachings of prominent revivalists like Phoebe Palmer, Charles Finney, and Dwight Moody, a punitive God was replaced by a loving God, willing and ready to console sinners and "meet [the] needs" of those who proactively chose redemption.[14] In this model, the individual was both active and passive in the process of salvation, where "a common image was that of an instrument . . . on which the savior plays."[15] The sinner first offered herself to God to "be filled" by His presence. Filled by the Holy Spirit, the believer was "freed not only from particular sinful acts but from the disease of sinful motives and the 'power' of sin."[16]

Such novel American Christianity was both personal and pragmatic, promoting the healed individual as the "[t]he best evidence for Christianity" and for "what God had done."[17] Since the world was already lost, the Christian's highest duty was to personal transformation and witness, rather than social uplift. This orientation provided a spiritual interpretation for socioeconomic distress. The poor became solely responsible for their own destitution and joblessness, and could ameliorate their circumstances by electing proximity to God, Christian living, and sobriety.[18] Through the success of holiness traditions like Pentecostalism and Pietism, this therapeutic message grew in popularity throughout the twentieth century. Its ascendancy was confirmed when the other dominant strand of evangelical Christianity, the militaristic and antimodern message promulgated by William Jennings Bryan and his "fundamentalists," met its decisive defeat in the Scopes trial of 1925.[19] Along with social conservatism, American evangelical Christianity was thus redefined by an emphasis on personal salvation, forgiveness, and love.

Modeled by Billy Graham and popular televangelists who followed, this evangelical consensus remains strong today. Since the 1960s, "expressive Christianity" has continued to define much of evangelical experience in the United States, emphasizing the immediate and personal benefits of embodied faith. Prominent evangelical leaders and writers like Oral Roberts, James Dobson, Jerry Falwell, and Joyce Meyer emphasize the spiritual essence of Christianity, highlighting how it transforms personal and interpersonal relationships, rather than its political applications. Organizations like Focus on the Family and the Promise Keepers promote the Bible as a "recipe" for Christian living, and as the only path toward well-being and "self-fulfillment."[20] Twentieth- and twenty-first-century evangelical Christianity thus embraces and reflects the contemporary therapeutic age, in which individual happiness and health remain paramount concerns. Scholars have documented the endurance and expansion of this therapeutic core of evangelical Christianity in both the US and global contexts.[21]

The current chapter highlights how migrant evangelical leaders repurpose this deep-rooted tradition. While the teachings of migrant pastors invoke centuries-old metaphors of "being filled by God" or "being played by God," the maladies they target remain specifically shaped by contemporary US migrant experience. Like nineteenth-century rural Americans, contemporary migrants in the US face profound uncertainty about their future. Their socioeconomic marginalization is compounded by legal exclusion, familial rupture, and linguistic and cultural isolation. It is unsurprising, then, that evangelical therapeutics have been embraced by a new segment of the American underclass. The hymns I heard Brazilian migrants sing with passion and conviction reflected tropes almost identical with those verses recited by the left-behind Americans of an earlier epoch, such as "I am a stranger here; within a foreign land; my home is far away, upon a golden stand; Ambassador to be of realms beyond the sea, I'm here on business for my king."[22] Considering migrant evangelical churches within the broader genealogy of American evangelical therapeutics illuminates how this phenomenon both rehearses and transcends a distinctly American tradition. While steeped in US history, migrant churches adapted evangelical therapeutics to the particular sufferers in their care.

Amor e Dor: A Theology of Personal Responsibility

Therapeutic Intimacy with God

Sitting in the living room of her small apartment where she lived alone, I asked Mônica about her relationship with God. Did she currently feel close to Him? How did she know when He was close, and when He was far? I met Mônica early on during my visits to the Pentecostal church. Unmarried and in her early forties, she struck me as warm, lighthearted, and friendly. Despite church formality, Mônica seemed down-to-earth, opting to wear pants and leave her hair curly, rather than conforming to the much more prevalent custom among women of wearing tailored skirts, colorful blouses, bold makeup, and straightened hair to worship services. Throughout fieldwork, many people encouraged me to hear Mônica's *testemunho*.[23] She "used to be" a lesbian and a drug addict, they told me in hushed voices, but God saved her.

In her response to my query, Mônica likened the intimacy between believer and God to the intimacy between father and child. She first described how feelings of closeness or distance between father and child depended on the child's behavior:

> If you make a bad decision, and commit wrongdoing, it will upset your father. And, if tomorrow you do more wrongdoing, and keep doing bad things that upset him, he will become despondent. He will fight for you, but it won't work, because you keep insisting on doing bad things. What will your father do? He will become upset, and begin to watch you from afar, understand? Then, you will become distant from him, and you will no longer feel the kind of protection from him that you once had. You will feel insecure, right?

After a period of distance, she commented, it would become harder to reach out to one's father in a time of need, because intimacy had attenuated. Likewise, God would withdraw His love and intimacy from adherents who knowingly transgressed His laws. Again returning to the relationship between father and child, she contrasted the distancing described above with how children could encourage intimacy with their fathers:

> And, when you do things that are pleasing to your father again and again, and you stop doing things that make him unhappy, then what will happen? He [your father] will be happy with you, and each time [you do something pleasing to him] he will become closer to you.

Leaving behind the analogy of father and child, Mônica then directly considered how God evaluated the efforts of believers and consequently bestowed His ultimate rewards on them—constant love and proximity:

> What counts in the end is not how many times you knelt on the floor, or how many times you prayed. Rather, how many times you said "no" to sin, "no" to the things of this world, because of your love (*amor*) for Him. This will make you feel closer (*mais próximo*) to Him, and you will see evidence of His caring (*os cuidados*) in your life.

Mônica's comments recalled a familiar rhetorical pairing that I heard repeatedly in churches and throughout numerous interviews with congregants. Living righteously and according to God's precepts produced greater feelings of *amor* (love) for God, self, and others, as well as greater evidence of God's love for the believer. In contrast, wrongdoing produced feelings of distance, bitterness, and hardship, encapsulated by the term *dor* (pain). To maximize intimacy with God, and the positive consequences associated with divine love, including happiness, peace, and security, adherents strived to be actively close to God. According to Mônica and other evangelicals I met, such intimacy was achieved through rejecting "things of the world" and instead pursuing a life of prayer, Bible study, worship, good works, and Christian fellowship. The model of therapeutic intimacy that Mônica elaborated and churches espoused placed the burden of living in *amor* versus *dor* squarely on the individual's shoulders. If Mônica successfully resisted temptation—in her case, women and drugs— she would enjoy the fruits of God's love. If she succumbed to temptation, she would palpably feel God's withdrawal as pain.

Mônica's conversion narrative, dependent on the opposition of *amor/dor*, exemplified migrant evangelical churches' theology of personal responsibility for affective states. Mônica had resumed drug use as a new migrant in the United States after several years of being clean in Brazil. She found herself desperately yearning for sobriety but did not know how to overcome addiction, explaining, "I didn't know how to stop." Evangelical friends encouraged her to turn to God for help, telling her that God wanted to use her as "a train to bring multitudes" (*locomotiva para trazer multidões*) to Him. She began attending midnight prayer vigils with other young Brazilian migrants searching for liberation and "began to feel something different," God's intimate presence. This proximity, she asserted, transformed her desires. "I began to want to go to church more. To seek out [God] more," she noted. God took away her desire for drugs, alcohol, and women. With a sweep of her arm, she exclaimed, "God took away everything [that displeased Him], like smoke, everything evaporated."

While Mônica experienced healing as a result of her active pursuit of God, she noted that therapeutic intimacy remained tenuous and depended upon constant vigilance. Mônica reported sensing God withdraw, for instance, when she casually watched movies featuring two women in romantic partnership. Distancing would lead to her preconversion life associated with loneliness, drugs, and depression. As Mônica explained it, love for and love from God depended on her ability to restrain and discipline her desires.

The Labor of Love

Clergy regularly invoked the fundamental opposition between love and pain to implore individuals to try harder, to "search more" (*buscar mais*), in order to tap into God's therapeutic love. Although God's love was indeed eternal, and ever-present, pastors explained that it was incumbent upon individuals to both access and maintain it. Living in the aura of God's love, therefore, was framed as an individual choice.

Frequently, adherents and pastors formulated this choice as actively returning to one's *primeiro amor* (first love) for and with God. This phrase elicited the following narrative. When adherents first entered the church, they literally "fell in love with God" (*se apaixonaram com Deus*). Suddenly freed from the pain they had suffered in their secular lives, they experienced overpowering and complete transformation through God's love, inspiring them to plunge enthusiastically into devout religious life. In this initial moment of being "saved," new converts fully experienced God as *Consolador* and church as *hospital*. Flooded by good feeling, new believers never missed worship, eagerly gave testimony, and voraciously read the Bible.

Mônica's account of her faith implied the healing potential of *primeiro amor*. As she became more fervent, God swept away her "sinful" desires and rewarded her with an embodied feeling of His presence. This experience, in turn, induced stronger faith, impelling her to give up alcohol, drugs, and dating women. In her telling, this "first love" brought about the end of acute suffering. As time went on, however, pastors warned that the feeling of *primeiro amor* dissipated, and adherents risked retreating back into a life of sin, and therefore of *dor*. Returning to this life of pain led to God's distancing and ultimate withdrawal from adherents' lives. The work of believers, I learned, was the constant pursuit and maintenance of this primary, original love.

In his encouragement for congregants to "turn back" to *primeiro amor* and the devotion with which they first approached God, Pastor Jeferson asserted each individual believer's responsibility to actively seek out and reflect God's love. He made this contention concrete during an evening Bible study, in which he noted that love was not a feeling (*sentimento*) but rather a decision (*decisão*). To witness the presence of God in one's life, he taught, it was first necessary to decide to embody God's love, and then to commit to the practice of loving others. He called the practice of loving others *exercício espiritual* (spiritual exercise). In the same way that one became stronger through lifting weights, one had to practice using one's "spiritual muscles" to strengthen them. Pastor Jeferson concluded by pointing us to 1 John 4:8, emphasizing that without the disciplined, consistent practice of love, it was impossible to know God.[24]

The evangelical discourse attached to *amor e dor* outlined a strategy by which adherents could view themselves as individually responsible for their own affective states. As detailed by Mônica's account of her faith and Pastor Jeferson's teachings, the experiences of love and pain were concretized as individual choices to be deliberated upon daily, rather than the unjust consequences of life as migrants in the United States. By working toward love and rejecting pain, migrants engaged in what Nikolas Rose considers the transformative goal par excellence of therapeutic projects, "the calculated attempt to bring the subject from one way of acting and being to another."[25] Through intimacy with God and faithful brotherhood, churches promised to move migrants from passivity, vulnerability, and distress into activity, power, and health. As such, these institutions engaged in the production of "the individual who is 'free to choose'"[26] and who is "apparently part of a profoundly emancipatory project of learning to be a self."[27] Rose's understanding of such therapeutic regimes reveals the daily mechanics involved in the kind of affective reorientation I witnessed in migrant churches. "Achieving freedom becomes a matter not of slogans nor of political revolution, but of slow, painstaking and detailed work on our own subjective and personal realities."[28]

In this framing, evangelical churches aimed to make good on their promise to be hospitals for those suffering distress, afflictions churches interpreted as primarily spiritual in nature. Pastor Jeferson, Juliana, and other church workers endeavored to teach believers how to choose love over pain, and happiness over suffering. As experts of the soul, they argued that sincere contentment was attainable for migrants through practiced devotion and Christian belonging.[29] This meant teaching believers to regularly experience God as *Consolador* and church as *hospital*. The promise of such affective therapeutics was return to "health," marked by the affective states of happiness, contentment, gratitude, peace, and liberation.

The Happiness of Believers

> The happiness duty is a positive duty to speak of what is good but can also be thought of as a negative duty not to speak of what is not good, not to speak from or out of unhappiness.
>
> —SARA AHMED[30]

According to church leaders, the outward mark of authentic faith and righteousness was *a felicidade dos crentes* (the happiness of believers), the first discursive tactic of affective therapeutics. I often encountered this phrase during sermons, prayer meetings, and interviews to describe the affective state and social mores elicited by acceptance of Jesus as one's savior, and the practice of active, daily communion with God. By filling one's thoughts and activities with the divine, I heard repeatedly, there would be no room for negative impulses or feelings. Instead, believers would become "Christ-like," and emanate the love, light, and peace of Jesus. As such, Pastor Jeferson insisted that "the word [of God] was like a vaccine" against unhappiness, illness, and tragedy. It simultaneously cured existing maladies and protected against future threats to health.

In the following discussion, I briefly situate migrant evangelicals' concern for happiness within the broader contemporary "happiness turn." Then, according to my ethnographic findings, I examine happiness as a central component of affective therapeutics in migrant evangelical churches. The Pentecostal women's book group I attended at Juliana's house over four months became a prime venue to understand what clergy and congregants meant when they evoked *a felicidade dos crentes*. I learned the key components of this ideal disposition, including positivity and gratitude, and understood how happiness related to churches' ideology of personal responsibility for affective states.

Happiness Discourse

Evangelical churches' concern with "happiness" (*alegria, felicidade*) and good feeling is not unique. Instead, such rhetoric joins and reflects a broader cultural concern in both the United States and beyond with happiness. Scholars have identified the growing preoccupation with happiness in media, psychology, politics, business, and religion as a novel "happiness turn" that promotes "feeling good" as an ultimate end of the "good life." Yet, happiness is not value neutral. Instead, it clusters around normative values and institutions, such that "the face of happiness . . . looks rather like the face of privilege."[31] Certain configurations, such as the heteronormative family, financial success, or attainment of citizenship, embody "happy objects" through which individuals most often find happiness.[32] While "feeling bad" indicates personal failure and errant striving, "feeling good" coheres to personal success and normative striving.[33]

The churches I visited reflected this concern with happiness, making faith, and devotion to God and congregation, the ultimate happy object—that which promised migrants the experience of feeling good. Desiring and pursuing intimacy with Jesus and Christian community promised eternal happiness and well-being. Nothing else in this world could guarantee happiness and well-being besides God, Juliana often asserted while leading book group. At Sunday school, Pastor Jeferson made this promise even more concrete. The *fruto do espírito* (fruit of the spirit) righteousness offered, he lectured, were manifold: peace (*paz*), happiness (*alegria*), self-control (*domínio próprio*), good sense (*bom senso*). In accepting Jesus, and reorganizing one's life according to Jesus's teachings, he preached during another lesson, congregants would take on *uma nova natureza* (a new nature), "a nature of peace, love, and enjoyment." Pastor Jeferson promised that faith would make believers slower to react, able to let things go, and more patient in the endurance of suffering (*longanimidade*). Simply put, they would learn to feel good. To attain this happiness, however, believers must first be happy. Positive attitude and positive feeling begot greater blessing from God, and therefore greater happiness, whereas negative feeling indicated an absence of God's favor.[34]

Be Positive

I found myself looking forward to Tuesday evenings at Juliana's house. As we sat on plush leather couches in her immaculate living room, sipping tea and eating cake, I almost felt that I, too, belonged. Like me, many of the women in attendance were in their twenties and thirties, newly married, and contemplating having a family. Despite this sense of familiarity, however, the very real challenges these women faced as undocumented migrants frequently burst to the fore to remind me of my privilege: their parents, siblings, and sometimes children remained out of reach; their ability to communicate and move freely was deeply constrained; their workdays were long, lonely, and often exploitative.

What was the nature of the solace and guidance Juliana's evangelical teachings offered in response to the concrete forms of bodily and psychic distress these women so frequently endured? As long as they remained in the United States without documents, these women could expect very little to change in the infrastructure of their everyday lives. Even if they were to acquire those eagerly sought-after green cards, as some of them eventually did through marriage, employment, or temporary amnesty,[35] the limitations they experienced regarding employment, language, and mobility would still shape their circumstances.

As women discussed their ongoing frustrations with life in the United States, Juliana adeptly shifted the conversation away from the women's structural circumstances to their affective landscapes. Throughout the four months of book club meetings, I never once heard Juliana offer concrete employment, medical, or legal advice in response to women's difficulties with their jobs, medical care, or immigration status. She never provided public advice, for instance, as to the navigation of the American legal system, or free health-care clinics or English classes for migrants, despite a plethora of these free or low-cost resources in the area.[36] She never once announced events taking place at the Brazilian consulate in Washington, DC, or other public events intended to alleviate migrants' everyday financial, legal, and employment burdens. Given the self-contained universe in which the church ensconced itself, perhaps Juliana simply did not know about these events. This is doubtful, however. More importantly, Juliana seemed to assume, evidenced through her omissions, that these institutions and services could at best provide momentary and superficial relief for the ailments that plagued her congregants. During the book club, Juliana helped women to recognize such ailments as primarily spiritual in nature, rather than political or economic.

Rejecting the capacity of secular society to solve migrant women's problems, Juliana instead framed women's distress as stemming from "spiritual weakness" (*fraqueza espiritual*) or "spiritual laziness" (*preguiça espiritual*). Both of these ailments emerged from inactivity. In the first, women failed to effectively curb their negative thoughts, feelings, and impulses. In the second, women failed to tenaciously pursue God's love through spiritual practices such as churchgoing, fasting, prayer, and Bible study. These spiritual maladies and shortcomings produced domestic and interpersonal discord by compromising a woman's ability to control her own interior world and embody the correct disposition of Jesus's followers: happiness.

Juliana utilized a Portuguese translation of Joyce Meyer's best-selling Christian self-help book, *The Battlefield of the Mind* (*O campo da batalha da mente*) as our discussion text.[37] She also added her own commentary by introducing biblical passages, personal anecdotes, and anonymous testimonies, to encourage women to transform their emotional responses to external stimuli. Most significantly, these included their relationships with family members, friends, employers, and church members.

During these weekly meetings, Juliana explained the obstacles to attaining *a felicidade dos crentes,* defining both the origin and the impact of negative emotions for the women in attendance. She began one meeting, for example, by discussing chapter 5 of Meyer's book, "Be Positive" ('Seja positiva'). To complement Meyer's message that positivity emanated from faith in God and attracted divine blessing, she recounted the parable of two builders described in Matthew 7:24–29. One man builds his home on sand, while the other builds his home on rock. The home that rests on rock, symbolizing Jesus's teachings, can weather any storm, whereas the home built on sand, symbolizing a willful rejection of Jesus's authority as the son of God, falls apart at the slightest sign of bad weather.

Our emotional worlds, Juliana contended, were akin to these homes. If we built our lives according to Jesus's teachings and cleaved to His Word, she explained, we could maintain good humor, confidence, and resilience in the face of adversity and become the *pessoa positiva*. Without our eyes lifted to God, however, we would become the *pessoa negativa,* noticing every flaw in ourselves and others, becoming angry, judgmental, jealous, and depressed at every provocation. The negative person repelled both God and humans because of an unsavory countenance, while the positive person attracted blessing and friendship. Juliana read from Meyer's descriptions of the two competing temperaments:

> the positive person can go ahead and decide to enjoy himself no matter what happens. The negative person never enjoys anything. A negative person is no fun to be with. He brings a gloomy overcast to every project. There is a "heaviness" about him. He is a complainer, a murmurer, and a faultfinder. No matter how many good things are going on, he always seems to spot the one thing that could be a potential problem.[38]

Asking the other women to read passages aloud from Meyer's text, Juliana emphasized the relationship between "positivity" and faith in God. Women read aloud: "The more positive you and I become, the more we will be in the flow of God. God is certainly positive, and to flow with Him, we must also be positive"[39] and "I can't promise you that you'll never be disappointed. But, even in disappointing times, if they do come, you can hope and be positive. Put yourself in God's miracle-working realm. Expect a miracle in your life. Expect good things!"[40]

Having read these passages, Juliana explained that God revealed His plan for our lives and bestowed blessings only when we actively looked for Him with a "glad heart" (*alegria do coração*) and a "ready mind" (*uma mente pronta*). God constantly provided opportunities for the faithful, but only for those who remained in active pursuit of blessing by vigilantly warding off negativity.

Juliana asserted that negativity stemmed from the absence of faith, obedience, and devotion. By truly recognizing Jesus, and believing in personal salvation, it was possible to say, according to Juliana, "I'm a child of God. My name is written in the Book of Life" (Sou uma filha de Jesus. Meu nome está no Livro da Vida). Without proper attentiveness to God, however, humans elevated their own knowledge above divine wisdom. Owing to such arrogance, they judged others, took justice into their own hands, questioned their lives, became angry and impatient, rejected their spouses, mistreated their children, and resented their circumstances. The failure to build one's house on the "rock" of faith led individuals to become immersed in the external world, the "lost" world, and its problems. One of the primary tasks of believers, then, was to discern the will of God and conform to it. Juliana thus recast the problems women faced as symptomatic of spiritual inadequacy, redressed solely through attentiveness toward one's inner life.

Gratitude

By doing the work of the *pessoa positiva*, it was possible to avoid familial disputes, particularly between spouses. Often, the book discussions would prompt women to ask Juliana specific questions pertaining to their intimate relationships outside of church, providing her with the opportunity to concretize her advice. During one meeting concerning the importance of women's submission to their husbands, Paula, a young convert introduced in chapter 2, became visibly upset. *Must* she submit to her husband's will, she asked Juliana, even if she knew that he was ultimately wrong? Several other women eagerly echoed this specific complaint: their husbands behaved irrationally or impulsively, and women simply knew better! Shouldn't they assert themselves? Paula explained that her husband had become increasingly unhappy living in the United States and decided that they would soon return to Brazil. Paula preferred life in the United States. Despite living far away from her brother, extended family, and close friends, she feared returning to a country she now perceived to be "very dangerous." Paula was pregnant with her first child and worried about raising a family amid crime and instability. After listening attentively, Juliana answered that all Paula could do was pray and fast to understand God's will. If she learned that God wanted her to stay in the United States, she should then pray for God to change her husband's mind. If God did not change her husband's mind, however, it was clear that He in fact wanted them to return to Brazil. Juliana then warned the group against being "headstrong" (*brava*), and pitting themselves against their husbands, who were divinely elected as heads of their households. As a caveat, she shared another couple's misfortunes. Despite "hearing from God" that they should remain in the United States, the wife forced her husband to return to Brazil. Soon after they arrived, cascading misfortunes befell the couple, ultimately leading them to divorce. This result demonstrated God's disapproval with the wife's willful decision.

Juliana, an assertive, charismatic, and intense woman in her own right, appeared determined to leave the women feeling empowered rather than discouraged at the end of meetings. She followed her commentary on the importance of "submission" (*submissão*) with reflections on "women's power" (*o poder da mulher*). Women had greater "spiritual sensitivity" than men, Juliana continued, and must use this "gift" to their advantage in "winning" arguments against their husbands. While God enjoined women to be submissive, He also granted them greater access to His power. Through fervent devotion and intimacy with God, women could "work on" (*trabalhar em*) their husbands without words.

"We have great authority in our lives!" Juliana insisted. Women had authority over their homes and children. They had authority over their language and thought patterns. And, they had authority over their Bible study, faith, and communion with God. All these spheres of influence, she asserted, constituted "a great power" (*um grande poder*) and profound individual responsibility.

Perhaps as a gentle rebuke to Paula, and other women who complained about their husbands, Juliana concluded the meeting by urging the group to "be grateful" (*seja grata*). She affirmed, "We are all married, our husbands don't beat us, and our children are not sick! We don't have any problems (*a gente não tem problemas*)!" When her children complained, she reported, she urged them to think about children in Africa who ate only one meal a day and often went without shoes on their feet.[41] What could they, as immigrants living in the wealthiest country in the world, possibly complain about?

To punctuate her point concerning the importance of gratitude, Juliana then showed the group a YouTube clip from the television show *American Idol* on her iPhone. In the video, a young man serenades his wheelchair-bound fiancée on stage, in front of a large screen projecting photos of the couple before the young woman's disfiguring car accident. She had sustained extensive brain damage, preventing her from ever walking, speaking, or feeding herself again. The young man explained to the audience that before the accident, he had asked her to marry him before God, and so he would honor his vows, remaining steadfast until the day he died.[42] As the women watched huddled together on the black leather couch, tears sprang to their eyes. At the end of the video, Juliana again repeated her refrain: "What problems do we have? We don't have any problems!"

According to Juliana's teachings, the happiness of believers stemmed from the "happiness of salvation" (*a felicidade da salvação*). With the true recognition that Jesus had died for the sins of humanity, Juliana asserted, it became impossible to complain, or to be anything but positive and grateful. The young man who had expressed unwavering commitment and faith to his fiancée, despite her tragic accident, was emblematic of this ideal. Rather than bitterly asking God, "Why?" or despairing when confronted with suffering and adversity, believers should remain "grateful" (*grata*), "positive" (*positiva*), and "faithful" (*cheia de fé*).

During a Sunday Bible study with the same group of women, Juliana asserted that the Bible constituted a "recipe for peaceful and saintly living" (*receita da paz e vida santa*). By meditating on the Bible's "eternal things," Juliana asserted that women could liberate themselves from the "futilities" (*futilidades*) of the external world that bred negativity, such as television, music, fashion, and material goods. American culture in particular, she explained, compelled people to invest more time and energy in what they *had* (*ter*) rather than in what they *were* (*ser*), leading to high rates of depression (*depressão*) and phobias (*fobias*) among migrants. In contrast, believers who read the Bible as a "recipe for holy living" maintained equanimity and peace regardless of circumstance. As an example, Juliana recalled an *irmã* who visited her soon after the birth of her first child. The saintly woman arrived with a Bible tucked securely under her arm and spent the next several hours reciting Bible verses. Everything that came out of her mouth, Juliana attested, was "an extremely beautiful thing" (*uma coisa lindíssima*) because it came directly from God. As she relayed this story, Juliana's eyes gleamed and her smile brightened. "What a beautiful thing!" she repeated. If the women filled themselves up only with God's Word, like this saintly woman, she continued, "You would never have to think! All of your words would be the words of God!"

Through her teachings, Juliana articulated the ideal emotional disposition of the happiness of believers, and described the components of this state: positivity, gratitude, and abundant faith. Through her exclusive focus on individual emotional control, Juliana implied that it was irrational to entrust politicians with immigration reform, or to assume that one's employer would suddenly become kind and generous, or to believe that the everyday humiliations and injustices of undocumented migrant life would one day disappear. What each woman could do, Juliana asserted, was to reform her own internal landscape, converting anger, judgment, jealousy, pride, and resentment into love for the divine, from which love for others, and love from others, emanated. In creating themselves as new kinds of affective subjects, women could win souls (*ganhar almas*) solely through the example of their unshakeable equanimity, satisfaction, and joy. Strangers on the street, Juliana asserted, would see their enviable way of being (*o jeito*), and ask, "Why is she so happy? What does she know? Where does she go to church?"

"Be God's Vessel": Feeling States as Evidence of God

One Thursday evening, in front of a small group of congregants, Pastor Jeferson demonstrated how God's "light" (*luz*) worked to purify the internal constitution of devotees. The pastor placed a clear glass on the podium and explained that human beings were like empty *vasos* (vessels). They would reflect whatever force dominated them. If they allowed themselves to be filled by the evil forces of God's enemy, o Satanás (Satan), there would be no room for God's love and light.

Here, he turned to Galatians 5:19–21 to enumerate the many temptations to which humans could succumb: prostitution (*prostituição*), impurity (*impureza*), lasciviousness (*libertinagem*), idolatry (*idolatria*), witchcraft (*feitiçaria*), antipathy (*ódio*), drunkenness (*embriaguez*), divisiveness (*discórdia*), and jealousy (*ciúmes*), among others.[43] As Pastor Jeferson named each sin, he placed a small yellow ping-pong ball into the empty glass. Congregants watched as the "sins" gradually filled up its entirety. By inviting God into one's life, and actively pursuing intimacy with God and through prayer, Bible study, churchgoing, and good works, humans could combat dark forces and reflect God's divine nature.

Taking a pitcher of water, representing God's presence, Pastor Jeferson slowly poured the liquid into the glass, watching with satisfaction as the water level rose, bringing each of the plastic yellow balls to the surface where they swiftly spilled out into the basin below. Delighted, the congregants nodded, clapped, and affirmed the demonstration with effusive fist pumps accompanied by shouts of "Glória ao Deus!" Pastor Jeferson reiterated the clear message illustrated by his crowd-pleasing trick: allowing oneself to be filled up by God enabled human beings to take on a divine nature, a nature of love and a nature of peace (*uma natureza de amor e uma natureza de paz*). With God's presence, all satanic content of the human body and mind would simply be "washed away" (*ser lavado*) in the blood of Jesus.

———

Seja o vaso de Deus (be God's vessel) comprised the second key tactic of Brazilian evangelical churches' affective therapeutics. Through teachings like Pastor Jeferson's ping-pong ball demonstration, clergy members and church workers implored adherents to "empty" and "clean" their hearts, minds, and souls. Such language encouraged migrants to dismiss negative thoughts and feelings in order to ready themselves to hear and feel God. Combined with a framing of God that privileged feeling over knowing, the mandate to be God's vessel encouraged migrants to intensely monitor their interiority as indicative of God's presence in, or absence from, their bodies. Such teachings further promoted internal affective experience as the terrain of individual responsibility and migrant healing.

The Evangelical God as "Empty Concept"

For the Brazilian migrants with whom I spoke, who was this God who promised to "fill them up" with peace, love, and contentment? While I attempted to answer this question by documenting how church members talked about the attributes and physicality of God both in and out of church, I soon realized through many frustrated attempts that this query was misguided. For the believers I interviewed and spent time among, God was simply God. Either you knew Him or you did not. Either you lived in His presence, aware of Him daily, or you did not. When I asked people to describe God, therefore, interviewees often repeated hackneyed and rehearsed phrases such as God is love (*Deus é amor*); God is peace (*Deus é paz*); and God is everything (*Deus é tudo*). Or they paused, and reflected, "It's impossible to describe to someone . . . ," leaving me to complete their thought: "who does not know God." Their descriptions more often than not ended in ellipses.

I came to understand the God of the evangelical imagination to be akin to what Pascal Boyer calls an "empty concept," an integral and prevalent notion placed at the "very heart" of a discursive system and yet wholly diffuse and abstract.[44] Despite extensive time observing and studying Brazilian evangelicals' personal and collective engagement with this God, my sense of who and of what this entity consisted remained sketchy at best. My field notes, interview transcripts, and survey responses reflected this intangibility.

In contrast, believers became much more animated and descriptive when explaining how God made them feel. Pastor Jeferson's demonstration described above helped me to understand the discrepancy between adherents' difficulty in describing God as something objective, external, and independent, and the much more vivid accounts believers offered of the feeling states evoked by this God. According to church teachings, individuals came to know God through "discerning" His presence, a process involving the correct reading and interpreting of their own feeling states and thoughts. Pastor Jeferson suggested the prerequisite to accurate discernment through the ping-pong ball example: believers must make themselves available to God as vessels (*vasos*) readied to be filled. Such readiness amounted to taking personal responsibility for one's affective experience, and then scrutinizing one's own feelings, thoughts, and emotions as indicative of God's activity in one's body.

"I Can Feel That He's There with Me"

I asked Felipe and Viviane, Neusa's son and daughter-in-law who were prominent church leaders, to describe how they knew that God was present and how God appeared to them. Having observed their deep faith over the course of the year, I expected each of them to share vivid accounts that would help me to understand who God was in the context of their church and faith community. Instead of describing God as an entity independent and external from them, both Felipe and Viviane resorted to describing their own sense perceptions, linking the knowledge of God's presence, and intimacy with God, to particular feeling states in their own bodies. In English, Felipe explained:

> I guess intimacy with God to me, it means that even though I have so many flaws and I sin a lot, it means whenever I kneel down and pray, I can feel that He's there with me. . . . There's been times when I'm praying and the Holy Spirit just fills my heart, and I really feel that God is present wherever in the room that I am in. . . . I'm intimate with God in the way that I allow Him to use me whenever he wants. I'm like *um vaso na mão de Deus* (a vessel in God's hands). Like, I just want Him to do whatever He wants with me.

Following Felipe's account, I turned to Viviane, who also answered in English:

> I think it's something that . . . you just can't control your emotions, you can't control yourself when you know that God is there, when you are really

in His presence. You can't control yourself. . . . You don't know if you cry, you don't know if you laugh.

Both Felipe and Viviane highlighted the extent to which their sensations brought about awareness of God. Felipe described a more diffuse feeling state, invoking Pastor Jeferson's metaphor of the vessel in God's hands to convey how he allowed God to "fill him up." In this account, Felipe noted that he experienced God by somehow evacuating himself and making room to receive God. Through prayer, he could become the clear, pure glass of Pastor Jeferson's demonstration. Viviane, on the other hand, identified God's activity with the intensification of feeling—the experience of intense sensation suddenly washing over her and making her lose "control."

When I pushed Felipe to share an example of feeling God's presence, he recounted an episode of speaking in tongues, indicative of baptism by the Holy Spirit.[45] As he was driving home from work, Felipe reported, he was "worshipping Him [God] really hard" and soon became lost in devotion, hearing strange words pour from his mouth. When he arrived home, he was overcome, recalling, "I was just crying so much, and I went to my room . . . and I was just, for at least an hour or so, just crying and crying." When I asked Felipe how crying related to his perception of God, he reflected, "It's just a feeling like . . . if you die today, you know you're going to go to Heaven. And that's really hard to have, because we sin every day." Felipe's powerful response, according to his narrative, proved not only God's presence but also God's love, protection, and approval.

Felipe's account illustrated the two-step approach to knowing God that clergy taught and adherents strived to master. First, believers must empty themselves of corrupting thoughts and behaviors of the flesh. This constituted abstaining from behavioral and psychological sin and embodying the *pessoa positiva* and *felicidade dos crentes* described in the previous section. Through these principles, adherents strived to embody pure vessels ready to receive God's presence. Believers then succumbed to the powerful external force that stormed through their feelings, and brought about deep sensations of healing, love, peace, acceptance, and joy. Such sensation promised to transform migrant affective experience. Instead of an imprint of distress marked by loneliness, feeling stuck, depression, anxiety, bitterness, and worry, believers would experience the imprint of God marked by happiness, contentment, gratitude, and peace.

Viviane's comments corroborated Felipe's description. She knew when God was present by the sensation of being overpowered and out of control. In these moments, God physically "filled her up," enabling her to identify something foreign operating within her own body. When I asked her to share an example, she too described speaking in tongues. For almost a year, Viviane told me, she had attempted to suppress the impulse to speak in tongues. She explained, "I started doubting, and I said, 'This is crazy. This is something from my head, you know it's just crazy.'" One day, feeling the urge to speak in tongues, she silently prayed to God for confirmation of this "spiritual gift" (*dom de poder*), explaining, "I said, 'God if this is true, then show me, give me a sign, do something, so that I know that it's not from my head.'" Shortly after forming this thought, the pastor approached, placed his hand on Viviane's head, and instructed, "Speak!" Following this "confirmation," Viviane no longer stifled these spiritual urges or struggled with doubt. She concluded, "I still think whenever it happens, I think it's crazy, but I know that it's not from me anymore, I know that it's . . . God."

Unlike Adam and Eve, whom Pastor Jeferson described during one Sunday evening sermon as having the luxury of physically "walking and talking with God daily," contemporary believers learned to subtly identify the activity of God in their lives. If they could not encounter God "face to face" like Adam and Eve, or Moses, how could believers feel God's presence? They would have to constantly work to forge intimacy and closeness, he offered, by *buscando ao Deus* (seeking out God) and discerning His presence in their everyday realities. Ultimately, this work entailed scrutinizing one's internal feelings, and discovering evidence of God in the stuff of the emotions.

Siblings in Christ: Relationships of Care and Obligation

In addition to inducing affective transformation by promoting "happy" dispositions and self-scrutiny for the purpose of divine intimacy, migrant evangelical churches combatted suffering by offering ready-made communities of care. Promoting church community as a "brotherhood" and "family" in Christ constituted the third tactic of affective therapeutics.

As Pastor Jeferson explained during our formal interview at his home, the church taught migrants to "get closer to people" (*aproximar mais as pessoas*) and stimulated such intimacy by hosting frequent *aproximações*—opportunities to get close. In the context of migration, church communities offered places of socialization, information exchange, job assistance, and psychological support. The practical and emotional benefits of these relationships became essential to migrants and enabled them, in Pastor Jeferson's words, to *se esforçar* (endure) in the face of continued adversity. Deep sociality and intimacy remained essential to churches' understanding of their function as "hospitals." Through mutual recognition, support, and conviviality, church communities combatted loneliness, despair, and isolation.

The benefits of this dense sociality of care explicitly motivated many individuals to seek out church communities while in the United States. In light of the deep loneliness many migrants experienced confined by language, work, and geography in the suburbs of Washington, DC, the ready-made community and self-defined *família* of evangelical churches provided refuge. For those migrants who had already been committed church members in Brazil, finding a new church community was among the first requirements of life in the United States. For those who had lived outside of a faith community, or remained less involved in their home churches, the extensive migrant social network Brazilian evangelical churches afforded compelled greater adherence and regularity. Below, I consider the therapeutics of deep social engagement fostered by evangelical churches, including the reimagining of family and the practice of mutual recognition.

Family Restored

When I walked into the Pentecostal church one Sunday evening in late autumn, the room was abuzz with expectation and nervousness. The men stood to the side conversing in low tones, while the women sat together in the front pews, trading knowing smiles and gestures. As I walked down the aisle to meet the group, one of the women clued me into what was happening: Viviane, Felipe's wife, had gone into labor early that morning on the way back from worshipping at a sister congregation in Virginia. As I looked around, I noticed the absence of many prominent congregants, including Felipe's parents, Neusa and Rubém, brother, Frederico, and sister-in-law, Luana. While present when I arrived, Juliana, the pastor's wife, left for the hospital as soon as she finished teaching Sunday school.

Throughout the evening, the congregation's normal formality was temporarily suspended. The women to my left and right pulled out their phones, displayed text messages from the *irmãs* currently at the hospital, and excitedly recalled their own labors and deliveries. Throughout the Sunday Bible lesson, Juliana updated the group: Viviane was now six centimeters dilated. She was doing well. The doctors would see her at 8:30 p.m. to check her progress.

After the lesson, more women left to attend to Viviane at the hospital. Pastor Jeferson's updates from the pulpit became more regular and grew increasingly concerned: after the doctors last checked Viviane, they determined that the baby, Daniel, was in distress and Viviane had a fever. Pastor Jeferson prayed over Viviane, Felipe, and their soon-to-be-born son, beseeching God to protect them and usher the baby safely into the world. He urged the congregants to pray fervently as well. Seemingly all at once, everyone leapt to their feet with arms and hands outstretched in the air. The electricity in the room was overwhelming. While the congregation this evening was thin, those present unleashed prayer unlike I had seen before. Eyes pressed tightly, mouths moved rapidly, hands and feet pumped and stomped, tears streamed. Their prayer *would* reach God's ears. They *would* bring this baby into the world safely. The next morning, I received a text message from Juliana informing me that Viviane had given birth to Daniel via Cesarean section a few hours after services had concluded and they were both healthy and happy.

During the following weeks and months, the *irmãs* continued to offer support, advice, and companionship to Viviane as she adjusted to new motherhood. When she returned to work full-time as an administrative assistant at a doctor's office a mere month after Daniel's birth, Juliana cared for the baby alongside her own school-aged children. Given Pastor Jeferson's comparatively stable income as a salaried pastor, Juliana was able to stay home full-time, an unknown luxury for most of the migrant women I knew. At Juliana's house during book club or prayer circle, it was normal to see the other women passing around the baby, cooing over his newborn wiggles and squirms. When Juliana had another commitment, another *irmã* would assume this responsibility. Soon, I stopped being surprised when I would see Baby Daniel everywhere—at Juliana's house on Monday, at Marilza's house on Wednesday, at Neusa's house on Friday. The care of the baby, I learned, was a collective responsibility.

In each of the evangelical congregations I visited, I observed similar multifaceted relationships of care and obligation among the self-defined *irmãos em Cristo* (siblings in Christ). In addition to the formal time spent together in and outside of church worshipping, studying, praying, and fasting, congregants cared for each other's children; worked together in construction and housecleaning; lived together; shared rides; celebrated birthdays, baby showers, Thanksgiving, Christmas, and New Year's Eve; played soccer; enjoyed *churrascos*; went out for pizza. When relatives visited from Brazil, congregants shared the responsibility of hosting them. For instance, fourteen years after she had left Brazil, and one year after the unexpected death of her mother, Celina's father was finally approved to visit the United States on a tourist visa. He stayed for one month. While Celina worked full-time throughout his visit, church members shared in showing her father around Washington, DC, and the surrounding areas. When Pastor Jeferson was unexpectedly called to Florida by the church *sede* (headquarters) located there, he brought Celina's father with him on an impromptu road trip. Such relationships comprised a renewed and keenly felt experience of family.

Mara, a sixty-year-old widow and mother of three I met at the Adventist church, utilized the language of family to articulate the significance of social relationships she had forged through the church. A devout Adventist from the time she was twenty, Mara sought out an Adventist community during the first week she spent in the United States. Sixteen years later, Mara identified the church community as her family in the United States. She explained, "As immigrants here, we don't have a large family to be with (*pra ficar*). So our family is the church (*então a nossa família é a igreja*), where we spend every Saturday." When she had free time, she would seek out friends from church or attend community events. Like many of the Brazilian faithful I met, she celebrated birthdays and holidays with her church family. She underscored the importance of regular encounters within a space where "everyone knows you" (*todos sabem de você*). She took the responsibilities of this family seriously, noting that they were the same as the obligations of blood kin: "To help, to visit the sick . . . to help whoever is spiritually weak. I think the objective of the family is this. The objective of the church is this."

Mutual Recognition

Pastor João, the leader of the Adventist church and prominent member of the consulate's Conselho de Cidadãos (Citizens' Council), eloquently articulated the transformative psychological impact of church community on new migrants. While profoundly religious and committed to his faith, Pastor João surprisingly spoke little about God in his analysis of his church's ability to ease migrant distress during our formal interview at his home in a leafy neighborhood of Montgomery County. Instead, he emphasized the emotional and psychological pain that his congregation aimed to address, primarily through providing a regular space for community gathering, companionship, and recognition:

> During the week, these people [Brazilian migrants] live very much alone (*vivem muito sozinhas*). Because they are working without talking, without understanding. Therefore, when they arrive at the end of the week and enter our church . . . my gosh! (*Nossa!*), to hear your language and even be able to speak! During the week if you see these people, they are saying, "You're not really seeing me, I'm not this person" (*Não está me vendo. Não sou essa pessoa*). But when they come to church in their good clothes, high heels, ties, then, "Now, look at me. Now I'm me. I was such-and-such leader of this church in Brazil. There I did this. There I was a professor. There I was an engineer. I was even a pastor there . . . I wasn't who you saw over there during the week."

According to Pastor João, churchgoing among Brazilian migrants constituted a performance in which individuals asserted their premigrant selves, enabling them to reembody affects and dispositions they had habitually suspended throughout the week. The engineer-turned-construction-worker demanded respect; the teacher-turned-house-cleaner asserted dignity. Through joining together, migrants constructed an alternative universe to their daily realities in which to recognize one another as full social selves, "seeing" one another for who they truly felt themselves to be. Pastor João's commitment to fostering such healing relationships explicitly informed the church's motto, emblazoned on all institutional materials: "You're not alone, we're your family" (*Você não está só, somos sua família*).

Angela, a single woman in her early thirties whom I met at the Baptist church, echoed Pastor João's words in recounting to me what drove her to first attend church soon after arriving in the United States to work as a live-in domestic worker for a Brazilian diplomatic couple:

> When I arrived, I did not know anyone, only them [my employers]. I did not have any contact with any Brazilians, *zero* contact. And then the woman that did my boss's nails was Brazilian, and she went to this church [the Baptist church]. We started talking, and she said, "Let's go to church on Sunday. I'll come to pick you up." And I said, I don't know anyone, it will be good to meet Brazilians.

Angela continued attending services regularly, becoming enmeshed in the community, and ultimately was baptized. Although she had been born into a

Pentecostal congregation in Brazil, she had never undergone baptism. Once in the United States, however, she felt differently. Angela's mother, still in Brazil, was surprised at her decision. Angela shared how she responded to her mother's incredulity:

> I explained to her, when you are here, without your family, without any friends, you feel alone (*se sente só*), and look for something to hold on to (*vai buscar alguma coisa para se agarrar*) so I began to attend the church, I began to convert, I was baptized, and it was the best decision I ever made in my life.

Life amid others who spoke Portuguese, gathered several times a week to worship a deeply intimate and all-powerful God, and endured similar challenges and degradations of migrant life in the United States provided Angela with "something to hold on to." Rather than know no one, be known by no one, and suffer from "zero contact," Angela and many migrants like her found recognition and care within the context of evangelical churches.

The profound significance of mutual "seeing" and "recognizing" within the church encounter among migrants who otherwise experienced alienation, marginalization, and loneliness can be better understood by considering what Angela Garcia calls "commensurability" and "watchfulness,"[46] forms of care she identifies among heroin users in the New Mexican Española Valley. According to Garcia, care involves not only "watching over" someone who suffers but rather "watching *with*" them.[47] Caring from this perspective necessitates commensurability, a form of shared vulnerability. She writes, "It is a practice that opens up the possibility of being-together. . . . In the midst of loss, insecurity, and abandonment, the healing potential of social commensurability, of keeping watch with one another, remains vital."[48] In his writings on xenophobia in Britain post–September 11, Paul Gilroy similarly considers the forms of sociality that emerge from, and may potentially overcome, broader contexts of rupture.[49] The key to overcoming hate-filled narratives of division, according to Gilroy, depends on daily intimacy among diverse individuals, what he terms "conviviality," living life together.[50]

I observed similar forms of therapeutic sociality within migrant evangelical churches. From their common experience of loneliness, vulnerability, and invisibility, migrants forged dense everyday sociality within the context of evangelical churches. Churches encouraged migrants to care for one another in part by witnessing, empathizing, and recognizing the ways in which daily life constituted injury, and enabled migrants to heal through social restoration stimulated by multiple ways of being together.

A Note on Exclusion

Despite their promise to be all-embracing and all-inclusive communities of care, several migrants I met throughout my fieldwork experienced upset, exclusion, and disappointment at the hands of these institutions. The tight-knit intimacy of the core members of the congregation, and the beneficial multilayered sociality such intimacy afforded, seemed to depend on an equally well defined "outside." It was particularly easy to distinguish visitors and casual churchgoers in the Pentecostal church by where they sat and how they dressed. The core church members often wore similar colors and sat in the pews nearest to the pulpit, demarcating themselves as leaders and participants, while non-members generally wore more casual attire and sat near the back of the church.

Given the sheer centrality of these churches in the lives of migrants, rejecting or being rejected from such spaces carried especially weighty consequences. Churches were often the only regular spaces in which migrants felt they belonged—where they heard their language, where their status was never questioned, where they freely traded advice and information, where they enjoyed the company of being together and the dignity of being seen. Exclusion from such spaces often resulted in migrants experiencing increased loneliness, marginality, and isolation. Despite these exclusions, however, I found that personal faith among migrants remained hardy and steadfast, a conclusion I examine more fully at the end of the book.

Against a Hermeneutics of Suspicion

Through affective therapeutics, migrant evangelical churches offered attractive and accessible solutions to the kinds of distress migrants commonly faced as a result of deeply ingrained structural constraints. By adeptly and comprehensively recasting the problems migrants encountered as individual and spiritual in nature, rather than collective and systemic, churches contended that reforming one's interior landscape through intimacy with God and Christian community enabled enduring happiness, peace, contentment, and liberation. Migrants learned to "cure" their own afflictions in these churches by embodying love (*amor*) rather than pain (*dor*), choosing happiness and positivity over bitterness and negativity, and viewing themselves as vessels of God's transformative love. The deep intimacy, mutual recognition, and relationships of care fostered by evangelical churches reinforced these good feelings and their therapeutic outcome. Through these tactics and the promise of God's consoling embrace, churches cast themselves as hospitals for migrant sufferers.

Critical theorists point to the power dynamics inherent in the kind of therapeutics I witnessed in migrant evangelical churches and have outlined above.[51] These scholars raise important questions regarding the potential costs of discourses of happiness and healing. For instance, what kinds of migrant feelings and experiences do churches erase by emphasizing happiness? What broader power regimes do such erasures serve, such as profit maximization for the elite?[52] While individuals may perceive good feelings to result from their healing, critical theorists argue that larger structures, namely, the neoliberal order, configure these convenient and profitable affects. The pursuit and internalization of happy feelings, and the rejection of negative feelings, these theorists assert, reproduce prevailing structures of privilege, injustice, and harm.

It would be easy to apply this reading, a hermeneutics of suspicion, to the material I have presented at the exclusion of all other interpretations.[53] By producing happy believers, such a hermeneutics would suggest, evangelical churches neutralized the political mobility of Brazilian migrants by orienting them toward private feeling rather than civic engagement, and absorbing them into the Western world's ceaseless pursuit of individual happiness, often to the detriment of collective equity, justice, and uplift. "Happy" migrants, accordingly, become law-abiding individualists, grateful to be in the United States, and largely disinterested in structural change.[54]

This reading, born from suspicion, is not wrong. It raises critical insights about the power and politics of religious institutions, how churches become sites of production and exclusion, and how evangelical Christianity reflects and bolsters the neoliberal order. Yet, asserting this narrative at the exclusion of all other interpretations misses an equally significant, and frequently overlooked, consequence of evangelical belonging among migrants. This therapeutics, while apparently depoliticizing and conservative, can also be understood as imbuing migrants with a significant and consequential feeling of potentiality, what Cheryl Mattingly identifies as the "radical hope" embedded in "trying to create lives worth living even in the midst of suffering."[55] Rejecting a hermeneutics of suspicion, and instead employing a hermeneutics of understanding, I argue that evangelical therapeutics enabled migrants to project hopeful and liberatory "imagined futures" within intimate community. These imagined futures remained particularly meaning-laden because they were understood as divinely conceived.

4

Hopeful Migrants,
Confident Christians

SPIRITUAL DISCIPLINES AND
EVANGELICAL EFFICACY

AS I WALKED into church on one of my final days of fieldwork in July 2014, an air of despair greeted me. The usually jubilant and energetic congregants spoke to one another in hushed tones, and many dabbed visibly wet eyes. As the worship service got under way, a new kind of wail pierced the congregation. I had learned to recognize the usual sounds of spiritual ecstasy over the prior fifteen months, the cries of encounter with divinity and "being slayed" in the Holy Spirit, but *this* cry sounded altogether different—an uncontrollable, guttural utterance of absolute desperation. As I scanned the chapel, I found the wail emanated from Neide, a woman in her midforties. Juliana, the pastor's wife, rushed to Neide's side and ushered her to the corner, where Neide then collapsed into her embrace. Neide's two daughters, aged sixteen and five, hurried to be with their mother. Absent was David, the girls' father. As I watched, I wondered, what had befallen him?

After services, I asked Neusa what had happened. With eyes downcast, she explained that he had been arrested while on vacation in Ocean City, a popular beach community in Maryland. The police pulled him over, she surmised, because he had a prominently displayed Brazilian flag bumper sticker, making him an easy target for racial profiling. Having received a deportation notice years earlier after crossing the Mexican border, and failing to appear at immigration court, he was now at risk for expedited deportation. David, Neide, and their elder daughter had lived in the United States for almost a decade, and Carina, their younger daughter, had been born in Maryland.

Deportation would upend their family life regardless of whichever impossible choice they made: either prolonged separation while mother and daughters remained in the US and David returned to Brazil, or an unwanted return to Brazil, a country neither child considered home.

At the time of services, David had been detained for two weeks. At the end of my fieldwork, a month later, his status remained uncertain. When I asked Neusa what would happen, she shook her head and said that everyone continued to pray. She invoked Acts 12:12–17, the biblical story of Peter, who miraculously escaped prison the night his friends and neighbors gathered to pray for his release. Like Peter, she explained, David's fate was left *nas mãos de Deus*, in God's hands.

Several weeks and even months later, David's teenage daughter, Jênifer, conveyed a similar faithful resolve on her Facebook page. In one resolute message, she wrote, "My lawyer is my Lord, he defends me in front of my accuser. I put my fate in His hands, so I can rest my heart." Months later, after fieldwork concluded, I learned through Facebook that David had returned home. It is easy to imagine how the family would understand this terrifying experience through the lens of evangelical faith. They had prayed and God had listened. They had put their lives, and their loved one's life, in the hands of God. Their reward was David's safe return home, and the preservation of the life they had become accustomed to in the United States. Neide and Jênifer's faith in the face of David's detainment revealed the power and persistence of evangelical hope for migrants. More so, it revealed how such steadfast resolve and dogged optimism emerged precisely from believers' precarity as undocumented migrants in the United States.

How, and to what extent, did affective therapeutics "work"? How did evangelical discourse and practice not only compel migrants to convert and intensify their commitments to churches, pastors, and cobelievers but also fundamentally alter their broader experience as migrants? How can this account satisfy the skeptical reader who might subscribe to the hermeneutics of suspicion, and view migrant believers as dupes of cunning pastors, or as "happy" subjects of the neoliberal order?

The phrase Jênifer used in English to convey her absolute conviction in her father's return, "in His hands," meaning "in the hands of God," and which Neusa spoke in Portuguese, "nas mãos de Deus," to communicate the same, offers an answer to each of these questions, and to the broader question of efficacy. Rather than amount to escapism or apathy, the disciplined practices and real-world consequences of putting oneself *nas mãos de Deus* meaningfully alleviated the specific forms of distress migrants encountered, including loneliness, anxiety, despair, and feeling stuck. The twin processes encapsulated in the evocative phrase *nas mãos de Deus*—the spiritual disciplines and real-world applications of affective therapeutics—are the focus of this chapter.

Evangelical Potentiality and the Problem with Politics

I learned early on what other anthropologists of Christianity have often reported: that my research subject (evangelical Christianity) and analysis (that evangelical Christianity warranted serious consideration) made many colleagues, family members, and friends deeply uncomfortable.[1] Often repelled by the heteronormative, patriarchal, and politically conservative nature of evangelical Christianity in the United States, individuals failed to suppress knee-jerk reactions to my inquiry, or my sympathetic rendering of those who practiced conservative Christianity. Over dinner one night in Palo Alto, California, for instance, a visiting scholar openly mocked my project, remarking, "Of all the Brazilians you could have studied, you chose the *least* fun and the *most* backward!" Another time, a friend's mother shook her head disapprovingly when she learned of my project. She lamented how her Brazilian housecleaner consistently "threw away" her paycheck to her church. She wondered if I might intercede in Portuguese to convince the woman not to "waste" her money.

Academic colleagues found my ethnographic writing unsettling. While writing about undocumented migrants (an accepted anthropological trope that engages what Joel Robbins terms the "suffering slot"[2]), I also explored the "efficacy" of conservative Christianity, and how it significantly reshaped migrant interiority and experience. Several interlocutors found this approach troubling. Wasn't evangelical Christianity simply "brainwashing" migrants, they wondered, numbing very real pain, and making them blind to the structural conditions that produced their distress? Worse, wasn't the church simply transforming them into willing cogs in the churning wheel of American capitalism and state-sanctioned violence against ethnic, racial, and religious "others"?

Rebecca Lester's commentary on an essay I authored regarding these subjects succinctly articulates these suspicions, giving voice to those who would see evangelical faith among migrants purely as a contemporary "opiate" of the masses.[3] Lester writes:

> a cynical perspective might suggest that, in this regard, such churches function at least in part as defusing stations, where migrants are provided a sense of home and community and an amelioration of their potentially

disruptive affects, while they are increasingly socialized into subjects will-ing to accept the meager—and sometimes cruel—dispensations of the various bureaucratic systems in which they are embedded.[4]

While Lester, herself a scholar of religious interiority and its therapeutic ef-fects, takes belief and its ameliorative capacity seriously, she forcefully evokes the suspicions that such research often generates.[5]

As I repeatedly encountered such questions, I learned that the pervasive discomfort and at times open suspicion of evangelical subjectivity among mi-grants reflected deeply entrenched cultural assumptions regarding what counts as efficacy, agency, and freedom. This tendency is as true in popular discourse as it is in academic literature, where considerations of religious efficacy, particularly among marginalized and subaltern communities, have often become muddled with questions of political agency.[6] Evaluations of po-litical agency in writings on religion have been especially pronounced with regard to Latin American Christianity. Such scholarship examines whether evangelical conversion promotes or hinders political mobilization and self-determination among formerly Catholic populations.[7] This literature, which often focuses on the rural and urban poor, often conjoins the question of po-litical influence and self-esteem, assuming that those with greater self-assurance and self-love are more likely to organize, protest, and agitate for change.[8]

Two opposing poles have come to define the terrain of this debate. While some scholars argue that the broad evangelization (or "Protestantization" and "Pentecostalization") of Latin America signals the region's adoption of liberal cultural values such as individualism, democracy, and modernity, others suggest that Protestant denominations, especially charismatic and Pentecostal groups, perpetuate the entrenched hierarchy of the hacienda system, whereby power remains concentrated in the hands of elites.[9] These opposing views have led to contradicting conclusions regarding the political consequences of conversion. Champions of the former consider the evangelical turn of Latin America to be an agent-producing social movement, whereas advocates of the latter highlight the religious movement's tendency to produce political apathy and withdrawal.[10] Embedded in both of these opposing positions, however, remains the central question of how religious belief impacts liberal concep-tions of agency and freedom.

The search for, and evaluation of, an individually bounded and willful po-litical self in these framings betrays the extent to which such studies remain influenced by Enlightenment framings of freedom produced in Europe and North America.[11] Such studies suggest that the political arena, defined by electoral politics, community organizing, legislative action, and public mobilization, remains the primary arena within which to witness and evaluate agency. Furthermore, agents ought to clearly demonstrate their freedoms through specific kinds of self-initiated public actions, namely, voting, speaking, protesting, organizing. To be considered truly "free" under such scrutiny, such agents must be strictly bounded individuals who act according to their own personal will, reason, and desires.

How can we evaluate religious movements born from distinctly nonliberal traditions, and the kinds of subjectivities and intersubjectivities they shape?[12] This chapter demonstrates how apparently submissive evangelical disciplines, including prayer, discernment, and testimony, generate modes of self-realization, freedom, and agency among migrants, despite being divorced from liberal assumptions of "autonomous will" and an "emancipatory politics."[13]

———

JBR: Are you involved or interested in political debates concerning immigration reform?

GLÁUCIA: I really leave them *nas mãos de Deus,* because in the first place, I can't do anything. I can read, right? And, I can wait. But, especially for me, I'm in the hands of God. They could pass a law, and maybe I wouldn't be eligible [for amnesty] under this law, you know what I mean? Therefore, I always think, "My life is in the hands of God." I love living here. But if God wants me to leave, I'm under God's will (*de baixo da vontade de Deus*). Wherever God directs me, I will go. Therefore, I don't get worried, because we can't become worried about what comes tomorrow. Because tomorrow belongs to God. We make our plans, we have to make our plans. It's just that, I'm not going to be, you know, nervous, worried. This is in the hands of God. The most I can do, which I always try to do, is pray to God to give direction to the governors . . . to those who are involved with this. That it will be God's will, that God touches their hearts (*que Deus toque o coração deles*) and that we can be blessed.

———

Like most of the migrant believers I met, Gláucia aimed to submit wholly to God. In order to make decisions and act, therefore, Gláucia engaged in spiritual practices meant to perform her dependency on God, and illuminate God's will, rather than her own. Detached from the liberal trappings of autonomy and individual freedom, agency in this case becomes, according to Saba Mahmood, "a capacity for action that specific relations of subordination create and enable." This capacity remains "predicated on [the] ability to be taught . . . a condition classically referred to as 'docility.'"[14]

What could Gláucia do about the injustices that migrants faced in the United States? In her words, the "most" she could do was pray to God to change the hearts of those in positions of power. Other than that, she "[left] them *nas mãos de Deus.*" According to liberal assumptions about agency, this orientation would be interpreted as self-effacing, passive, and apathetic, signaling an absence or abnegation of freedom. Yet, I learned that "leaving things in the hands of God" entailed choice, work, and proactivity that ultimately expanded migrants' sense of their own potentiality—of what they could accomplish, imagine, and become both within and outside of the United States. In large part, such feelings of potentiality among migrant believers resulted from the forms of sociality and intimacy evangelical Christianity afforded. Instead of the individualistic, bounded, and self-determining protagonists of political liberalism, evangelical performances of submission and dependency fostered deeply relational and porous subjects, defined by multifaceted and embodied intimacy among migrants, clergy, and God.

In lieu of political or economic power, migrant believers deployed their devotion to transform their felt and lived realities. The practices of prayer, discernment, and testimony enabled migrants to feel responsible for the tenor of their lives in the United States. Not only did migrant believers report feeling less despair and greater hope as a result of their faith, but they also demonstrated how such spiritual practices enabled them to obtain tangible goods that improved their daily lives, such as legal documents, better employment, reliable housing, and financial assistance.

Sincerity, Meaning, and Materialism

What does it mean for spiritual disciplines to "work"? This question cuts to the heart of age-old debates in anthropology and religious studies concerning why people believe, and what believing accomplishes for them. Answers to these questions have generally fallen into two categories: intellectualism and materialism. According to intellectualists, religion works when it reorients how adherents view the world, and, as a result, imbues adherents with newfound feelings of well-being, resolve, contentment, purpose, and peace. Materialists, alternatively, suggest that religion works when it enables adherents to secure worldly goods or concrete advantages from belief, such as money, power, and prestige.[15] This latter view of religious efficacy is often denigrated as "functionalist" or "utilitarian," whereas the former would correspond to "sincere" conversion triggered by authentic internal transformation. Affective therapeutics, I observed, worked for migrants by accomplishing both of these goals simultaneously. The discursive tactics discussed in chapter 3 imbued migrants with a sense of choice, purpose, and divine partnership. This chapter considers how migrants shored up these good feelings and parlayed them into consequential action.

First, evangelical discourse and practice reoriented migrants to their daily experience. Striving to place themselves *nas mãos de Deus*, in the hands of God, as Jênifer, Neusa, and Gláucia relate, meant trusting wholly in God's plans and short-circuiting their own mortal reactivity. Such wholehearted submission relieved migrant distress, transforming perception of self and experience. In this sense, affective therapeutics supports an intellectualist framing of religion. Evangelical Christianity worked by making migrants feel better about themselves and the world around them.

Second, and just as significantly, this transformed sense of self and world spurred novel forms of activity. Migrants did not just feel anew; they also acted anew. Placing themselves in God's hands enabled migrants to more proactively pursue concrete goods that would meaningfully improve their daily lives and mitigate marginality. These goods of migration included green cards, driver's licenses, stable housing, secure employment, and visas for loved ones. Affective therapeutics thus also supports a materialist framing of religion.

This chapter delves into the deep entanglement of these two modes of religious efficacy. When religious conversion confers material rewards, observers question the "sincerity" of those who profess belief. The ideology of sincerity insists that one's words must correlate to one's inner intentions, and furthermore must be divorced from material pursuits.[16] The evaluation of religious conversion, by clergy and scholars alike, has often hinged on such questions. What I learned from the migrants I met refuted this simple binary. Their experience in the world, largely shaped by the forms of distress and dispossession they experienced, motivated their religious seeking and intensified their yearning for intimacy with God, pastors, and cobelievers. In turn, faith practices and deeply held convictions emboldened their action in the secular realm and informed how they interpreted everyday events. For the migrants I met, intellectualism and materialism converged, for so too did faith and daily life.

Spiritual Disciplines: Prayer and Discernment

Migrant believers worked to place themselves in the hands of God through the twin practices of prayer and discernment. Despite the churches' differing approaches to prayer, each of the three congregations I studied promoted prayer as the primary way to know and act upon God's will.[17] Through these practices, migrants asserted their capacity and responsibility to make God hear their prayers, and to prove righteous enough to warrant God's response. Through practiced and disciplined prayer, adherents acted upon their environment as confident Christians rather than as marginalized migrants.

Open-Scripted Prayer

The migrant believers I met described three distinct modes of open-scripted prayer: *falando com Deus* (informally chatting with God), *oração* (formal prayer), and *louvor* (formal group worship and praise). Each kind of prayer remained open-scripted in that believers spoke extemporaneously to God, rather than according to a predetermined liturgy. In the first mode, congregants reported "chatting" with God while driving, working, eating, and bathing. Such regular and lighthearted chatting remained integral for feelings of closeness with God to develop. The second mode, *oração*, occurred alone or in small groups. Unlike informal chatting, successful *oração* required privacy, quiet, and concentration. Migrants knelt, closed their eyes, and prayed somberly in the privacy of their own homes. In the third mode, migrants participated in group praise, *louvor*, during regular worship services.[18] Such prayer, often accompanied by music and guided by clergy, was frequently noisy. During group services in the Pentecostal church, believers stood with their hands extended upward, swayed side to side, shook their heads emphatically, and yelled their prayers aloud. While less pronounced, group prayer in both the Adventist and Baptist churches followed a similar format. Accompanied by music and guided by pastors, congregants prayed together with their intimates, often speaking their prayers out loud or in hushed tones. In each church, prayer entailed visible work. Adherents often wiped their eyes and brows following group prayer, helped each other to stand, and embraced. Their prayer had generated and demanded intense energy, focus, and commitment.

Pastor Jeferson explicitly encouraged loudness. He cited vocalized prayer as a formidable weapon against the Devil.[19] During a service to liberate believers from satanic forces (*culto de libertação*), he guided the group of thirty to feverish, high-pitched prayer by yelling from the pulpit, "Não fica calado! Abre a sua boca e grita!" (Don't stay quiet! Open your mouth and yell!). Silence was the tool of the Devil, he charged, while praying loudly demonstrated to God that you were vigorously *lutando* (fighting) evil.

Yet, for other migrants, praying alone and in silence best assured the safe arrival of one's prayers to God. Despite being a member of Pastor Jeferson's church, Gláucia insisted on leaving her most pressing requests to silent prayer. She told me, "When I want something specific, a response, for me to know that it's really God, I only pray in my mind. God has the power to know your thoughts. But the Devil, he doesn't have this power, but if you speak, he can hear it."

Gláucia's comment revealed the deliberate choice involved in style, volume, and form of prayer. Migrants determined how best to address God according to the particular prayer they had uttered and according to their desired result. As such, prayer constituted an important form of action for the migrants I met. Like Guatemalan Neo-Pentecostals or American congregants of the Vineyard church, Brazilian migrants practiced prayer to act on their interior and exterior worlds.[20]

Toward this end, the churches I attended organized numerous activities to engage migrants in prayer. The Pentecostal church hosted weekly prayer circles, monthly consecrations, and occasional all-night vigils. In each of these gatherings, men and women prayed on their knees for hours at a time. The Adventist and Baptist churches hosted prayer walks and morning prayer conference calls in addition to weekly services. The plethora of such prayer meetings suggests that, like their US counterparts, migrant evangelicals viewed prayer as a spiritual discipline to "train" through frequent engagement and devotion.[21]

The migrants I met described ideal prayer as an unfettered and uncensored stream of consciousness shared with God. Through constant divulgence, appeal, and giving thanks, God became friend, father, companion, and counselor. In response to the question "When you pray, how do you know when God is present?" adherents gave answers highlighting sensation in their body. For instance, one Baptist responded, "Through the peace I feel in my heart." An Adventist wrote, "Through the comfort God concedes me when I pray"; another Adventist answered, "I feel the emptying of my problems and the Holy Spirit giving me strength to confront daily fights."[22] Through responses that highlighted feeling states, believers identified their interior landscapes as indications of God's presence.

During one Thursday evening *culto de ensino* (theological study), Presbyter Rogério articulated the connection between heightened emotion called forth in prayer and God's presence. "Without sound, there is no revival!" (Sem som, não há avivamento!), he called. He then encouraged the group to cry, for crying facilitated proximity with God.[23] Rogério announced, "God is the Great Consoler. It's glorious to see someone cry in the presence of God. So, cry more (*chora mais*)! Cry, cry, cry! Those who cry are those who seek [God]." During the week, believers strived to both stimulate and simulate this emotional sensitivity by watching sermons and listening to popular music online, reading the Bible and Christian self-help books, and attending prayer meetings and Bible studies. The capacity to generate and interpret feeling, therefore, became a primary method to experience the presence of God.

Discernment

Through all three forms of prayer, believers strived for discernment—the ability to know God's will. While frequency and fervency of prayer allowed believers to literally feel divine presence in their lives, prayer also enabled individuals to understand and influence God's will. This divinely inspired "gift of discernment" (*o dom de discernimento*) allowed believers to understand the personal significance of biblical passages and prophecies, as well as gain insight into the origin of spiritual phenomena. Because believers considered the world to be animated equally by agents of God and the Devil, praying for and employing discernment remained crucial to safeguarding faith and pursuing righteousness.

Migrant churches were extremely self-conscious of charges of charlatanism, leading to frequent suspicion of claims of divine encounter or divine knowledge.[24] Much of the content I heard during sermons and Bible study was aimed at teaching believers to subject claims of personal experience of God to rigorous scrutiny. Above all, migrant believers emphasized biblical coherence and confirmation through other people's prayers. If the purported message diverged from the Word of God (e.g., "You should leave your husband for

Fulana's husband, whom I've prepared for you"), the message most certainly emanated from demonic forces rather than from God.[25]

Pastor Jeferson and Juliana frequently warned against the proliferation of "false prophets" (*profetas falsos*) and called discernment the "most important gift" God bestowed. To illustrate growing inauthenticity in Christianity, Juliana once criticized a migrant church in the region that routinely left out chairs for its resident "angels." The church members had most certainly lost their ability to discern the real from the unreal, she laughed. In another cautionary tale, Pastor Jeferson told the congregation about a woman who had claimed to be possessed by the Devil during every worship service. Detecting falsity in her flamboyant spiritual display, the pastor, with presumed divine ordinance, commanded her to stop. When she did not, he threw a glass of cold water on her. With an audible yelp, she immediately ceased speaking in tongues, proving she had manufactured her possession.

Different from distrust (*desconfiança*), which grew from human weakness and suspicion of others, discernment (*discernimento*) emerged from divine wisdom (*sabedoria*). When pastors, missionaries, or cobelievers delivered a prophecy (e.g., "God wants you to return to Brazil now," or "God is calling you to be a missionary in Africa," or "The man you are dating is/is not the man God prepared for you"), believers employed discernment to determine the origin of the message. Did it come from God or the Devil? The ability to discern enabled believers to interpret the events of their daily lives according to God's will (*a vontade de Deus*) and God's plan (*o plano de Deus*).

Following one Sunday school lesson, an older woman offered testimony concerning the importance of discernment. During the prior week, Eduarda reported feeling incredibly depressed over several days. She prayed to God, read her Bible, and fasted, hoping to discover what "to do" next to relieve her upset. The next morning, she awoke energized, ready to "fight" against what had upset her (she did not divulge the specific details of the situation). Then, the next evening, she heard a soft voice whispering, "Silêncio, silêncio." In this moment, Eduarda recalled to the group, she discerned that God wanted her to remain silent, and to wait for Him to act, rather than take matters into her own hands. Juliana nodded in agreement, noting that each believer should discern whether it was the Holy Spirit, or God's adversaries, moving them to action.

Eduarda's account and Juliana's response revealed important evangelical considerations on the limitations of human agency and free will. Rather than result in increased freedom, as theories of political liberalism would suggest, self-directed action, according to evangelical thought, amounted to enslaved action. Beyond merely misguided or willful, premature action and premature speech revealed possession by demonic forces, and risked eternal damnation. True liberation (*libertação*), migrant believers learned, depended on *silêncio* of the secular conception of "self," and in its place, submission to the will of God. Righteous submission almost always amounted to yielding to God and embodying divine patience. In mastering these techniques, however, adherents won God's favor and therefore enhanced His activity in their daily lives, a powerful action in its own right.

The Pursuit of Migrant Goods

Through the practices of prayer and discernment, migrant believers learned to experience themselves, and narrate themselves, as powerful beings able to impact the most pressing concerns of their daily lives. Rather than succumb to the feelings of being stuck with regard to the constantly shifting terrain of immigration reform and life without documents, prayer provided migrants with a pragmatic response.

Through its interpretive and generative power, prayer helped migrants obtain what I call the goods of migration: visas for loved ones, driver's licenses, green cards, housing contracts, and secure employment. These objects constituted "goods" in two senses. First, in the literal sense, they constituted concrete commodities that migrants exchanged and pursued. Second, they constituted the sought-after valuables that impacted migrant mobility and quality of life. Prayer conferred primary and secondary benefits with regard to these goods. First, prayer allowed believers to feel that they could impact bureaucracy through appealing to God. And second, because migrants felt that they could impact this domain despite their lack of status in the United States, prayer emboldened migrants to act pragmatically to obtain these goods. In both ways, migrants accessed and experienced potentiality through submission.

Migrant believers interpreted the general incidents of their lives through the quality of their prayer and the response they discerned from God. One's job, home, family, finances, and migration status depended on securing God's blessing, discerning His will, and enacting it. If migrants prayed enough, and if it was God's will, they would have the outcome they desired. Prayerful practices served to quell migrant anxiety and feelings of precariousness. What should migrants do to enhance the chances of visa approval for their loved ones in Brazil? How could they ensure the safety of their husbands and brothers who worked in construction year-round without any job protections or insurances against injury? How could migrants cope with the unknowable separation they faced from their families? The internal benefits and external consequences of regular prayer provided migrants with meaningful and productive ways to mitigate and overcome these brutally real circumstances.

A typical Monday evening prayer circle among *irmãs* highlighted the most pressing concerns for which migrants prayed, and demonstrated how migrants identified God in the mundane. During the two-hour prayer service, Juliana read aloud congregants' prayers over ailing loved ones, or those who had not yet accepted Jesus. She also read requests concerning visas, green cards, licenses, employment, and homes. After, the group of women gathered at the front of the church, where they provided accounts of the prayers from past weeks that had been answered.

During one such meeting, Paula thanked God for securing a tourist visa for her mother-in-law. With this document, she would be able to see her son for the first time in nine years and meet her daughter-in-law and newborn grand-daughter. Viviane's aunt and grandmother also secured visas, allowing them to see her and her mother for the first time in fourteen years. At another meeting, Maura testified about the small home where she lived. Despite being undocumented, she and her family found a freestanding home to lease with its own garage and yard. She had assumed she would have to live in the same concrete apartment complex where most congregants resided owing to its lenient leasing requirements for individuals without social security numbers.[26] According to these women, their good fortune was not arbitrary. Rather, God had recognized and rewarded their persistent devotion with increased mobility, visits from loved ones, and improved residences.

During our conversation at the large home where she worked as an au pair, Gláucia shared a recent example of her own efforts to increase God's work in her life. She had prayed daily that God find her a home, conversing with Him on her way to and from work, as well as in church. The couple she currently lived with intended to move out and could no longer take her on as a tenant. She found an encouraging listing on Craigslist, but when she asked God whether He intended this particular place for her, she discerned His response by randomly flipping to a biblical passage decrying "false gods." At first, she did not understand God's message. But, when she pulled up to the home, she saw a large statue of the Buddha prominently displayed on the front steps. With a visceral sense of foreboding, she immediately understood God's

warning, saying, "I felt something terrible in that house. And then I understood that God was telling me that this wasn't it. Because God is the All Powerful, there are no other gods." Despite her initial excitement, she left
immediately.

On her way home, feeling defeated, she stopped by a Portuguese store, and
spoke to the owner about her housing search. As another customer entered
the store, Gláucia heard the Holy Spirit speak to her, urging, "Keep talking.
Keep talking." So, she did. "The person that walked in heard me, and asked,
'Are you looking for a room to rent? I have a friend that has a basement, and
she's looking for someone.'" On the spot, the man called his friend, and offered
to take Gláucia directly to the home. Again, Gláucia felt God "working" in her.
She explained, "It was so clearly from God that God gave me peace in my heart
to follow him. I followed him, even though you shouldn't follow someone you
don't know, but the Holy Spirit gave me this peace in my heart."

At the home, Gláucia immediately felt she belonged. Yet, the owner asked
for $800 per month in rent, and Gláucia could only afford $600 per month.
She returned home and prayed that God "move" the woman to lower the rent.
Later that afternoon, the owner called and said, according to Gláucia, "I
thought about it, and I want you to live with me. I'm going to rent it to you for
$600." The woman encouraged Gláucia to invite her friends over from church,
to pray "loudly," and to "lift up the house in prayer."

Gláucia told me that she experienced profound happiness (*alegria*) every
time she arrived back at her new home, thinking to herself, "Wow! Look at
that beautiful house, Jesus!" The owner, a Christian woman whose children
had left for college, made her feel included in the family. When she needed
advice about the house, or about her personal life, or her faith, she conferred
with Gláucia. And this too, Gláucia noted, was the work of God: "God took
care of me . . . God sees that I am alone. Therefore, God wanted me to live in
a place where I could have a person to be my friend, to sit, converse, to watch
a movie together, and also to talk about God . . . so, I see the hand of God, it's
the answer to my prayers (*eu vejo assim a mão de Deus, é resposta de oração*)."

Through her active devotion, Gláucia had faith that God would hear her
prayers. The activities of prayer, Bible study, and church participation kept her
close to God, and in so doing, mitigated her anxieties related to her precarious
legal status. By following the instructions she discerned from Him, and praying
often, she felt confident in "being tied to" God, explaining, "When you stop
praying, when you stop reading the Word, you become distant (*se afasta*). Like

a plant, if you don't water the flower, it will keep withering (*vai murchando*) and it will die (*vai morrer*)."

Through the informal and formal activities of prayer, Gláucia nourished her relationship with God. In doing so, she remained assured and aware of God's constant presence and concern. Owing to this proximity, she was able to discern God's intense disapproval of the first home she visited, and quickly left. Again, she listened to God in the Portuguese store, continuing to talk about her housing search to the owner. When she found her current home, she remained confident that it was the answer to her prayers. God heard her prayers and delivered exactly what she had requested: a beautiful, safe, happy, Christian home. By "watering the plant" of her relationship with God, Gláucia ensured God's attentiveness.

When God Is Silent

Through prayer and discernment, migrants learned to convert waiting into a spiritual discipline. They practiced submitting to God's omnipotence and superior wisdom, and in doing so, yield to *o tempo de Deus* (God's time) rather than *o nosso tempo* (our time). "God's time is different from man's time," Pastor Jeferson frequently reminded the congregation. On several occasions, he pointed to Bible verses reinforcing this fact: Ecclesiastes 3, "There's a proper time for everything," and Daniel 2:21, "God moves the epochs and the seasons." God's time had no past and no future, he noted. You may pray for something today and receive His blessing in thirty years. Juliana echoed this message, saying, "God reveals things slowly." She suggested that God's slowness in revealing His plans for each believer was deliberate. As fallible humans, we could not tolerate God's wisdom to be revealed all at once. By accepting God's time, *crentes* worked to embody divine patience. Through this faithful and stoic posture, they asserted confidence in God's complete control of their lives.

Divine patience first required the intense work of complete submission to God. Juliana often criticized believers who sat in the pews every week but failed to seek out God on their own at home. Such congregants assumed faith was akin to *chiclete de segunda mão* (secondhand chewing gum). They erroneously believed they could get the same intensity of spiritual experience by digesting another's encounter with God. Instead, she urged the *irmãs* in her care to seek out their own intimacy with God. If they noticed an absence of blessing in their lives, whether at work, with their children, or in their marriage, it was likely due to insufficient prayer, study, and devotion. Pastor Jeferson also highlighted the activity involved in cultivating divine patience and submission, pointing to the story of Gideon (Judges 6). Believers should model themselves on this lowly farmer, who encountered God while he was alone, diligently and selflessly thrashing wheat in his field. "*Decide* to be born again!" Pastor Jeferson once thundered from the pulpit. "Change *now!*" (Mude agora!). God would lift up those who actively submitted themselves ("Se abaixe, Deus levanta").

Migrants frequently invoked *o tempo de Deus* when they expressed the uncertainty and precariousness of living without documents. Like Gláucia, migrants strived to put themselves completely in God's hands. When faced with denied visas and green cards, lack of health insurance, unstable employment, and possible deportation, adherents reminded themselves and others to pray, submit, and *wait*. For many years, Miriam, a Baptist woman in her late thirties, told me that she fought (*brigou*) with God about her immigration status. Over the course of two hours, Miriam divulged her eighteen-year saga applying for a green card. Despite the fact that her father, brother, stepmother, and sister had all attained US citizenship, her own application had been repeatedly denied.

When the application was finally approved after several years and multiple attempts, it came with the stipulation that she and her husband await their documentation in Brazil, where the process could take an additional decade to complete. A few weeks later, they received a deportation letter in the mail. Between 2006 and 2012, Miriam told me, she, her husband, and children appeared before an immigration court in Baltimore every year to appeal the deportation order. Miriam reported gathering letters from school psychologists, teachers, and lawyers to prove that her three US-born children would not only fail to thrive in Brazil, a country they did not know, but would also experience extreme hardship and psychological duress as a result of their parents' deportation. After six years of arbitration, the judge finally relented, and granted them an exception. Miriam and her husband could await documentation in the United States.

During these stressful and uncertain years, Miriam recalled she felt *revoltada* (revolted) by the legal system in the United States and exasperated by God's silence. She could not understand why each of her family members had acquired legal status, and the stability it afforded, while she continued to live on the margins. She felt unseen and unjustly persecuted by God. Over the last three years, however, her evangelical faith intensified and newly allowed her to reinterpret the turmoil surrounding her legal status in the United States as a divine gift. Miriam shared her new understanding with me:

> Today I can tell you that I'm calm and my heart is calm because I know that my green card is coming, maybe two or three years from now. But I'm calm, my heart is calm, because like I told you, God is planning. There's a purpose behind all of this (*tem um propósito em cima disso tudo*). Many things have happened in these years, and now I understand, "Okay, God still hasn't given me my green card because of everything that has happened here." If He had, if I had the green card in my hand during this period of my life, maybe this, this, or that would have happened in the wrong way.

When I pressed Miriam further, asking what exactly she thought could have happened had God granted the green card earlier, she pointed to her marital difficulties:

> Maybe, for example, if I had my green card three years ago, me and my husband wouldn't be together (*não estaríamos juntos*). To me, this is the greatest example of God working above everything. Today, I say, "Thank God I didn't have my green card three years ago. Thank God He didn't give it to me." Now my heart is calm. I wait. I wait for however long it will be.

If Miriam had acquired a green card three years ago, she conjectured, she likely would have returned to Brazil with her children and separated from her husband. God had deliberately withheld her documentation, she mused, to keep their family intact. In keeping with this newfound understanding, she awaited her documentation with patience, understanding it was "in God's time." During this divinely imposed waiting, Miriam explained, her family life had dramatically improved. Her marriage was now stable. She was in better control of her emotions. When she felt upset about her liminal status, instead of fighting with God or with her family, she prayed, saying, "God, calm the storm and make it pass" (*Deus, acalme a tempestade e faça passar*).

Through the activities of prayer and discernment, migrant believers mobilized their faith to cope with the enduring and open-ended nature of waiting without documents. Would they again see loved ones in Brazil? Would they receive amnesty from this administration or the next? Would they make it through deportation proceedings? Would they find document sponsorship through a family member or work? Would they ultimately become American citizens or return to Brazil? For many migrants, these unanswerable questions mounted as the years passed. The spiritual disciplines of evangelical faith transformed this enforced and mundane waiting into righteous and divine action.

Divine waiting, however, did not mean abdication from worldly activity, especially the kind of activity that might dramatically improve migrants' lives. Like Miriam, migrant believers pursued action in both the mundane and heavenly spheres. Rather than replace worldly strategies to secure relief, prayer, discernment, and testimony accompanied and emboldened such real-world pursuits. The faith practices described above imbued believers with a kind of divine confidence.

While Miriam prayed for her documents to arrive, she also showed up at immigration court for six years in a row, enlisted the help of a lawyer she worked for, and gathered the testimony of psychologists and school counselors to attest to the need for her entire family to stay in the United States. She came to see herself as partnered with God in this divine pursuit. She prayed *and* she wrote letters. She fasted *and* she gathered documents. When days and months turned into years, she strengthened her resolve by invoking "God's time," and "God's will." With a calm heart and mind, she prayed, she acted, and she waited.

I found such industriousness among migrant believers to be manifold. Migrants referenced Maryland's immigration laws, preferable to those of Virginia, providing insight into their residential choices. They tracked the apartment complexes that required social security numbers versus tax identification numbers. They encouraged family members in Brazil to apply for tourist visas at specific locations, learning about supposedly sympathetic consulate workers. They enrolled in local English classes and even recruited their resident anthropologist to provide them with lessons. They discovered free prenatal clinics and applied for medical assistance funds. They opened businesses and energetically marketed their services. And, they shared information of their successes and failures. Prayer informed and strengthened such secular activities by ensuring, in migrants' minds, that their earthly pursuits would be divinely blessed.

Testimony: The Social Currency of Migrant Faith

In addition to prayer and discernment, migrant evangelical practice depended on testimony. Through giving voice to God's miraculous answering of prayers during both formal and informal settings, believers bolstered their own, and each other's, faithfulness.[27] Similar to the practices of prayer and discernment, testimony enabled adherents to assert and enact agency predicated on religious devotion. While prayer and discernment emboldened migrants to act pragmatically by viewing themselves as partnered with God, testimony shored up migrants' confidence in their rightful place in the United States. Through the giving and receiving of such testimonies, migrants identified the meaning and purpose behind their own and others' journeys to the United States. Furthermore, this practice articulated and performed ideal evangelical selfhood in relation to God and Christian community.

In utilizing the practice of testimony to articulate an empowered sense of self, shore up collective solidarity, and claim rightful belonging in the United States, migrant believers mobilized an age-old "rights claiming" tradition that traverses religious and secular contexts in both the United States and across Latin America. As a "performative and public speech-act" long employed by marginalized communities to make visible violence, injustice, and despair, and simultaneously point toward redemptive possibility, the act of testifying remains deeply embedded in Latin American societies, where Indigenous and rural communities give testimony to "enact alternative visions of political and cultural participation," and to create "new cultures that influence how to do politics, defend rights, and engage with the state."[28]

In the United States, historically persecuted and disenfranchised populations, especially Black Americans, have long employed first-person narratives "witnessing" their dehumanization, abuse, and mistreatment for the purpose of decrying and rejecting injustice, mobilizing social support, and asserting alternative visions of just and inclusive futures.[29] Whether such testimonies occur in courtrooms, churches, or other public spaces, they serve to impact both the speaker and the listener by "broadening who participates in the creation of social memory and truth."[30] While the Brazilian migrants I met delivered exclusively religious testimonies, delivered in unequivocally religious settings, and couched in their intimate encounter with God, their engagement in testimony served ends similar to testimony delivered in courtrooms and truth and reconciliation commissions. Across these venues, testimony enabled the "harnessing of emotion and building it into a sense of collective solidarity and human dignity."[31]

Testimony as Self-Narrative and Self-Construction

One Friday in late March, Thaís invited me to attend a youth group meeting with her at a Baptist church different from the one where we had first met. On Friday nights, she attended this group, made up exclusively of young Brazilian migrants in their twenties and thirties, even though it was affiliated with a competing congregation. When I arrived around 8:30 p.m., I was struck by the size of the church, and the fact that the Brazilian congregation so visibly owned it. Unlike the Brazilian Pentecostal and Baptist churches where I had primarily conducted fieldwork, this church's name was proudly emblazoned above the door, marking its community and leadership as sufficiently established and well-resourced to buy permanent church space.[32] Plastered on its walls were photos of its own congregants, rather than the anonymous faces of strangers.

A group of young people casually socialized in the chapel as they awaited their peers and youth group leader, Norman. They joked around with one another, flirted, and played on their iPhones. As we waited, we placed chairs in a circle, preparing for the usual Bible study. In contrast with the Adventist and Pentecostal meetings I had attended, there was a lightness of mood, I noted as I relaxed into the informality of socializing with peers on a Friday night. When Norman arrived around 9 p.m., he also took note of the playful and easy mood among attendees and suggested that the group do something different. With only about fifteen people in attendance, and a few others trickling in, he aimed for something more "intimate." He suggested the group share their *testemunhos*—their "testimonies"—with one another.

Norman did not elaborate upon this concept. Rather, he assumed that his audience understood this word and invitation implicitly: to publicly share how God had blessed and transformed their lives, and in doing so, glorify God's greatness and give thanks (*dar graças*) for His blessings. Testimonies provided space for believers to detail, document, and distribute the ways in which they had experienced God's hand personally, and to reflect upon the impact of this encounter.

Testimonies were a central feature of all group religious practice in each of the evangelical churches I observed. Believers often retold especially evocative testimonies they had witnessed or heard about years before. I heard several stories repeated frequently: the woman who had stopped a gang shooting in São Paulo by marching into the middle of the street with a Bible tucked under her arm; the congregation that had forestalled torrential Amazonian rains with their fervent prayers; believers who had survived Hurricane Katrina unscathed while holding a prayer vigil in an exposed driveway while every other home succumbed to flood waters. Such testimonies inspired strong feelings in both listener and speaker, and served to "edify" (*edificar*) the faith of all in attendance, including the individual bearing witness to God's power in their own life.

Migrants deployed testimonies to situate themselves as divinely ordained to be in the United States. Such an assertion explicitly refuted, and worked to counteract, feelings of precariousness, doubt, and liminality broadly associated with migrant experience. In the act of announcing to others the divine purpose behind their departure from Brazil and arrival in the United States through testimony, migrants newly presented themselves as empowered and purposeful agents of God.[33]

On the evening of my visit to the Baptist youth group, the young men and women in the room offered testimonies that shared one striking feature. One after another, each young person asserted that God, the church, and their faith had enabled them to transcend misery, loneliness, and depression in the United States. Furthermore, they reflected new understanding about their central purpose in the United States: to truly *know* God (*conhecer o Deus*). Without God, a young man visiting from Boston asserted, he would have returned to Brazil long ago. Instead, he reported triumphantly, "I've now lived here for fourteen years!" Meeting God in the United States had revealed the purpose of his life: to stay and spread God's Word in this new land. Now, staying (*ficando*) in the face of struggle proved his enduring commitment to God and "God's mission."

Cláudio, another participant, articulated a similar conclusion. He shared that he had moved to the United States in the mid-1990s, but soon decided to return to Brazil. Once back in his home country, however, he embarked on several doomed ventures. He failed his driver's test. His business selling evangelical books and music floundered. In the face of these defeats, he began to have dreams about returning to the United States. Because he had overstayed his first tourist visa to the United States, friends and relatives warned him that he would never secure legal travel documents again.[34] And yet, miraculously— the first sign of God's hand at work—the US consulate approved his visa application.

As Cláudio waited to board the plane to Washington, DC, he prayed fervently, knowing it was unlikely that customs would allow him to reenter the country, especially if they discovered that he had previously overstayed his visa. While praying, an older woman befriended him and joined him in praying for his seamless entry. She sat in first class while he sat in economy. He recalled that she wore a beautiful white gown, smiled easily, and emanated a brilliant light. When they landed at the airport, he fortuitously ended up behind her in the customs line. She drew his elbow close to her, and when the officer checked her passport, the woman asserted, "He's with me" (Ele está comigo). The officer waved them both through without a second glance, and with that, Cláudio entered the United States for a second time.

An enormous smile spread across the man's face as he recalled this moment. Amid delighted laughter, he told the group that upon passing through security, he dropped to his knees and kissed the airport floor, exclaiming out loud, "Hallelujah!" In reflecting on his good fortune, Cláudio claimed that the woman who had enabled his smooth passage was most certainly an angel sent by God (*um anjo de Deus*). He later tried to thank her for her kindness, calling the number she had given him, and discovered that the line was disconnected, more evidence that she was God's agent. In the decade and a half since his return to the United States, Cláudio reported, he had found lucrative work, joined the church, and met his wife, who was seated beside him. Concluding his testimony, he commented that he now understood that God had ordained him to live in the United States.

Cláudio's wife, Tina, shared her testimony next. Like several other young women in the room, she had come to the United States as an au pair and found her entire life rapidly transformed. In Brazil, she noted, she was raised Catholic, but remained casual in her observance. At the time, Tina noted, she even made fun of *crentes*, assuming they were fanatics. She preferred to go out with friends, drink, and date. Yet, moving to the United States brought her into contact with the Brazilian Baptist church, where she soon met her future husband and decided to convert. Now, she reported feeling at peace (*com paz*) in her everyday life. Having accepted Jesus, she concluded, she came to understand that God brought her to the United States to find her husband, and most of all, to find Him.

The other young people seated in the circle shared testimonies with similar refrains. Through God, they had come to identify the primary purpose behind their presence in the United States. They did not simply come for adventure, work, language training, money, or education, as they had thought upon leaving Brazil. Rather, they had come to fulfill God's explicit purpose (*propósito*) for their lives—to serve Him in the United States. Through their testimonies, they interpreted their journeys to, and lives within, the United States as indicative of this powerful and transformative fact. When they received employment, it was because God provided this opportunity; when they found friends, spouses, and church groups, it was because God had directed them; when they found comfort during times of adversity, it was because God had revealed Himself to them. Such self-narration tempered the sensation of being stuck that so many migrants expressed. In the face of downward mobility, marginality, and precariousness, testifying allowed migrants to proclaim the power and purpose inherent in their daily lives. They asserted that God recognized their struggle and rewarded their effort.

Testimony as Encouragement

In addition to reorienting personal narratives from being stuck to being divinely ordained to live in the United States, the practice of testifying enabled individuals to encourage one another to endure adversity. In enjoining friends and family members to "stay" (*ficar*), believers asserted the positive theological value of remaining in the United States as God's chosen. During these moments, individual believers as well as clergy members equated enduring the hardship of migration with *cumprindo a missão de Deus* (fulfilling God's mission/plan for one's life). In this way, testimony provided migrants with important reservoirs of moral support from their peers, counteracting the adverse effects of loneliness, isolation, and alienation.

During the Friday night youth group, I was struck by the directness of veteran migrants' consoling words to their newly arrived peers. A young au pair explained that the American family she worked for frequently mistreated her. Norman, the youth group leader, as well as some of the other men who had just attested to God's activity in their lives, immediately reassured her. One man offered, "You may not know why you are passing through this now, but one day you will. God wants you *here*."

Toward the end of the meeting, two young men who had recently arrived from Brazil, Lucas and Alex, spoke about the unanticipated hardship they had confronted in the United States. Both men enjoyed what they described as good lives (*boas vidas*) in Brazil. They had both attained university degrees. After university, Lucas told the group, he had worked as a music producer in São Paulo, a symbol of his privilege and cosmopolitanism. They had left their partners and families to pursue "adventure" and "opportunity" in the United States. While at the time they vowed that they would never become like other migrants—working in manual labor, overstaying their visas, becoming depressed—they had succumbed to these very conditions soon after arriving.

The church, however, had alleviated their ballooning despair. As Lucas spoke about his deep gratitude for Norman and the other members of the church, his new "family," he was suddenly overcome with emotion, saying he could not continue without crying. Bruno, the visitor from Boston, offered impassioned encouragement, letting them know that they had the help and support of everyone there. They did not have to go through anything alone, he insisted, and while it would be difficult, they would persevere. God had brought them to this place for a reason, he concluded, so they must persevere.

Testimony as Institutional Performance

While migrants asserted the importance of staying and waiting in the United States to themselves and others through testimony ("God chose *me*, God chose *you* to be in the United States!"), the practice also provided churches with an important institutional tool to mark belonging, righteousness, and devotion. Adherents who diligently practiced the spiritual disciplines described above, prayer and discernment, and successfully underwent evangelical affective therapeutics were given the opportunity to publicly testify. Testimony thus allowed migrants to perform their belonging in a dense Christian brotherhood, and to mark themselves as fully "healed" from the traumas of migration.

Through spending time with Diana and observing her radical transformation from *visita* (visitor/outsider) to *irmã* (sister/insider), I came to understand how church leaders distributed the opportunity to testify. In telling her story to me and to the church, Diana communicated all three imperative aspects of testimony. First, she couched her experience in the United States in terms of God's plan for her life. Second, she addressed congregants as fellow undocumented migrants, both implicitly and explicitly encouraging others to persevere, like her, against all odds. And third, she marked her deep commitment to and acceptance within the church by publicly testifying, and thus representing the church's ideal congregant, transformed from distressed migrant to victorious *crente*.

When I first met Diana in early 2014, it was clear that she was struggling. I would see her often on Sunday nights, sitting alone in the back pews. She would habitually fall to her knees in sobs throughout services, visibly overcome by despair. As two young women who attended church on our own, we gradually became friendly, drinking coffee together after services, and chatting about what brought us to the congregation. I found it particularly comforting and easy to be with Diana. While she was devout and committed to God, she also remained accepting and knowledgeable about other belief systems and ways of life. Perhaps of greatest comfort to me, she seemed to understand my academic interest in the church without assuming, or even hoping, that I would one day convert. As we began to spend more time together, I considered her a good friend—someone with whom I would easily connect outside of the fieldwork context.

In her early thirties when we met, Diana had an advanced degree in business administration, and had worked as a financial analyst in a large bank in São Paulo. She had moved out of her parents' home during college and remained financially and emotionally independent from them. Unlike many of the migrants with whom I had spoken, Diana expressed little *saudade* (yearning) for her family in Brazil. While she missed her friends and the ease of communicating in her native tongue, she had been independent from her family for many years.

During our formal interview at a Starbucks near church, she told me that she had moved to the United States to be with her boyfriend, whom she had met online. While she enjoyed the increased security and decreased traffic that life outside of Washington, DC, afforded, her greatest challenge, she explained, was finding work while on a tourist visa, without a car, and with limited ability to communicate in English. Women at church had offered her work babysitting, waitressing, and cleaning homes, but she was not used to this kind of work. She found it *pesado* (weighty/burdensome). Diana explained that she trusted God to provide for her, because He had brought her specifically to the United States.

After a period of ten years *afastada da igreja* (distanced from the church), Diana returned to her evangelical congregation in São Paulo, seeking God's guidance (*direção de Deus*). Over the course of several visits, three different people repeated the same biblical verse to her, revealing God's will. Diana could not remember the exact verse, but she summarized God's message, as told to her by various missionaries, pastors, and believers:

> It's a passage in which Jesus asks his disciples to enter the boat and go to the other side. And the pastor there elaborated that Jesus is commanding you (*mandando você*) to go to the other side. . . . At different points, different people preaching read this same passage and preached the same thing [to me]. . . . "[God is] commanding you to go to the other side (*mandando você ir para o outro lado*). If He commanded you, he will take responsibility for everything. You can go in peace because everything will work out (*vai dar tudo certo*)."

After arriving in the United States, Diana continued to pray, asking for confirmation that God truly wanted her to stay. When I asked if she was now certain that she should stay in the United States, she responded, "[God's]

Word confirmed to me that God brought me here and He will take responsibility for everything" (Deus me trouxe aqui e ele vai responsibilizar por tudo).

Over the next few months, I noticed that Diana began to sit closer to the pulpit, eventually sitting in the front pews with Pastor Jeferson's *obreiros*. Rather than wear jeans and a casual top to services, she began appearing in tailored skirts and colorful blouses. She never missed Bible study or prayer circles, and no longer socialized as readily with me or other *visitas*.[35] After services, Pastor Jeferson often called her to confer with him privately ("Irmã Diana, vem aqui!"/ "Sister Diana, come here!"), or to sit at his table, where he included her in conversations with prominent church members, visiting pastors, and other personal guests. It became clear that Pastor Jeferson was taking her under his wing. Diana's intimacy with the church elite correlated with an ever-growing distance from me. In place of warm conversations or casual text messages about our families and daily lives, Diana greeted me politely, yet formally, at the beginning and end of services, "Paz do Senhor, Joana."

Soon after Diana formally *se membrou* (became a member) in the congregation, she began participating in services and women's ministries more robustly. At first, she joined Juliana, the pastor's wife, and the other *irmãs* in worship songs, or in preparing food for the *café* after services. Diana's true "coming out" as a full church insider, however, corresponded to her giving testimony from the pulpit one Sunday evening, only a month after we had spoken at Starbucks. Juliana chose Diana to initiate the monthly service led by women (*culto de mulheres*), a publicly recognized honor in the congregation. During our interactions over the past several months, I had experienced Diana as timid and reserved. I was curious to see how she spoke from the pulpit for the first time.

As soon as she began, her demeanor transformed. She gripped the lectern with both hands, and looked directly at the congregation, punctuating her remarks with feeling and conviction. Diana first explained the hardship she had faced moving to the United States earlier that year. She had worked in São Paulo as a financial analyst in a large bank, yet here, without a work permit or English fluency, she faced the daunting prospect of *trabalho duro* (manual labor), for which she soon realized she was ill prepared. While she attempted such employment, she often came home feeling exhausted and defeated. Crying nightly, she asked herself in the throes of desperation, "What am I going to do here? *What am I doing here?*" (O que vou fazer aqui? O que estou fazendo aqui?). She doubted her decision to move to the United States and considered returning to Brazil.

It was then, she told the congregation, amid a flood of tears, that she turned to God. She prayed for a consistent office job, or for God to confirm that she should return to Brazil. Soon after she began praying, she saw a friend's post on Facebook advertising an administrative position in a Brazilian landscaping company. She immediately responded. The next day the company interviewed her, and then hired her. God had answered her prayers, she asserted, and in doing so, had confirmed that He wanted her to remain in the United States, where he had brought her for a particular purpose, rather than by chance ("não foi por acaso"). As she concluded her testimony, she closed her eyes, raised her hands, and prayed over the congregation. With her face set in an expression of determination, she yelled loudly, and by my reckoning, uncharacteristically, into the microphone, reprehending any evil spirits in attendance, and praying that the congregation become a "ready bride" (*noiva preparada*) in anticipation of Jesus's imminent return.

Through her testimony, Diana both asserted the significance of her individual journey to the United States and performed her holiness in the eyes of the congregation. Both facts would serve to encourage her and her fellow congregants to persevere in the United States, despite the challenges they faced. When Diana and I spoke during our interview in March 2014, she told me that she would rather return to Brazil than overstay her visa and remain in the country without documents. She had even purchased a return ticket to Brazil in October 2014, when her ninety-day tourist visa expired. Yet, Diana did not return to Brazil. Instead, I learned the following year that Diana had married Anderson, a prominent *obreiro* from church, and subsequently had two children. Through their union and commencement of family life, Diana's commitments to and enmeshment in the church deepened. She remained even further in the "fold" of the church, assumed greater responsibility, and as a result, became more rooted to her life in the United States.

Through her public testimony, Diana powerfully integrated the three functions of testimony. First, she couched her experience in the United States in terms of God's plan for her life. Second, she addressed congregants as fellow undocumented migrants, both implicitly and explicitly encouraging others to persevere, like her, against all odds. And third, she marked her deep commitment to and acceptance within the church by publicly testifying, and thus representing the church's ideal congregant, transformed from distressed migrant to victorious *crente*. Through these three modes of testimony, Diana combatted the affective maladies of the US migrant experience. In asserting the theological imperative of *ficando* (staying), she redeemed dignity, confidence, and security to her status in the United States, despite her lack of documents. Rather than being stuck as a marginalized migrant, she asserted her divine election to work and reside in the United States as God's chosen.

And, she positioned herself securely within a righteous community of care, thus warding off loneliness. Diana embodied the success of affective therapeutics. Individually transformed and socially embedded, she encouraged other migrants to be like her, enduring and hopeful in their faith.

Soldiers, Citizens, and Ambassadors of God: A Compensatory Model of Belonging

> Put on the full armor of God, so that when the day of evil comes, you may be able to stand your ground, and after you have done everything, to stand. Stand firm then, with the belt of truth buckled around your waist, with the breastplate of righteousness in place, and with your feet fitted with the readiness that comes from the gospel of peace. In addition to all this, take up the shield of faith, with which you can extinguish all the flaming arrows of the evil one. Take the helmet of salvation and the sword of the Spirit, which is the word of God.[36]

During o Dia das Crianças (Children's Day in Brazil) on October 12, 2013, the Adventist Church staged a pageant dramatizing the above military metaphor of Christian faith. At the beginning of Sunday worship, thirty or so children filed into the chapel dressed in fatigues and combat boots. With dog chains around their necks and black makeup smudged under their eyes, they marched down the aisle to the delighted amusement of their parents and friends. Mothers and fathers giggled at their little soldiers and snapped pictures of their preschoolers performing Christian militancy.

After indulging in the reverie with his congregants for a few brief moments, Pastor João, otherwise affable and easygoing, abruptly ended the lighthearted display with a somber reminder: "Do not forget why you are here. Satan is real. Satan wants to destroy you, your marriage, your relationships, your children, and everything in your life. The only thing that can save you from this destruction is the 'armor of God': faith, prayer, and righteousness."

———

The spiritual discourses and practices of evangelical affective therapeutics, discussed in the previous and current chapter, culminated in an insistence of powerful Christian belonging over and above particular national allegiance. Viewing themselves and their children as soldiers in God's army, migrant believers aimed to prepare themselves for spiritual warfare and Jesus's Second Coming by assuming the *armadura de Deus,* the armor of God. Despite their great urgency for US markers of belonging, like driver's licenses and green cards, migrant believers, reoriented by affective therapeutics, reminded one another that such documents meant little in the Kingdom of God. Migrants instead emphasized a different order of belonging. They urged each other to be more concerned with being *soldados de Deus* (soldiers of God) and *cidadãos do Céu* (citizens of Heaven) than *cidadãos nos Estados Unidos* (citizens in the United States). In this pursuit, neither legal status nor wealth mattered. The rules dictating citizenship and belonging were immutable and could not be changed according to partisan agenda. Rather, the path to inclusion remained radically open to all.

You Are Not from Here

Pastor Vicente, a visiting Pentecostal pastor from Brazil, powerfully articulated this message to migrant believers during one Sunday worship. "You're not from here," he began. "You're not from the United States, and you're not from Brazil. You are from Heaven!" He explained that while Christians should abide by their host country's laws, respect for the law should not be confused for belonging. Christians must remember that they belonged only to God. To illustrate his premise, he spoke about driving, a pressing concern for migrants in sprawling Montgomery County. Pastor Vicente explained that he could not drive legally in the United States because he did not have a US driver's license. But, the fact of his law abidance—*not* driving illegally—did not amount to belonging to, or even wanting to belong, to the United States. Driving legally in Brazil, where he did hold a license, also did not amount to belonging. Instead, no matter where he traveled, he belonged only to God.

Pastor Vicente's message distinguishing between respect for the law and national belonging was uniquely suited to the mostly undocumented migrants in attendance. Living in the United States without documents for years, if not decades, these migrants had a muddled relationship with the notion of "legality" in the United States, what it meant, and what it afforded. Migrants like Neusa, her husband Rubém, and their two children, Felipe and Frederico, had lived in the United States for fourteen years without documents. Based on their "illegal" residence in the United States, they had at various points received, and ignored, deportation orders, thus flouting the law. Yet, they also assiduously followed the law. Living in Maryland, they attained legal driving licenses. Like many migrants I met, they reported paying their taxes yearly and never defaulting on monthly bills. They never cheated, stole, or lied to their neighbors, friends, or acquaintances, and they demanded the same from their children. To the best of their ability, they respected the law. As such, they were indignant at being deemed "illegal" by the US government and broad swaths of the American public.

Yet, Pastor Vicente's sermon made it clear that such law-abiding actions would never amount to true belonging or true citizenship for migrant believers in the United States, or any country for that matter. Perhaps more importantly, he implied that migrant believers should never aspire to such belonging. In his framing, the failure to belong in the United States was a mark of righteousness, rather than marginality. Migrant believers would never belong because they belonged only to God. Moreover, they should embrace and broadcast the immutable fact of their separateness.

As he continued, Pastor Vicente elaborated upon the transcendent citizenship available to all Christians, and the privileges and duties that cohered to such belonging. Unlike nonbelievers who could never adequately account for their earthly existence, Christians could emphatically answer the fundamental question that confronted all human beings: why are you here? No matter where they found themselves in the world, Christians affirmed the divine purpose (*propósito de Deus*) behind their existence. They were on God's great commission (*a grande comissão*) to spread the Gospel. "You did not come here to earn money or to get an education," Pastor Vicente asserted. "You came to fulfill a mission as an ambassador of God's Kingdom."

Migrant believers similarly minimized their exclusion from the United States and rationalized their distance from Brazil by criticizing both countries' relationship to Christ as tepid and insincere. Calling for *avivamento* (revival) from the pulpit, Neusa's eldest son, Felipe, charged that Christian faith in both the United States and Brazil had grown stale. While historically a great Christian nation, the United States had "distanced itself" (*se afastou*) from God. People were now ashamed of their parents' and grandparents' religion, he charged, evidenced by the removal of prayer from schools, and the insertion of secular music, dance, and gay marriage in churches. Felipe voiced similar condemnation of Christianity in Brazil, which he called "de homens" (manmade) rather than "de Deus." Evangelical Christianity had become big business in Brazil, where secular musicians could market themselves as gospel singers, fill stadiums, and sell millions of records. When he watched clips of Brazilian revival events, he "tested" their righteousness by watching clips without sound. When muted, the events and their participants appeared identical to secular concerts. Men and women were scantily clad and danced lewdly. Christianity in both countries, Felipe concluded, had been infiltrated by secularism.

This stark rejection of both Brazil and the United States enabled him to then cast his own migrant church as an exceptional and exemplary bastion of faith. Because they were leaders of true revival (*avivamento de verdade*), he encouraged the fifty or sixty migrant believers present to be like the Puritans of England, who swept through the United States bringing repentance (*arrependimento*) everywhere they went. "I want our church to be a point of reference for this nation!" he announced. When he encountered an acquaintance at the supermarket, he wanted to say, "I don't know what happens in *your* church, but here in *my* church, we have the *true* presence of God!" In order to invite this spirit of revival, however, migrants must be more concerned with being soldiers of God than citizens in the United States.

Like the practices of prayer, discernment, and testimony, the language of citizenship, mission, and soldiering provided an avenue to rehabilitate migrant believers' self-understanding against their daily realities. With citizenship in God's Kingdom, migrants diminished the importance of citizenship in the United States. More so, their marginalization and failure to belong became redeployed as a mark of distinction and righteousness. With the divine mission of evangelization and salvation, the fact of grueling and undercompensated migrant work remained part of God's larger plan for their life. With membership in God's army, the most powerful army in Heaven or on Earth, being undocumented in the US meant little. Placing oneself in the hands of God through prayer, discernment, and testimony promised profound power and meaning, the antidote to undocumented life.

Evangelical Efficacy

Evangelical affective therapeutics contravened the expectations of those professing a hermeneutics of suspicion. According to the ethnographic data discussed above, these churches did not produce self-serving individualists who proclaimed national citizenship to be the happy object par excellence, nor passive subjects simply waiting for God to materialize.[37] Instead, migrant churches explicitly diminished the importance of national citizenship and legality in the United States, and in its place, promulgated a Christian, transnational, relational, and transcendent vision of belonging. This vision confronted, and then embraced, the impossibility of legal belonging for most migrant believers in the United States, and in doing so, leveraged its own Christian critique of the category of "legality." At best, notions of humanmade legality were fragile, and at worst, overtly demonic. Rather than single-mindedly strive for US markers of belonging and security, migrants learned to shift their aspirations, and instead shore up their belonging as "soldiers," "citizens," and "ambassadors" in the Kingdom of Heaven. They assumed the *armadura de fé* through the spiritual disciplines of prayer, discernment, and testimony.

Through these practices, those without documents warded off the central maladies of migrant distress: loneliness and feeling stuck. Prayer provided migrants with an avenue for immediate recourse to their daily frustrations and indignations. Discernment enabled believers to understand the expansive purpose behind their seemingly constrained lives in the United States. And, finally, testimony provided migrants with the opportunity to present themselves as powerfully healed, and encourage the healing of others, within the context of intimate and watchful community.

Importantly, affective therapeutics, and its constitutive practices, encouraged frequent and ongoing engagement. Gláucia's divinely blessed housing search, Miriam's professed faith in her coming green card, and Diana's triumphant testimony did not end their engagement with spiritual disciplines, nor guarantee their insulation from future disappointment, doubt, or despair. Rather, affective therapeutics provided the blueprint for how to cope, reframe, and sublimate adversity and distress when it emerged. The frequency with which migrant adherents engaged in spiritual practices helped strengthen the efficacy of affective therapeutics and its ability to mitigate migrant distress.

These findings contribute to a growing body of evidence that spiritual disciplines paired with religious sociality can, in fact, consequentially alter subjective experience.[38] Such studies add nuance to the study of subjectivity within anthropology, a field that primarily considers how power, politics, surveillance, and control shape subjectivity.[39] If biopower wielded by experts can penetrate our beings and shape our most privately held desires, perceptions, and inhibitions, so too, this growing literature suggests, can practiced, joyful, and satisfying encounters with the divine. Furthermore, such studies confirm that the transformative potential of spiritual disciplines grows exponentially when practiced amid a like-minded community of devotees who jointly witness, encourage, and interpret these encounters.[40]

5

Affective Therapeutics in Comparative Perspective

CATHOLIC AND SPIRITIST
MIGRANT EXPERIENCE

WHEN LUIZA MOVED to the United States from Rio de Janeiro, she was thirty years old and in her third trimester with her first baby. She came to join the baby's father, Ulysses, whom she had been dating for two years. Very soon after arriving, she went into labor and delivered her son several weeks premature. During our meeting at her home in a residential area of Rockville, Maryland, she described the first months with her infant son, Nicholas, as incredibly lonely, exhausting, and trying. Ulysses, and the few Brazilian friends she knew in Maryland at the time, left at 4 a.m. each day for work, and returned after 10 p.m. Luiza spoke little English and had no prior experience with babies. She highlighted the tenuousness of this period by vividly describing her terror when Nicholas's umbilical cord abruptly fell off:

> I said, "My God! What's happening, bleeding is coming from his stomach!" I had never been alone with a baby, so everything was very new. In this moment, I remember, I said, "My God, what am I going to do?" I didn't speak English well. I'm going to call 911, and say what? It was here that God calmed me (*me acalmava*), "I'm going to take care of you. Everything will be okay." It was me and God all day long.

Luiza's deep Catholic faith buoyed her in the early months of new motherhood in a foreign country. In Brazil, her social life had revolved around her lively parish. After confirmation at the age of seventeen, Luiza taught Sunday school, prepared children for first communion, and led Bible study for adults. When not at work as an airport administrator in Rio de Janeiro, she volunteered at a Catholic nursing home, leading prayer circles for the elderly.

After Nicholas's birth, she and her husband desperately sought out a similar faith community in Maryland, especially in which to baptize their still fragile baby. Luiza and Ulysses worried over Nicholas's health as well as his soul should he not survive. They took seriously Catholicism's teaching that infants who die before baptism cannot proceed to Heaven. When Nicholas was four months old, they sought out a priest from a nearby Catholic parish that served Brazilian migrants to perform the sacrament. Luiza described her grave disappointment (*decepção*) with the priest over what she perceived to be his frigid and aloof demeanor. She recalled:

> We went and asked to speak with [the priest] after Mass, and he said that he didn't have time. So, I called, and I said, "I want to baptize my son." And he said, "But have you paid your tithe?" I said, "I don't pay the tithe because I'm not a *dizimista*, I'm not a member of your church. I attend, we go, but I'm not a member." From there, he charged us a fee of $170 for the baptism. After, I learned that you don't do this. You don't charge for baptism.

Determined to ensure the salvation of their son, Luiza and Ulysses paid the fee. While they experienced relief following the baptism, knowing that their son would "go into Jesus's arms" should some tragedy afflict him, their opinion of the Catholic Church had changed irrevocably.

They had sought out the church in a moment of deep vulnerability, expecting comfort and embrace. Instead, they felt dismissed, rejected, and turned away. Luiza articulated her and her husband's profound disappointment:

> We lost our desire to go to this church. Because when people go to church, especially people who are immigrants, we look for a word of comfort, for the priest to console us, help us in moments of affliction, and not that he won't have time to speak with us, or only talks about money the whole Mass. We were disheartened (*desanimados*).

Although they stopped going to that parish, Luiza and Ulysses continued to strongly identify as Catholic, so they continued to search for a Catholic congregation. For a time, they attended an English-language parish, but there, too, felt alienated and lost. "We couldn't understand," Luiza noted. She described being unable to follow along during the central prayer of the liturgy, "Our Father," in English. "It was like a movie that we were watching without much emotion. It was beautiful, it was enjoyable, you see people in communion, but we couldn't connect." After leaving this parish, they tried a third parish, another Catholic church serving Brazilians. But soon after they began to attend, this parish moved to a new location two hours from their home. "This won't work anymore, we're not going," she and her husband concluded. As a devout Catholic, Luiza had tried to bring her young family to three separate parishes. Yet, each had disappointed her in some way.

Then, Nicholas's Brazilian babysitter invited her to a Brazilian Baptist church for an event. For about a year and a half, she went with her children to church events, enjoying the atmosphere and getting to know members of the congregation. She went to baptisms and parties, but resisted going to Sunday services because, she explained, "We were Catholic, so I'm not going to attend a Baptist church." When evangelical relatives visited from Brazil, they spent New Year's Eve at the Baptist church. After the service, they kept attending. "Our visitors left, but we said, 'No, we're going to keep going. Because it was so enjoyable, it was so *good!*'"

The following year, Luiza began teaching Sunday school and organizing refreshments after services. A friend invited her and her husband to join a weekly Bible study that met at her home. Luiza found herself enjoying reading and debating the Bible, and speaking directly to God, rather than calling on the saints or Mary to intercede on her behalf. She discovered an even deeper intimacy with God. After another year attending the congregation, she and her husband were baptized. At the time I met them, three years later, Luiza and Ulysses were active and devoted church members who often mentored other migrants who had yet to convert.

Luiza was not alone in her experience of feeling disappointed by the Catholic Church, nor in her desire to seek out an alternative faith community after an upsetting encounter. I heard multiple versions of the same narrative among Brazilians who had been devout Catholics in Brazil yet found the institution and faith community to be deeply lacking in the United States. Almost one-quarter of survey respondents indicated that they had left the Catholic Church after arriving in the United States. During formal interviews, one-fifth of the migrants I spoke with shared that they had left Catholicism after arriving in the United States. These findings, while impressionistic, were further corroborated by numerous informal conversations, leading me to conclude that Luiza's experience provides important insights into broader patterns of migrant flight from the Catholic Church, particularly among Latin Americans.[1]

Seeking comfort and familiarity once in the United States, migrants consistently recounted their deep disappointment (*decepção*) with the absence of empathy, intelligibility, and warmth they experienced in Catholic parishes, both those serving Brazilians specifically and those they called "American." They described the Mass and parish social life in the United States as "traditional," "cold," "distant," "outdated," "dry," and "impersonal." While migrants associated Catholicism in Brazil with levity, music, and rich community life, American Catholicism struck them as overly solemn and solitary. After Mass in the United States, migrants told me with dismay, parishioners *ran* to their cars. Others, like Luiza, recoiled at the place of money in the Catholic Church, with one woman exclaiming, "It's like a business we're dealing with!" Many former Catholic migrants, like Luiza, made multiple attempts to find community and care in Catholic parishes in the United States. When such attempts failed, however, migrants sought out alternative religious communities. For the most part, migrants found receptive spiritual homes in the much more visible and robust Brazilian evangelical churches in the region. Several former Catholic migrants also found spiritual fulfillment within Spiritist centers.

Vera, a woman in her midfifties, shared that she and her husband, Tiago, had attended a Catholic church in Baltimore for three years, in the hopes of finding comfort and community after arriving in the US and starting a family. Tiago, Vera told me, had suffered from severe depression, and they struggled to cope with his difficulties and raise their young daughter while far from their families in Brazil. Vera recounted her horror when the priest of their parish mocked her request for help understanding how to use an English-language Catholic devotional. She had been feeling vulnerable and alone, and desperate for human warmth and religious inspiration. She explained that she had "wanted to open her heart" to the priest. "I said, how do I use this book? And he said, 'You take this finger, and you . . .' He was very sarcastic and ironic. . . . I had a kid in my hands, I had a baby in my hands." Vera and Tiago looked elsewhere, ultimately finding comfort in a Spiritist center. Instead of encountering a "wall," as in the Catholic parish, Vera described their feeling at the Spiritist center as total "peace." Apart from the consoling Spiritist message, Vera's husband felt soothed by being near other Brazilian migrants. She reported that his mental well-being improved after two weeks attending the Spiritist center.

Unlike Luiza and Vera, Juçara never found an alternative to the Catholic Church once she moved to the United States. Instead, she felt a gaping hole in her life, sharing, "I miss it, yes. I miss it a lot." A young woman in her early thirties, Juçara had stayed in the United States after working as an au pair and studying English after she met and married an American man. In Brazil, she had attended what she described as "extremely" devout Catholic schools for her entire education and attended Mass several times per week. In Brazil, she had considered faith to be absolutely *fundamental* and *no primero lugar* (her first priority). Once in the United States, however, every church left her feeling disappointed. "I didn't find a church where I felt peace," Juçara explained. She had visited both Brazilian and American parishes, and neither compelled her to return. While Juçara continued to recite the Catholic liturgy and read from Catholic devotionals at home, she witnessed her Catholic identity slowly erode. She surmised, "I think that little by little, with the passage of time, I left a little bit of being Catholic. I'm not the same person that I was living in Brazil. Because here it's not the same thing."

Despite her intense religious upbringing and urgent desire for spiritual satiation, Juçara remained disillusioned with Catholicism in the US. The church could not hold her. It did not provide her with what she desperately sought out, what she termed "peace." Juçara's experience struck me as particularly telling. If the Catholic Church alienated migrants who maintained long-held, nurtured, and cherished Catholic identities, as she did, how could it survive among migrants?

To understand the grave alienation and disappointment former Catholics expressed, I studied the Catholic Church's general approach toward migrants. How, if at all, did the Catholic Church attempt to embrace, retain, and incorporate Brazilian Catholics within its dioceses in Greater Washington, DC? And, to what extent did its approach to Brazilian migrants differ markedly from what I had observed among the comparatively robust Brazilian evangelical churches? I also inquired into the success of the smaller yet vibrant Spiritist movement in the region, where I met many former Catholics. How did the Spiritist approach to migrants compare to evangelical and Catholic strategies?

In addition to considering the approach of religious institutions, I also considered the religious experiences of individual migrants. To what extent did Catholic and Spiritist migrants, like evangelicals, imbue their migratory experiences with religious meaning? And, how did nonevangelical migrants evaluate the healing efficacy of their faiths? Toward these ends, I routinely attended two Catholic parishes and two Spiritist centers. In addition, I formally interviewed fourteen Catholics and ten Spiritists, including both leaders and members, and collected surveys from eight Catholics and seven Spiritists.

Such comparative analysis enabled me to interrogate the particularity of migrant evangelical churches' affective therapeutic model, and their success in addressing and transforming migrant distress. In the first two sections, I outline these findings. First, the Catholic Church's emphasis on "culture" revealed an orientation toward collective need and uplift. Second, Spiritist centers offered teachings regarding emotion and behavior that remained strikingly similar to the evangelical message. As a result, Spiritist centers, like evangelical churches, attracted new members to their ranks, while the Catholic Church weathered significant membership loss among migrants.

Unity in Diversity: The Catholic Church's Reductive Approach to Culture

Finding, meeting, and gaining access to Brazilian Catholic groups and their members proved surprisingly difficult. This fact immediately struck me as a significant divergence from Brazilian evangelical congregations, which I easily identified owing to their visibility and prominence in the region. While I visited local evangelical congregations unannounced, I needed to navigate the regional bureaucracy of the Catholic Church to identify Brazilian migrant Catholic communities. I found the Multicultural Ministry of the Diocese of Arlington through web research, which listed a "Brazilian Catholic Community" among its many "multicultural" groups. Correspondence with the American director of this entity, Margaret, led to a second Brazilian Catholic group, organized by the Diocese of Washington, DC, in Montgomery County and overseen by the Scalabrini mission, a Catholic order founded specifically to attend to migrants and refugees.

Many of my initial emails and phone calls to the local priests and administrators of these groups went unanswered for weeks. Several times, I considered dropping the comparative piece of my study altogether. When Cláudia, a prominent member of the Brazilian Catholic group in Montgomery County, failed to show up to our meeting after postponing several times already, I was particularly discouraged. I had driven forty-five minutes, attended the Sunday morning Portuguese Mass, waited awkwardly in the chapel, and inquired eagerly about Cláudia's whereabouts, only to be told by curious parishioners that she was not in attendance. Even more troubling from the standpoint of my research, every person I spoke with after Mass was from Portugal, not Brazil! While tickled by my Brazilian Portuguese accent, these parishioners were dismayed about the focus of my study. Why would I study Brazilian Catholics, they inquired, when Brazilians made up such a small segment of the Portuguese-speaking parish population? I should instead research Portuguese and Cape Verdean migrants, they insisted.

While I eventually identified a number of devout Brazilian Catholics who were willing to speak with me, my general impression remained unchanged. Formal groups of devout Brazilian Catholics remained small, private, and exceedingly hard to find. In light of this experience, it was not surprising to me that many Brazilian migrants felt alienated from the Catholic Church in the United States. Often, I found that former Catholics, and even those who maintained Catholic identities outside of an institutional home, had never heard of these small and dispersed Brazilian Catholic groups.

The Arlington community met only once per month, when a Portuguese-speaking priest (there were two: one American, one Brazilian) traveled from neighboring parishes to host Mass in a beautiful wooded retreat center owned by the diocese. During my three visits to these events, most attendees were Brazilian women above forty who had lived in the region since the 1980s. Congregants were highly educated, well-off, and documented. Many of the women I met had attained US citizenship decades earlier. Nilma, who had petitioned Bishop Loverde for a Brazilian Portuguese Mass, had received her doctorate in economics in the United States and subsequently taught Portuguese to diplomats. Another woman I interviewed worked at the World Bank. A third active member held law and business degrees from the presti-gious University of São Paulo and currently directed an NGO in Northern Virginia. Some regular attendees were devoted Catholics, attending English-language parishes the rest of the month. Others, however, considered them-selves to be casual in their faith and often experimented with other religions. In addition to members of this Brazilian group, I interviewed the director of the Multicultural Ministry and attended the diocese-wide Multicultural Mass.

The second Brazilian Catholic group I eventually identified, located in Montgomery County, held most of its events, including weekly prayer circles, holiday meals, and fundraisers, together with other Portuguese-speaking mi-grants. I attended four weekly Monday prayer meetings and four Portuguese Masses and formally interviewed six members and the parish priest. The group operated in Montgomery County, where I had conducted the majority of fieldwork on migrant evangelical churches. Catholic migrants at this parish shared profiles similar to those of the evangelical migrants I met. They worked in the domestic service industry as babysitters and housecleaners, had lived undocumented in the United States for many years, and regularly experienced the forms of migrant distress I discuss in chapter 2. On average, however, like Catholics in Northern Virginia, the Catholic migrants I met were older, had lived in the United States longer, and had more often regularized their status through employment sponsorship or amnesty. As in Northern Virginia, the group was made up almost entirely of women. The two men I met and interviewed were married to active members.

Through fieldwork, two central aspects of the Catholic Church's approach to migrants emerged that shed light on membership attrition among Brazilian migrants. First, the Catholic Church's reductionist understanding of "culture" left Brazilian migrants feeling misunderstood and out of place. Second, the church's emphasis on migrant "integration" and universal "liberation," rather than personal "healing," encouraged Brazilian flight from the Catholic Church. In contrast to the intimate, person-based, and consequential affective therapeutics of evangelical churches, the Catholic Church repelled Brazilian migrants by failing to address the particular needs of each individual.[2]

The Reification of "Culture" in the Multicultural Ministry

I met Margaret, the director of the Diocese of Arlington's Multicultural Ministry, in her office at the diocese's headquarters in Northern Virginia. In a large and sprawling parking lot, the formidable tan high-rise sat next to a Catholic primary school. A Catholic social services building, and the main Cathedral of the Diocese, shared the expansive site. In this small corner of Northern Virginia, the Catholic Church reigned supreme. Having never visited a diocese headquarters before, and having conducted most of my research in small migrant evangelical congregations that most often rented space from more established churches, I immediately felt the formidable nature of the Catholic Church as a sprawling, complex, and enduring institution.

After making my way up to the eighth floor, which housed the Multicultural Ministry as well as the Spanish Apostolate, I leafed through pamphlets featuring a diverse array of smiling children. A petite and energetic woman, Margaret met me with both warmth and seriousness. Learning that I was not Catholic, she used our meeting as an opportunity to orient me to the structure and history of the Catholic Church in the region. Margaret explained that Paul Loverde, Bishop of the Diocese of Arlington from 1999 to 2016, initiated the Multicultural Ministry in 2005, having recognized the growing prevalence of what she termed "nonwhite" Catholics in the region. While the Spanish Apostolate had been organized in 1970 to support Catholic Latinos, the Multicultural Ministry had a broader mission—to foster and facilitate Catholic faith in all "cultural" groups by providing native-language Masses and events, and to create "unity" across diverse populations. As such, Bishop Loverde defined the ministry with the motto Unity in Diversity.

Margaret explained that the Multicultural Ministry's approach to culture was not new. Instead, the Catholic Church had issued "pastoral statements" concerning the particular needs of various "cultural groups" since the 1970s, when it released its first "cultural" statement in regard to "African and African-American Catholics." As she showed me the original pamphlet cover featuring a stereotypical cartoon drawing of a dark-skinned, curly-haired, grinning child, she self-consciously noted the pamphlet needed an update. When I inquired with poorly veiled skepticism into the church's painfully simplistic grouping of Africans and African Americans into a single culture, she responded simply that the church had joined these "brothers and sisters together" owing to shared "cultural" heritage.

Margaret explained that the Catholic Church in the United States was organized into six "cultural families": European; African and African-American; Hispanic and Latino; Asian and Pacific Islander; Native American; and Migrant, Refugee, and All Others. While the sacraments and Catholic liturgy remained uniform across these six groups, Catholics within each category, she asserted, maintained distinct "cultural traditions" that impacted stylistic preference as well as the importance of particular saints and feast days. Catholics were most comfortable, she asserted, worshipping within their own "cultural family."

To illustrate the working of these "cultural groups" for the church's policy toward migrants, she returned to my particular research focus and the reason for our meeting: Brazilian Catholics in the region. Because Brazilian migrants spoke Portuguese, and remained historically distinct from both Spanish-speaking Latin American migrants and Portuguese-speaking migrants from Portugal, Cape Verde, or Mozambique, the church had placed them into the Migrant, Refugee, and All Others category. As such, Brazilians would not belong to the same cultural family as other Portuguese-speaking migrants, such as Portuguese (European), or Angolan and Mozambican (African and African-American), or other Latin American migrants (Hispanic and Latino). Brazilian migrants, according to Margaret, required their own Mass to facilitate their particular Catholic traditions, such as more participatory music during worship, and a prominent place for Mary as Nossa Senhora de Aparecida.[3]

Although Margaret presented the church's logic as a way to respectfully include Brazilian migrants and their particular culture in the church, the classification of Brazilian migrants as "Migrant, Refugee, and All Others" struck me as both awkward and potentially offensive. It seemed that inclusion in the catch-all cultural category would corroborate Brazilians' collective sense that they remained generally unintelligible in the United States, where they failed to fit neatly into American racial, cultural, or ethnic categories.[4] The consideration of Brazilians as "Migrant, Refugee, and All Others" would provide confirmation that the Catholic Church, too, did not quite know what to do with Brazilian migrants.

A week earlier, I had witnessed the performance of these "cultural families" during the Diocese of Arlington's annual Multicultural Mass held in the middle of June, a kind of pageant for its Unity in Diversity initiative. Hundreds of Catholics processed into the large chapel according to these prescribed "cultural" groups. African parishioners, predominantly from Ghana, I learned, wore *kente* cloth and adorned themselves with headscarves, jewelry, and boldly colored makeup. Asian parishioners, generally from Vietnam and China, I learned, wore bright red and orange ceremonial attire. Spanish-speaking congregants, grouped together, according to Margaret, in the "Hispanic and Latino cultural family," remained casually dressed, wearing jeans and t-shirts, despite making up the largest "cultural group" in the audience. What were the visible symbols of their "culture"? And, I wondered, what did the "European family" look like, and where were their representatives?

During his homily, Bishop Loverde further revealed the Catholic Church's overly simplistic representation of culture as a material, bounded, and identifiable thing in the world. He aimed his remarks at articulating the "good" versus "bad" content of culture. While some aspects of culture should be celebrated and used to enrich Catholic traditions and values, other aspects must be discarded owing to the threat they posed. Culture, he warned, could corrupt. To illustrate his remarks, he pointed to Jesus's engagement with what he alternately called "Hebraic" and "Jewish" culture. While washing guests' feet constituted an admirable ritual embedded within "Jewish culture," he noted, corruption and power also remained fundamental to the biblical "culture of Judaism." In order to preach the Gospel, Bishop Loverde concluded, Jesus thus had to *overcome* his native culture. Contemporary Catholics, Bishop

Loverde asserted, must be equally discerning in regard to their cultural heritage, preserving the "good" and overcoming the "bad."

The event, as the most visible performance of the Multicultural Ministry, pointed to the reification of the church's understanding of culture and related approach to migrants. Parishioners who looked alike sat together in their colorful "cultural" garb. After Mass, they performed "cultural" dances and songs, and served typical foods in front of booths emblazoned with images from their nations of origin. Despite its designation as multicultural, I observed little interaction among Catholics across these so-called cultural families. Further, I noted a paucity of representatives from what Bishop Loverde euphemistically termed the "Anglo" or "European community" or "family."[5] There were no booths representing migrant populations from Europe, nor non-Hispanic, white American Catholics. The few white faces at the event belonged to the bishops and priests on the altar, and church workers and administrators, like Margaret. I was also surprised by the apparent absence of Brazilians from the event. During the Mass, one woman read a prayer in Brazilian Portuguese, but there was no Brazil booth announcing the group's presence.

My findings recall John Burdick's earlier study of evangelical and Catholic religiosity among Brazilians of African descent, whom Burdick refers to as "Afro-Brazilians."[6] While evangelical churches valorized the feelings, problems, and experiences of Afro-Brazilians as individuals, the Catholic Church, he found, aimed to appeal to Afro-Brazilians by incorporating Afro-Brazilian "culture" into what the church termed the "inculturated Mass" (*Missa inculturado*). While perhaps well-intentioned, such an attempt ultimately alienated Afro-Brazilians who failed to recognize themselves in the church's highly stereotypical, performative, and reductionist account of Black Brazilian culture. Conveying her unease with the cultural display at the inculturated Mass, one woman related her offense, saying, "I think we need a Mass which encourages the *negro* to be any way he wants, not take him out of one box and put him into another."[7]

The Multicultural Mass I witnessed, coupled with Margaret's explanation of the Multicultural Ministry, suggested that the Catholic Church's notion of culture had not evolved much since Burdick's study almost twenty years earlier. The church's notion appeared akin to long discredited anthropological theories associated with the same term. Early "arm-chair" anthropologists such as James Frazer[8] and E. B. Tylor,[9] for instance, promulgated an "evolutionary" theory of human behavior, suggesting that the arbitrary, magical, and nonrational practices of peoples in "lower" stages of evolution would ultimately give way to "civilization." The task of anthropologists, Tylor and Frazer argued, was to document these "primitive" practices, under the heading of "human culture." As the postcolonial theorist Edward Said noted, "culture" thus came to signify "ethnic," "primitive," and "Other," while "whiteness" connoted *culture-less* "civilized" societies, steeped in science and rationality.[10] The culture concept has continued to vex the discipline of anthropology, despite deliberate attempts to transcend its colonial and imperial legacy.[11]

In reducing such complex categories as "nationality," "race," "ethnicity," and "linguistic group" to "cultural family," the Catholic Church revealed its profound inability to address and include diverse migrant populations. The institution's performance of culture rehearsed troubling assumptions, such as the idea that some groups, generally non-Western and nonwhite, had more culture than others. While it glossed over difference, it simultaneously ghettoized minority practitioners along artificial "cultural lines." In doing so, the church failed to create meaningful alliances across the boundaries it had instituted, and risked alienating entire Catholic populations, such as Brazilians, who might recoil at the church's blanket designation, such as "Migrant, Refugee, and All Others." The church's awkward and reductionist approach to culture provides important context for migrants' experiences of alienation and disappointment.

The Pursuit of Universal Uplift at the Expense of Individual Healing

The Catholic Church's general handling of migration concerns revealed a similar uncritical and outdated approach to culture. Unlike the Diocese of Arlington, which explicitly emphasized issues of culture rather than migration, the second Brazilian Catholic community I studied, located in the Washington Diocese in Montgomery County, maintained an overt focus on the particular needs of migrants. As part of the Scalabrini mission, the parish explicitly served migrant populations.[12] Consistent with the Diocese of Arlington's approach to culture, the Montgomery County parish rarely engaged with individual difference or individual need. In contrast to evangelical churches' intense emphasis on individual healing, the priest identified "integration" in American society as the central goal of pastoral care. Rather than work to reshape migrant interiority through therapeutic divine encounter, the church presented abstract notions of justice, equality, and dignity as the subject of religious reflection.

I met with Father Bernardo, the priest of the Scalabrini congregation, in a small conference room attached to his administrative office. In contrast with the Diocese of Arlington headquarters, as well as the small and well-kept parish that the Brazilian community used in Northern Virginia, the building seemed old, dark, and underresourced. Although born in Brazil, Father Bernardo had served Catholics in North America since the 1970s. When I inquired into his own Brazilian identity, and whether he considered himself to be a migrant, he shook his head vigorously, replying, "No," and sharing that his grandparents were Italian immigrants to Brazil. In his sixties when we met, he had lived abroad for most of his adult life, serving English-, Portuguese-, and Spanish-speaking populations.

The Catholic population of Montgomery County, he explained, began to shift in the 1990s, with the influx of migrants from Latin America, and the subsequent "white flight" of white American families to more affluent suburbs. Owing to this demographic shift, the parish witnessed increasingly low participation, inciting the diocese to ultimately close its doors. Father Bernardo petitioned the diocese to reopen the parish as part of the Scalabrini mission in 1992, offering weekly Masses in Spanish and Portuguese, and instituting an explicit focus on the well-being of migrants. Above all, Father Bernardo emphasized that the Scalabrini mission's aim was to help migrants "integrate." To achieve this aim, the church assisted migrants in learning the "language and culture" of America. Father Bernardo had learned, he told me, that if the church tried to "force" migrants to rapidly discard their own language and culture, they would more forcefully reject the United States. The Scalabrini mission subscribed to the Catholic Church's Unity in Diversity motto, providing migrants with opportunities to engage with their own traditions through events like the Multicultural Mass, bilingual Sunday school, and culturally specific feast days and celebrations.[13]

Although the parish provided access to a mobile health-care clinic run by nuns and occasionally provided migrants with employment information, Father Bernardo emphasized that it rarely offered personal assistance. Cláudia, the organizer of the Brazilian community in Montgomery County, confirmed Father Bernardo's comments and emphasized the church's limitations in assisting individual migrants. I asked if the parish aided migrants with difficulties associated with being undocumented, such as legal counsel or financial aid. Cláudia immediately shook her head, explaining, "If [the church] were to help Brazilians, it would have to help Hispanics too. And they are many. And they have daily problems with immigration (ICE). They're deported. So, if Father Bernardo opened his hand for one, he'd have to open his hand for many." She compared the Catholic Church's limited response to Brazilian migrants to evangelical churches, which she viewed as much more expansive in their aid. She suggested that this fact drew many Brazilian Catholics away from the church, and instead toward evangelical churches, where they went, she conjectured, "in search of one thing or another" (*em busca de alguma coisa*).

In keeping with its mission to uplift migrants collectively through integration, rather than individually through personal assistance, the parish championed abstract moral principles rather than specific affective therapeutics aimed at migrants' feelings and perceptions. Whereas evangelical church workers taught individuals to identify and redirect their negative feelings to achieve intimacy with God, and subsequent good feeling, Father Bernardo emphasized universal moral goods such as justice, equality, and human dignity, rather than interior affective states such as happiness, peace, and contentment.

Unlike evangelical pastors who generally refrained from speaking about current events from the pulpit, Father Bernardo often incorporated significant world affairs into his teachings. On December 15, 2013, for instance, he spoke at length about Nelson Mandela, who had died ten days earlier. He named, along with Mandela, Martin Luther King Jr., Mahatma Gandhi, and John F. Kennedy as exemplars and "modern-day prophets" fighting to eradicate slavery and safeguard universal human rights. These men, Father Bernardo pronounced, had worked to publicize and manifest Jesus's message of "justice, equality, and peace, for all." As he concluded Mass, Father Bernardo prayed over migrant parishioners, calling God to protect their dignity and ensure their security in a foreign land. Father Bernardo often reiterated this liberatory benediction. As he opened *terço* (praying the rosary) one Monday evening, for instance, he asked God to protect undocumented migrants who suffered without "basic rights" like health care or legal representation.

In his call for freedom and justice and engagement of current affairs, from the altar, Father Bernardo's language struck me as profoundly different from what I had encountered in migrant evangelical churches. In his remarks, Father Bernardo argued that faith and religion provided humanity with universal and collective moral principles. Individual Catholics offered collective transformation by embodying this unchanging Catholic morality. Rather than striving toward collective principles of justice, freedom, and human dignity for all, evangelical pastors targeted personal behavior and feeling as the terrain of religious transformation. Unlike the outward gaze Farther Bernardo detailed, such evangelical work was directed inward.

Additionally, evangelical clergy very rarely invoked current events during their sermons. Instead, they shared testimony of personal struggle and divine uplift, intended to connect with the migrants in their pews, and infuse their own migrant-related distress with religious significance. God, they insisted, had personally chosen each and every migrant to come to the United States for a particular purpose: to know Him, and to spread God's Word to others. While Father Bernardo recognized migrant suffering, and insisted upon God's unique protection of the marginalized, he never imbued migrants' journey with divine purpose. The comparative growth of evangelical religiosity and decline of Catholic adherence among Brazilians in the United States suggests that the person- and emotion-centered model of affective therapeutics resonated deeply with migrants and effectively assuaged their migrant-related distress.

"It's Good to Be Good": Spiritism as an Alternative Affective Therapeutics

Although it was small relative to the much larger evangelical congregations I visited, I was struck by the robustness of the Spiritist movement among Brazilians in Greater Washington, DC. Spiritism was particularly popular among professional, highly educated, and documented Brazilians, though center directors also emphasized the movement's popularity among undocumented migrants.

In contrast to my deliberate search for Brazilian Catholics discussed above, I happened upon Spiritists accidentally. Rosa, the sister of one of my first Portuguese instructors, was among the first Brazilians I interviewed for this project. When I asked her about her religious identity, she told me she was an *espiritista*, a Spiritist. At the time, I had never encountered the word, nor heard of Allan Kardec, the French philosopher-medium who inspired the movement in the nineteenth century. I had expected Rosa to tell me about Catholicism or evangelical Christianity, rehearsing familiar narratives I had come to expect. Instead, she described her beliefs using words I had never associated with Brazilian religious experience—Spiritism as a "philosophy" and "science," God as "energy," and life as an "incarnation."

I learned that, like evangelical migrants, many Spiritists had come to their faith in the United States following disappointment in the Catholic Church. Of the ten Spiritists I formally interviewed, four had left the Catholic Church once in the United States. The other six remarked on the dramatic intensification of their Spiritist faith and practice once in the United States. Given these facts, I investigated what made Spiritism, like evangelical Christianity, an attractive religious movement to migrants.

I chose two centers as main Spiritist field sites, the Center of Healing and Peace, which conducted its meetings exclusively in English, and the Washington Kardecistas, which conducted meetings predominantly in Brazilian Portuguese.[14] These two centers represented the main camps of the Spiritist movement in the United States. The Center of Healing and Peace advocated holding its meetings in English in order to appeal to a broader American audience and to encourage "acculturation" among Brazilian migrants. The Washington Kardecistas was representative of more established Spiritist centers in the United States, almost exclusively served Brazilian migrants, and conducted meetings in Brazilian Portuguese.

Spiritist centers, like evangelical churches, attracted Brazilians by specifically addressing and seeking to alleviate migrant distress.[15] Spiritist centers similarly emphasized individual behavior and emotion as the locus of migrant transformation, and recognized the acute suffering migrants endured. Below, I consider how Spiritists, like evangelicals, emphasized happy dispositions, calm minds, and turning inward. Spiritist centers also explicitly imbued migrants' flight from Brazil with divine meaning and purpose. These teachings help explain the appeal of Spiritism among migrants, and especially among former Catholics.[16] In theology and style, however, Spiritist centers remained distinct, ultimately limiting reach among migrants.

Peace and You: World Transformation through Feeling "Good"

At the end of March 2014, Spiritists gathered at the National Museum of Women in the Arts in Washington, DC, for the fourth Peace and You event in the United States. Organized around the theme "The Science and Spirituality of Doing Good," the evening's program included lectures by the Peace and You awardee, Dr. Steven Post, and Peace and You founder Divaldo Franco, and introductory remarks by local center presidents. Each of these addresses confirmed the centrality of affect regulation in Spiritist teachings. Despite being theologically distinct from evangelical Christianity,[17] Spiritist teachings revealed a strikingly similar orientation toward individual transformation, personal responsibility, and affective regulation.

As I rounded the busy corner of New York Avenue in downtown Washington, DC, where the museum sits, I was greeted by several smiling ushers wearing white blouses with blue handkerchiefs tied around their necks. Outside of the auditorium, attendees dropped off paper bags filled with groceries to donate, and then perused tables lined with free Spiritist texts.[18] Inside the auditorium, speakers and attendees wore the typical uniform of American professionalism—suits, ties, ironed shirts, high heels, skirts, and understated jewelry. Over one hundred people were in attendance, having traveled from centers around DC, as well as New York and Philadelphia. I recognized several people from the Spiritist centers I visited regularly in the region, as well as a number of Brazilians I had spoken with over the course of my research, including members of Catholic organizations and the Brazilian consulate's Citizens' Council.

With varying degrees of commitment to Spiritism, they all had traveled to Washington, DC, to see Divaldo Franco, a celebrity Brazilian medium, bestselling author, and perhaps the most recognizable face of Spiritism worldwide. At eighty-six years old, Divaldo maintained an impressive and commanding presence. With a full head of dark hair, piercing eyes, and an expressive face, he electrified the audience. People hung on his every word as he spoke without notes for well over an hour. Attendees swarmed the lobby during intermission to hug Divaldo, kiss him, and request his autograph. With his gentle yet penetrating charisma, he embodied the tenets and promises of Spiritism—everlasting vibrancy, equanimity, health, and joy.

Speaking in the soft and lilting cadence that defined Spiritist prayer, Sílvia, the president of a local center, delivered the opening benediction. She invited the audience to "attune our minds" to the "highest vibrations" of the spirit world, readying ourselves for communing with "something bigger than ourselves." Regina, another president of a local center, then explained the origins of the Peace and You movement. Divaldo Franco founded the program in 1998, she explained, to promote peace and harmony, regardless of religion or politics. Regina noted that the movement championed "universal ethics" of what she called "good customs," such as love, kindness, fraternity, charity, and tranquility among all human beings. Divaldo Franco, she continued, traveled throughout the world to spread the Spiritist message, using his celebrity to forward "Christ consciousness," and the core principles of Jesus's teachings.[19] Besides bringing Divaldo to new audiences, the organization sponsored lectures by Peace and You awardees—scientists whose research resonated with core Spiritist tenets. In 2014, the organization named Steven Post, a researcher at Stony Brook University who studied the biological benefits of altruism, its annual awardee. As Regina turned the microphone over to Dr. Post for his keynote address, she reminded the audience that, like all Spiritist events, the evening's program amounted to a "therapeutic session" for everyone who attended.

Dr. Post's lecture, entitled "RX: It's Good to Be Good," presented evidence drawn from his scientific research that giving to others dramatically improved mental and physical well-being. Citing studies with older adults who suffered from loneliness and depression, he argued that altruistic activities, such as volunteering and donating, triggered biological processes that made individuals feel better emotionally and physically. Through philanthropic activities, he explained, individuals stimulated the release of oxytocin ("the compassion hormone") and stymied cortisol ("the stress hormone"). As a result, altruistic people experienced what he called "inner peace." In addition to simply "feeling good," Post explained, these "positive feelings" carried important long-term health consequences. "Good" feeling "turned off" the dangerous biological effects of "bad" feeling, like stress and anger, which lead to the buildup of fatty acids in the arteries and, ultimately, an increased likelihood of heart attack.

In listening to Dr. Post's lecture, the resonance between his scientific findings and Spiritist teachings became evident. His research championed the same conclusions that Spiritists taught, only with explicitly scientific, rather than theological or philosophical, language. While Dr. Post argued that altruistic works improved individual health by undoing the impact of stress on the body, Spiritists taught the same lesson through the language of "energy." For Spiritists, individuals should "attune to higher vibrations" (the spirits) and "send good energy" to those around them in order to magnify "good" feeling and cast away "bad" feeling. Dr. Post's talk reflected the circular logic inherent in Spiritist thinking, and endemic to evangelical therapeutics, which Sarah Ahmed identifies as the "promise of happiness": one must *be* happy in order to *be* happy.[20]

Divaldo Franco further revealed the centrality of emotion work in Spiritist teachings during his remarks at the close of the Peace and You event. After taking the podium, he gravely told the story of an Armenian nurse whom a Turkish soldier raped during the Armenian genocide. Although the woman survived, she witnessed the massacre of her entire family. Several years later, he continued, the former soldier arrived for treatment in her clinic. The doctors and other nurses turned their backs on him, knowing the horrific atrocities the man had committed. Even though the nurse—his former victim—recognized him right away, she still treated him. When she revealed her identity, the man was stunned, asking, "Why didn't you kill me?" In Divaldo's narration, the woman responded with faithful resolve, "Because the Gospel of Jesus told us to forgive. I have no other option. I forgive you with all of my heart." After relaying this story in unsettling detail, Divaldo pointed to the woman as an exemplar of Jesus's primary emotions: unconditional love and radical forgiveness. Such emotional orientations, he stressed, resulted in true happiness, which he called "the substance of love." Furthermore, Divaldo explained, cultivating these emotional dispositions interrupted the baser emotions of anger and fear.

Spiritism teaches that feeling good enables personal evolution and enhanced proximity to the "higher minds," including spirits and God. As with the evangelicals I met, Spiritists strived to control their internal thoughts and feelings as evidence of spiritual progress, enlightenment, and intimacy with the Spirit realm. Both accounts considered affective maladies like depression and loneliness to be treatable through spiritual disciplines and individual efforts at rewiring interiority. While evangelicals resorted to prayer, discernment, and testimony to act on and in accordance with God's will, Spiritists "sent energy" to improve the world, heal relationships, and alter circumstances. The language of "moving energy" invoked one of Spiritism's central tenets, a principle adherents called "universal cosmic fluid."

As Marcos, the president of the Center of Healing and Peace, explained during one Sunday afternoon lecture, universal cosmic fluid connected every person, place, and thing in the universe. Because the whole world was immersed in this mystical connective tissue, moving energy in one place carried significant "ripple effects" throughout the cosmos. Therefore, it was possible to send energy to particular locations as well as to the world writ large. During another lesson, Marcos exclaimed, "It's like skipping stones in a river without banks," portraying prayer as hugely consequential mental activity that produced unending "waves" of peace and well-being for all humankind. These positive "ripples," he continued, joined with energetically similar waves sent by other "intelligent beings," gaining in force and impact, like a gathering avalanche.

While distinct in language and doctrine from evangelical Christianity, the Spiritist conception of the universe similarly equated prayer with meaningful and consequential action. By "manipulating" the cosmic fluid through concentrated thought, Spiritists understood themselves to be impacting their surroundings in specific ways. At the end of Marcos's teaching, Vera, a devoted Spiritist in her fifties, spoke passionately about the efficacy of prayer, illustrating how Spiritists viewed prayer as imbuing individuals with meaningful agentive potential. In the small group of ten to fifteen attendees, Vera shared that she had observed how sending energy had eased her husband's severe depression and anxiety. Because of this experience, she practiced "sending positive energy" anytime she sensed pain, suffering, and difficulty around her. When she passed through what she termed "bad" neighborhoods that "looked terrible" in Baltimore, Maryland, where many people lived in what she called "poverty and ignorance," she prayed for them, "knowing that it makes a difference." While Vera's words struck me as both condescending and unwittingly racist,[21] they revealed a shared logic with migrant evangelical Christianity. For both groups of migrant believers, spontaneous open-scripted prayer remained the gateway to internal well-being and consequential action on the world.

Lucília, an expert medium, long-time treasurer, and founder of the Washington Kardecistas, further revealed the similarities between evangelical and Spiritist discourse regarding affect, behavior, and agency. I interviewed Lucília in her luxury corner apartment in downtown Washington, DC. The child of German immigrants to Brazil, and living outside of Brazil since the 1970s, Lucília told me she had never thought of herself as an "immigrant" in the United States. Her husband worked for the World Bank and other prestigious international organizations. The entire family had become US citizens, and enjoyed every privilege and ease of American life, she asserted. In many ways, Lucília epitomized the distinction I discovered between many Brazilian Spiritists and Catholics, who appeared to belong to the cosmopolitan Washingtonian elite, and the Brazilian evangelicals I met, who overwhelmingly constituted the suburban and undocumented migrant underclass that cleaned the elite's homes, prepared their food, maintained their lawns, and cared for their children.

Despite these differences, Lucília's understanding of the universe struck me as deeply resonant with what "immigrants" she distinguished herself from also professed. At the end of our conversation, I asked Lucília how Spiritists accounted for the terrible events that afflicted the world. At the time of our meeting in July 2014, the Islamic State had taken charge of large swaths of the Middle East, wreaking havoc in their wake, and thousands of undocumented migrant children were placed indefinitely in detention camps at the southern border. When considering these events, Lucília reflected, "It's a horror to watch what is going on. But, for us Spiritists, Jesus is at the wheel of this planet. Nothing happens here that is not permitted by God and supervised by Jesus. So, we must accept." I thought of the many evangelical migrants I had interviewed, all of whom insisted on placing themselves *nas mãos de Deus* when confronting adversity and the unknown. Here again, in the words of a well-off Brazilian Spiritist, I was confronted with the same rationale. One must submit to God and practice wholehearted acceptance. Such emotional discipline constituted meaningful and powerful action.

Continuing her remarks, Lucília added, "And, that's not to say that I will sit back, and be passive. I try to be a good citizen, I try to help where I can, but I do not become desperate when I see the things that are happening." In order to bring about a "new world order," Spiritists learned to regulate their individual behavior. Lucília explained that the Earth was in a "great transition," progressing from a planet where evil reigned to one where good reigned. Violence and upheaval marked this transition, during which time each individual spirit would choose whether to undergo inner reform, and therefore progress with the Earth, or to be exiled to "lower" planets subsumed in "primitive ways." While Spiritists rejected the idea of Heaven and Hell, the notion of the Great Transition contained familiar apocalyptic connotations. Lucília explained, "We have free will, and according to free will, we will reap the consequences. But looking at what exists now, it's like a smorgasbord of choices. And, according to your choices you will be inheriting this [the evolved Earth] or that [primitive] place." Later, Lucília explained that Spiritists worked to bring about this new order by embodying "living examples of faith, twenty-four hours a day."

Like migrant evangelicals, Spiritists suggested that "peace" and "happiness" followed from personal choice, including the choice to assume correct behavior informed by theological principles and encouraged by spiritual disciplines. When applied to migrants in the United States, Spiritism largely echoed the evangelical message I heard. According to both belief systems, individual migrants remained wholly responsible for their experiences and feelings. The particular components of this teaching, however, remained distinct. First, Spiritists counseled migrants to immerse themselves in American society and culture, and second, Spiritists taught that migration experience in the United States, often demeaning and isolating, comprised "atonement" for debts incurred in past lives.

Spiritist Therapy for the Migrant (Part I): "Forget Brazil"

Like the Scalabrini mission in the Catholic Church, many Spiritists I interviewed identified "acculturation" or "integration" as a requirement for migrant success in the United States. Although the organization offers spiritual guidance, comfort, and healing to Brazilian migrants, these leaders, often representing the younger segment of the Spiritist population, argued that Spiritism in the United States should cast off the markings of Brazil and instead wholeheartedly embrace and disseminate English and US culture. Otherwise, they explained, centers would prolong and intensify the pain of the migratory experience. Regina, the president of a third Spiritist center in the region and one of the founders of the English-language movement within US Spiritism, explained the unintentional harm centers perpetrated by conducting their affairs in Portuguese:

> Look, if you keep doing this in Portuguese, you're not helping [the migrants] either. Because, whenever they come to the center, they feel like it's Brazil. When they leave the center, every meeting, they have a wake-up call, like you're not in Brazil, so they are sad, and upset, and . . . you're just feeding the anger, the frustration . . . you know?

Language acquisition and cultural fluency, Spiritists insisted, were essential to both survive and thrive in the United States. Although acculturation was difficult, Regina insisted that it remained the only path to contentment for migrants. "You have to go through this process to be happy," she concluded.

During separate conversations, Regina and Diego, who presided over the Center of Healing and Peace, noted that their personal experiences as migrants had informed their fervent views concerning the importance of teaching Spiritism in English. When she moved to the United States, Regina had to change her name, condensing two first names and two last names to one first name and one last name. To her, this epitomized the transformation she underwent through migration. She also altered the way she dressed, having discovered that her Brazilian clothing was considered "tight" and "sexy" by US standards.

Reflecting on his initial "culture shock" and subsequent adaptation, Diego told me his ultimate advice for Brazilian migrants. He urged, "Forget Brazil. You're not going to find Brazil here. Do what the American does. First step, learn the language. If you do this, the doors are now open but if you try to find a 'Brazilian way' here, you're going to be miserable." In keeping with this advice, Diego studiously observed the gestures, rhetoric, and preferences of Americans. At bars during graduate school, he ordered drinks by parroting his classmates, practicing the phrase, "I would like," and deliberately cultivated a passion for American football. Noting these deliberate behavioral modifications, Diego stressed, "I'm living *here* now. I can't be here thinking about the Brazilian way. I need to find the good. I need to follow what people like. You need to find a way to survive."

As a result of their personal experiences, Regina and Diego promoted English at all Spiritist meetings in the United States. Beginning in 2007, they organized national meetings where all speakers were required to lecture in English, regardless of the composition of the audience. Regina mandated that Spiritist centers affiliated with the English-language movement display the American flag, serve "American-style" refreshments rather than Brazilian pastries, and distribute Spiritist texts in English rather than in Portuguese. During regional events, she and other leaders incorporated American history and culture into the conference, aiming to teach Brazilians about the United States and draw more Americans into Spiritism. Toward this end, meetings like the Peace and You event described above began with the playing of the American national anthem.

The three Brazilian evangelical churches I attended conducted all church events, including worship, ministry, study, and outreach, exclusively in Brazilian Portuguese. In doing so, they implied the theological necessity of speaking to God in one's native tongue. Migrant adherents broadly reflected this orientation, asserting that praying to God in Portuguese and among Brazilians remained imperative to their religious identity. Pastor Jeferson and his wife, Juliana, gently chastised congregants they heard conversing in English. Juliana asserted that Brazilian migrants strayed from righteousness and faith in American-led churches because they could neither participate in church life nor communicate adequately to God speaking English. Migrants who attended such churches, she asserted, were deliberately "hiding" from God. They also insisted on the importance of educating children in Portuguese and teaching them about Brazil. Failing to do so amounted to neglect, for without Brazilian Portuguese comprehension and Brazilian identity, children would not understand the Bible as it was discussed in church.

In contrast, Spiritist centers following Regina and Diego's "English only" mandate deliberately decoupled religious and cultural identity. Regina explained that Brazilians would always be welcome, and she would never refuse to provide counsel in Portuguese to those who requested it, but she reminded Brazilians who came looking for "Little Brazil" in Spiritist centers that they would be sorely disappointed.

Spiritist Therapy for the Migrant (Part II):
Migration as "Atonement" for Past Lives

As I began to inquire into Spiritism, I encountered Regina's name everywhere. Everyone I spoke with told me that if I really wanted to understand Spiritism and its relationship to Brazilian migrants, I had to interview Regina. Not only had she founded the Center of Healing and Peace when she was a young postdoctoral researcher, but she was also the president of another regional Spiritist center, the editor of a prominent Spiritist publication, and the founder of an English-language podcast about Spiritism. Beyond these activities, Regina was well known in the international Spiritist community for her prolific writings and lectures on Spiritism. She was a personal friend of Divaldo Franco, the famous Brazilian medium discussed above, and, I was told, she descended from an impressive lineage of Spiritist mediums going back five generations. Most relevant for my research, she had developed a workshop entitled "Spiritist Therapy for the Immigrant," in which she applied Spiritist teachings to migrants in the United States, in the hopes of easing their transition. After several unanswered emails, I finally met Regina in person at Divaldo Franco's talk in Washington, DC, at the end of March 2014. Months later, she invited me to visit her at home in Northern Virginia, where she lived with her husband and young daughter.

When I arrived at Regina's large home at 8:30 on a Friday night, the house was completely dark and I saw no cars in the driveway. After a few tentative knocks, Regina greeted me in sweatpants and a t-shirt, and smiled broadly. The baby had just gone to sleep, and she was eager to talk. From the moment we sat in her living room and I began recording, I barely asked Regina any questions. She interviewed herself, adeptly incorporating her personal narrative with her observations on migration, culture, and faith.

Regina told me she had developed "Spiritist Therapy for the Immigrant" after discovering that Brazilian migrants were a particularly "conflicted" group. While lecturing across the United States about the imperative of teaching Spiritism in English, she encountered what she termed "extreme resistance" from Brazilian migrants, who preferred teaching, socializing, and studying in Portuguese. Regina remarked, "There were people who hated us to death!" As a result of this unsettling experience, she consulted with her spirit mentor, Joseph, asking him how she could publicize Spiritist beliefs in English when Brazilians remained deeply resistant.[22] According to Regina, Joseph encouraged her to "scientifically" study the Brazilian population by developing a survey. Only by understanding the demographic, emotional, and spiritual profile of Brazilians in the United States, he told her, would she better understand how to help Brazilians "transition" to their new lives. Between 2005 and 2010, Regina solicited responses from Spiritist centers across the United States. At the time of our conversation, Regina planned to publish her findings in the English-language *Spiritist Magazine*, but at the time of writing still had not done so.

Through the survey, Regina explained, she better understood the "unbelievable resistance" she had encountered among Brazilians:

> People come [to the United States] mostly because of work, because of money. . . . So, the priority is *not* to immerse themselves in the culture at all . . . and precisely fifty percent of them said, "We don't want to stay." So, how can you ever disseminate Spiritism, if you are working with people who are deeply conflicted about staying here, being here, living here? So many of them embrace Spiritism because they were here, and they were in need, not necessarily because they were Spiritists in Brazil. The majority of people became Spiritist here, because of their sufferings, their emotional needs, something was missing, then they found Spiritism.

As a result of these findings, Regina developed a program to specifically address migrant suffering and migrant ambivalence in the United States. In her retelling, Joseph, her spirit mentor, instructed, "Create a program, and go to each and every center, giving workshops in which you can raise awareness about [the migrant's] emotional life, their profile, raise awareness in regards to culture."[23]

Regina launched the program in 2008. The workshop aimed to teach migrants to consider their time in the United States differently. Regina taught migrants to evaluate their journeys according to Spiritist teachings, rather than to the amount of fast money they could earn. She explained, "Spiritually speaking, there's a *reason* why we are where we are." She applied central Spiritist teachings regarding reincarnation and causality to explain the difficulties Brazilian migrants faced in America, and to help them cope with emotional distress. Regina explained:

> Divaldo Franco, in an interview they have in the *Spiritist Magazine*, says most immigrants who come back, who move to a country, are usually people who are like, they *owe* something to that country. So, one of the ideas that we are sharing in the workshop is that idea. Like, no wonder you are here [with] underprivileged status, it's almost like an atonement, you know. You took

something from the country in another life, now you have to give it back. But you're giving back in a way where you feel like you're an immigrant, second-class citizen. Some people really have language barriers, resistance.

Like Brazilian evangelicals, Brazilian Spiritists wholly rejected the possibility of chance. Instead of attributing all experiences to "God's plan," however, the Spiritist sense of divine design was tied to ideas of reincarnation and causality. One's current incarnation, Spiritist doctrine taught, depended upon one's spiritual progress in past lives. Because the entire universe in Spiritist cosmology tended toward progress and evolution, in contrast to Christian eschatology of apocalypse, every human being represented a different stage along the way to enlightenment, culminating in the end of earthly reincarnations and living with God and the highest minds in the "spirit realm." Even the most violent criminals, Spiritists reminded one another, would eventually reach the highest spirit realm. It would just take more lifetimes for them to get there. As Cláudia described this cosmology, she noted that Spiritists believe that "life is a learning school."

Comparative Therapeutics and Evangelical Efficacy

When applied to the case of migrants in the United States, Regina's teachings struck me as quite similar to what I had identified as distinctly evangelical affective therapeutics. By grounding Brazilian migrants' presence in the United States theologically, "Spiritist Therapy for the Immigrant" taught migrants that they belonged in the United States to fulfill a higher purpose. These teachings similarly considered the interior landscape of feeling to be the locus of individual transformation. The workshop, and the broader Spiritist doctrine it expressed, encouraged Brazilians to work toward acceptance and peace.

Gabriela, a young Spiritist who had encountered severe loneliness and depression in the United States, suggested to me the centrality of "acceptance" in Spiritist teachings. She explained that Spiritism's emphasis on divine order and progress helped her cope with the adversity she had faced. Rather than succumbing to frustration or resentment at the events that had come to pass, she learned through Spiritism to embrace her life. She explained:

That's why I came back to the [Spiritist] center, because it really gives me another perspective of things. It gives me more motivation. And a lot more hope . . . that things are going to be okay. That they *needed* to be this way, or whatever it is that they say, and it's so nice what they say, and I believe it.

Gabriela explained Spiritism as a source of deep comfort. Nothing happened by chance, everything was divinely ordained. As such, she tried to embrace the difficult aspects of her life, viewing them as necessary to spiritual growth. Reflecting on her tumultuous marriage to an American man, she noted, "Yeah . . . how many times that [my husband] and I tried to break up! And we couldn't get away. So, we might as well accept it. So, I guess that gives me a lot of that acceptance that I need."

Sílvia, the president of Washington Kardecistas, invoked these ideal emotional dispositions when detailing to me the kind of "spiritual counseling" that she and other mediums offered migrants. In general, she explained that Brazilian migrants sought treatment for anxiety wrought from family separation. Faced with loved ones' distress in Brazil, Brazilians here in the United States sought relief from extreme guilt, worry, and powerlessness. When I asked how she and the other mediums helped, she noted that mediums reminded migrants of the "Spiritist perspective." Sílvia explained the main tenets of such advice:

> If you are doing everything correct, you are not the cause of all of this, and there is nothing that you can do. There is no need for you to feel anxious, because you're not going to help. You have to be *good* in order to help. Many times I give them the example of when you are on the airplane, and they say you have to put the mask on yourself first.

Sílvia's emphasis on "putting the mask on yourself first" again indicated the Spiritist emphasis on personal well-being, contentment, and tranquility. In order to help those around them, individuals first needed to feel "good" in themselves. The way individuals learned to feel good, Sílvia explained, was through "letting go" of worry and doubt.

During a Sunday meeting at the Center of Healing and Peace, Débora, the speaker, underscored the centrality of this Spiritist teaching. Through the "Law of Consequence," she explained, every "effect" has an "intelligent cause." Like a "boomerang," she noted, "what we put out into the world comes back at us." The challenges each person faced, she continued, amounted to the personal "debts" individuals incurred through past lives, and must repay through good acts and enlightenment. Similar to evangelicals, Débora insisted, "Everything happens according to God's will." Rather than meet this fact with resistance and resentment, Spiritists practiced acceptance and resignation, recognizing God's superior wisdom and mindfully "doing nothing." In her counseling sessions, Sílvia employed this strategy. Like Regina, she wanted to help migrants see the divine meaning behind their presence in the United States. She explained, "[As] immigrants . . . the meaning is not just [get] here and work . . . there is another meaning."

Through mindfulness, equilibrium, and contentment, migrants would "attune to the vibrations of higher minds," and thus invite good "energy" into their lives, regardless of their legal status, employment, or language ability. Such Spiritist terminology remained distinct from the familiar evangelical phrases I encountered (see chapter 3)—*felicidade dos crentes* (happiness of believers), *seja positiva* (be positive), *seja o vaso de Deus* (be God's vessel)—yet the sum of such affective principles remained the same. Spiritist leaders, like their evangelical counterparts, taught migrants to invite divine blessing into their lives by being "happy," "positive," and "open."

While evangelical churches preached that God brought Brazilian migrants to the United States in order to accept Jesus, save friends and family members, or become missionaries, the Spiritist message uniquely positioned migration as a form of atonement for errors made in past lives, and as a kind of learning for future reincarnations. As such, Spiritists took an even more radical position than evangelicals concerning the theological function of migrant distress. Migrants, who lived as "second-class citizens" in the United States, had to "repay a debt" from a previous life. Like evangelical churches, Spiritists directly addressed the difficulties migrants faced in the United States, and offered specific teachings for how to cope with the negative feelings associated with distress. And, also like evangelical churches, this orientation positioned individual migrants, in relationship with the divine, as wholly responsible for their experience.

While also attracting many former Brazilian Catholics in the United States, especially among the well-educated and upwardly mobile, Spiritism remained dwarfed by evangelical religiosity in the region. Owing to its unconventional beliefs regarding spirit communication and reincarnation, many Brazilians regarded the movement skeptically. Spiritist growth was further constrained by the fact that unlike evangelical Christianity, the movement rejected proselytization. Finally, Spiritism's growing emphasis on English language and American culture undoubtedly dissuaded many Brazilian migrants from attending. In offering affective therapeutics in an entrenched and accepted Christian idiom, and immersed in a celebration of Brazilian language, culture, and exceptionalism, evangelical churches most effectively and comprehensively satisfied migrant yearnings.

6

The Evangelization of God among Migrants

INTIMATE FAITH AND EMBODIED
EXPERIENCE ACROSS DENOMINATIONS

If I thought I had faith while in Brazil, I didn't. Now I have true faith.

—MIRTES, 38, CATHOLIC

Many immigrants commit suicide. I, thank God, never thought about it. I always loved my life and I'm very happy here. But they arrive here and they're all alone, understand? If it wasn't for the church that embraces them . . .

—ROSALI, 55, CATHOLIC

WHILE INTERVIEWING evangelical migrants, I came to expect a standard conversion narrative from believers. Migrants reproduced the narrative arc that scholars of evangelical Christianity have long considered fundamental to the genre, regardless of geography or epoch.[1] Like evangelical believers elsewhere, Brazilian migrants equated their preconversion experience with generalized illness and despair, while they associated their postconversion lives with expansive health and happiness.[2]

Such uniformity, however, is not surprising. At its very core, evangelical theology depends upon the promise of radical rebirth in the wake of "meeting," "knowing," and "accepting" Jesus as one's personal savior. This recognition allows God to "wash away" human sin and purify the believer's soul such that it becomes "whiter than snow." The refrain from a popular Brazilian hymn, sung weekly with gusto in the migrant churches I attended, vividly illustrated this radical and alluring promise:

Salvos do mal nós estamos	Saved from evil we are
Por tua graça e teu favor	By your grace and favor
Pois sim mais alvo que a neve	Now turned whiter than snow
O teu sangue nos torna Senhor	By your blood, Our Lord
Alvo mais que a neve	Whiter even than snow
Alvo mais que a neve	Whiter even than snow
Sim, nesse sangue lavado	Yes, washed in blood
Mais alvo que a neve serei	Whiter than snow I will be

In accounting for their own arrival at sincere faith, migrant believers reproduced this theological core of evangelical Christianity. Their lives began in sinfulness, peaked in personal encounter with God, and culminated in radical rebirth.

In addition to reflecting the familiar tropes of affective and physical "discontinuity," migrants' conversion narratives highlighted the religious significance of spatial discontinuity.[3] Migrants converted, reconverted, or intensified their devotion to evangelical Christianity *after* their migrations to the United States. Several studies have documented the coincidence of growing evangelical commitment and migration across diverse populations and geographies, including Brazilians in Japan, Brazilians, Ghanaians, and Jamaicans in England, and Koreans and Salvadorans in the US.[4] The spatial rupture, and the fragmentation of lifeworlds it provoked, such literature concludes, impelled migrants to find comfort in evangelical belonging. To combat loneliness, marginality, and the deep sensation of what Suma Ikeuchi calls "the suspension of life," and what I document as "feeling stuck," migrants immersed themselves in devout, embodied, and socially embedded Christianity.[5] Such religious faith and belonging compensated migrants for the multiple losses they endured in their new societies. Brazilian factory workers in Japan found a way to "be modern again in spiritual, if not in economic terms,"[6] while Ghanaian migrants claimed moral superiority over their host nation, thereby asserting their "virtuous citizenship" and rightful belonging in Britain.[7]

Similarly, Brazilian migrants wed together their religious and migratory narratives into a single "unified process of subject formation."[8] They invoked evangelical theology not only to "make a complete break with the past," but to make moral sense of the past.[9] In their narration, migrants imbued their experience of dislocation, downward mobility, and marginalization with

Christian significance, coherence, and meaning. They transformed otherwise random events into meaning-laden occurrences, all "pointed towards the same goal."[10] In their telling, God was both origin and endpoint, for God had brought them to the United States to fulfill His plan.

While I came to expect such conversion narratives from the Adventist, Baptist, and Pentecostal migrants I met, I was surprised to hear strikingly similar language from committed Spiritist and Catholic migrants, especially since they vociferously critiqued evangelical churches. The nonevangelical migrants I met vocalized distinctly evangelical interpretations, even if they did not identify them as such. Like their evangelical counterparts, Catholic and Spiritist migrants asserted that their journeys to and lives within the United States prompted them to seek out the divine and pursue embodied intimacy with this entity. In their narrations, nonevangelical migrants attested to the power of their faith through employing tropes of the stage model of conversion discussed above. Like Mirtes, whose words open the chapter, many nonevangelical migrants repeated this refrain: "If I thought I had faith while in Brazil, I didn't. Now I have true faith."

While maintaining theologically distinct perspectives, Spiritist and Catholic migrants spoke of the motivations and consequences of faith in terms very similar to those used by evangelical migrants. Loneliness and distress wrought from living in the United States, they insisted, had impelled them to seek out religious comfort in God and community. In reflecting on their accounts of religious belonging and divine encounter, Catholic and Spiritist migrants emphasized novel intimacy and bodily knowledge of God as well as significant relationships with cobelievers. And, they also made sense of their migrations in theological terms: God had a particular reason for choosing *them* to live in the United States. In interweaving affective, embodied, religious, and spatial ruptures, their accounts resembled typical evangelical conversion narratives. This chapter considers how, and to what end, nonevangelical migrants' reflections approximated typical evangelical conversion narratives. Such narrative convergence reveals the evangelization of religious experience in migration. Migration impelled Brazilians to search for God differently, and to search for a different kind of God.

In the first section, I analyze a typical evangelical conversion narrative, noting the conjuncture of spiritual and spatial discontinuities. Through Laura's narration, I underscore key elements of evangelical conversion narratives, and the distinctive subjectivity they perform. In the remainder of the chapter, I consider how nonevangelical migrants, such as those who left evangelical churches, or who identified as Spiritist or Catholic, expressed evangelical-inflected religiosity. Despite overt criticisms of evangelical theology and churches, Catholic and Spiritist migrants relayed strikingly evangelical conversion narratives.

At the outset of this discussion on self-narration and faith, it is important to briefly note that whether or not migrants objectively and accurately told the "truth" of what they experienced or of what they felt does not interest me. Rather than accurately recount objective events, telling the "right" kind of conversion narrative itself constitutes an essential moment of faith and belonging, where the telling itself constitutes "a central element of conversion"[11] or, in my reading, of faith and religious subjectivity. Both in performance and structure, conversion narratives indexed the "total transformation of the person by the power of God."[12] Whether or not the person telling them has been perfectly transformed in the exact way they suggest remains beside the point.[13] Rather, migrants told a certain kind of totalizing story, one that knitted their past and present experiences into a coherent, meaning-laden account.

Evangelical Markers in Migrant Conversion Narratives

Laura's conversion narrative exemplifies the convergence of spiritual and spatial discontinuities in evangelical migrants' accountings of faith. I interviewed Laura in 2014, after meeting her the previous autumn at the Baptist church I attended. Laura had moved to the United States in 2002 at the age of twenty-four and converted three months later. A warm and lively mother of two, Laura invited me to her home to spend the evening with her family and to hear her testimony. After learning of my research, she actively sought me out, exclaiming, "I have so much to tell you!"

Laura lived in a sprawling and concrete apartment complex in leafy Montgomery County. She lived in a small three-bedroom corner duplex with her husband, Tião, and her two young children. Laura told me that she and her husband scraped together the $1,300 per month in rent from her husband's employment in construction, and her own part-time work as a day-care provider and party planner. Although Laura and Tião had lived in the United States for over a decade without documents, she noted, they were currently awaiting their green cards, sponsored by Tião's employer. While her children played with Angela, her best friend, whom she had met at church, I asked Laura why she had originally left São Paulo and moved to Washington, DC.

From the beginning of her narrative, Laura wed together her religious and migratory journeys, noting that she left Brazil because she was feeling "unmotivated" (*desmotivada*), "without a future" (*não tem futuro*), and "in the wind" (*no vento*). Laura explained that she had been the most popular of her friends in Brazil. She had loved drinking, partying, and going to bars, and would encourage the group to stay out late "to have fun" (*pra bagunçar*). Having recently graduated from college, however, and newly separated from her boyfriend, she "lost the ground beneath [her]" (*perdi meu chão*). The convergence of these two events plunged her into a deep depressive state. Laura illustrated her preconversion and premigration state by graphically recounting bodily and psychic breakdown. She recalled:

> I started to go crazy (*comecei a ficar doida*). I didn't want to go out, I would stay in my room . . . I wouldn't call anyone. And I vomited. Everything I ate, I vomited. When my mom found out, I went to the psychiatrist and took medicine that didn't help but made me worse . . . I was like this [mimics state of being heavily sedated] all day long.

Laura's parents were desperate for her to improve and encouraged her to join her brother in the United States, where he worked as a landscaper and secured Laura a job babysitting. Laura shared that her father was particularly "crazy for her to go, because he saw that there in Brazil, I was . . . you know . . . *no vento* (in the wind)." Realizing that her life had stalled in Brazil, where she had "no future," she opted to leave. Like Laura, most migrant believers I met layered geography onto standard preconversion and postconversion tropes. Of their preconversion and premigration lives in Brazil, migrants detailed stories of drinking, drugs, family conflict, financial woe, illness, or generally feeling, as Laura described, *no vento*—literally, floating in the wind, purposeless.

At first, upon her arrival in the United States, things worsened. While Laura had weaned herself off heavy medication, she remained fragile. Aside from her brother and sister-in-law, she knew no one. Despite learning English in school, she could not understand a word anyone spoke, including her employer. During her first three months, Laura reflected, "I was totally lost. I was just crying and crying." Her mother worried that she would experience a relapse of severe depression and bulimia. Out of desperation, Laura told me, she accepted her sister-in-law's invitation to go to church as a way to meet others. Laura recalled, "I entered the church and they were beginning to worship. I sat down. Those songs, you know, that the people were singing. They began to enter my heart in a way that made me cry. And I just cried and cried. God was breaking (*quebrantando*) my heart right there in that moment. I converted right then and there."

In order to escape the existential and physical malaise that Laura and others associated with Brazil, migrants contended that it was essential to leave their *zona de conforto,* comfort zone. Célia, a youth-group leader at the Baptist church, described over coffee one afternoon how intimacy with God depended on physical distance from Brazil. She explained, "Leaving Brazil is leaving a comfort zone. There is your home. You walk with your eyes closed. You know how to do everything. Here, you have to learn to do everything anew." She noted how her isolation as an undocumented migrant in the United States forced her to depend only on God. Célia remarked, "I experienced many difficult situations that I couldn't overcome on my own, with my own contacts, my own will, my own money. From two options, I had only one. Either trust totally in God or give up (*desistir*) and return to Brazil." Célia's and Laura's narratives suggested that their spiritual awakening depended upon a "dark night of the soul,"[14] whereupon they found themselves newly alone, far from their moorings, and fully aware of their dependence on God. Through the lens of evangelical faith, migrants reinterpreted their flight from Brazil and specific hardships they faced as migrants in the United States as preconditions to divine encounter.

In reflecting on her postconversion and postmigration self, Laura described newfound states of joy, calm, and contentment in everyday life. She felt freed from the worry and despair that had gripped her in Brazil. She explained, "My life transformed in a way that there would be no way *not to* believe." She no longer felt alone, or fearful about living in a foreign land. Laura described the powerful assurance intimacy with God had evoked:

> When I converted, God became such a strong presence in my life that I felt that I could go to Japan, where I don't speak Japanese, where no one would understand English, or Portuguese. But if I was with God, I could go *anyplace,* you know? I could confront *anything.* This is the sensation that I began to have after I started to attend church.

Soon after she converted, Laura told me, she asked God to eradicate her eating disorder. Medication and psychiatry had not succeeded in healing her. In the United States, her vomiting had become so severe that she occasionally spewed blood. Fearing that she had given herself cancer, she begged God for healing.

Laura recounted a particularly vivid encounter with God while accompanying her brother to his new Pentecostal church. At the end of her sermon, a visiting *pastora* from Brazil offered to lay hands on those who needed healing. At first Laura demurred. Then, an older woman pushed her forward urging, "Go! Go! Go, so she can pray for you!" While irritated at the stranger's brazenness, Laura acquiesced. According to her retelling, the *pastora* delivered a prescient message from God:

> My daughter, I have taken care of you up until now. It was my plan that you are here. It was me that brought you here. I know that you are feeling alone. But I have plans for you! You will have a family here! In this place! You will marry and have your family here. You have to wait. Know how to wait. Everything has its time. *I have even freed you from your cancer.*

In that moment, Laura recounted feeling God remove her eating disorder and restore her to health. Like the many migrants whose stories I recount in previous chapters, Laura came to understand her presence in the United States as fulfilling God's plan for her life. In order to be free from physical and psychic pain, in order to have a family, in order to find God, she had to first migrate to, and suffer within, this particular foreign land.

Laura's narrative reflects the key markers of what I consider to be typical evangelical conversion narratives among migrants, detached from denominational specificity. These key markers include the following elements of narration: (1) positioning conversion, reconversion, or religious intensification in the United States as directly inspired by personal encounter with God; (2) recalling specific and recurrent embodied intimacy with God; and (3) asserting a complete reorientation to everyday life according to "God's plan" following conversion and postmigration. Notably, these key markers do not include specific theological orientations evangelical Christians promulgate, such as biblical inerrancy and the mission to evangelize. The migrants I met rarely emphasized the more formal teachings of evangelical Christianity, especially in personal interviews. Instead, migrant conversion narratives underscored feeling, relationship, and practice.[15]

In evaluating the immediacy and whole-life impact of her postmigration conversion, Laura considered denominational affiliation, and even the terms "religion" (*religião*) and "evangelical" (*evangélico*), to be problematic. Her conversion, she insisted, was not inspired by Bible classes or the pastor's sermon, but instead by devotional music that "spoke deep into [her] heart." This was not a matter of religion, but rather of "having Jesus." Laura reported that her brother and sister-in-law scoffed at this distinction and reminded her of the formal requirements of Christian belonging. Yet, Laura remained insistent on the validity of her "immediate conversion." She related the exchange:

> My brother said to my sister-in-law, "What is this girl drinking today?" And my sister-in-law said, "Look, you know you're going to have to take baptism classes, these kinds of things." And I said, "Look, bureaucracy doesn't interest me. If I have to do it, I'll do it. But my heart belongs to Jesus, I already gave it to him. So, if I have to do a class, or if I don't have to do a class, it doesn't matter. What is important is that now I want to have this relationship together with God, with Jesus.

She then distinguished between "religion" and "having Jesus":

> I resolved to convert, not because of religion, I'm not going to be like, "Ah, now I am going to be *crente*, now I'm going to be Baptist." I said, "No. Now I'm going to follow Jesus." And that's still what I think today. A lot of people ask, "What's your religion?" I don't like to say that I have a religion. I like to say that I have Jesus in my heart (*tenho Jesus no meu coração*). If I have to have a denomination, then I'm evangelical (*evangélico*), but that's it. I have Jesus.

Laura's conversion narrative hinged on her repeated insistence of the personal, intimate, and embodied relationship she discovered with Jesus as a migrant in the United States. This was not about "mere" religion, she explained, a system created and perpetuated by humans and an affront to true personal faith. In her telling, Laura did not *work* to find this relationship, nor pursue it intentionally. Rather, the desperation and despair she experienced as a migrant drove her to church, simply as something to do and somewhere to be. Once there, she felt God physically enter her body and break her heart. It was clear and simple—a total life transformation initiated in an instant.

An Echo across Faiths: Evangelical Rhetoric and Religiosity among Nonevangelicals

Demographic Considerations

The Spiritist and Catholic migrants I met maintained greater resources than their evangelical counterparts, thus protecting them from certain forms of migrant distress. Within the small Catholic prayer group I attended in Montgomery County, for instance, the six members I interviewed had lived in the

United States between ten and thirty years. On average, group members were older than evangelicals—in their forties and fifties rather than their twenties and thirties. And, four of the six had obtained green cards or US citizenship through employment, family sponsorship, or amnesty. In the Arlington diocese, the three women I formally interviewed also had attained US citizenship and had lived in the US for over twenty years. In addition, these women had earned advanced degrees from renowned Brazilian and American universities, and worked in so-called skilled professions, occupying positions in policy, international organizations, and higher education.

Spiritists also maintained greater educational, financial, and professional resources than evangelicals. Of the ten Spiritists I formally interviewed, seven had moved to the United States for educational or professional opportunities and continued to work in the industries of their training and education. Nine of the ten reported that they had acquired green cards or citizenship. Like Catholics from the well-resourced Arlington diocese, most Spiritists I met spoke English fluently.

Each of these factors, unsurprisingly, lessened the vulnerability Catholics and Spiritists faced as migrants in the United States. With citizenship or green cards, these migrants lived without daily fear of apprehension or deportation, and without heightened barriers to health insurance, equitable housing, affordable public higher education, or basic job protections. They often traveled back and forth to Brazil, easing the pain of family separation, and somewhat mitigating the sensation of being stuck.

These migrants seemed uninterested in Brazilian evangelical groups and the robust affective therapeutics they offered. Often, Catholic and Spiritist migrants pointedly criticized such churches, both in Brazil and in the United States. Portraying them as opportunistic, money-hungry institutions, Spiritists and Catholics charged that evangelical pastors exploited migrants' despair for personal gain. Recurrent media exposés of rampant corruption, sexual scandal, and fraud among famous Brazilian pastors emboldened such rhetoric.[16]

Exploitation, Insincerity, and Utilitarianism: Migrant Critiques of Evangelical Churches

Cláudia, a devout Catholic in her midfifties, articulated the most common criticisms of evangelical churches I encountered. Like other Catholics I met, Cláudia referred to evangelical converts as *católicos não-praticantes*, nonpracticing Catholics, thus refusing to acknowledge their self-identification as *evangélicos, cristãos,* or *crentes.* Such language reflected the Catholic Church's official position referring to evangelical converts as "former Catholics" who had been seduced by evangelical promises of "health and wealth." When I asked why she thought so many migrants converted in the United States when they had been critical of evangelical churches in Brazil, Cláudia commented on the financial assistance that evangelical churches offered:

> I think they [Brazilian migrants] go there in search of help. This is the reason that many convert. . . . They convert because they think, "Oh, if I go there, I will be cured." In reality they don't have any faith. They think if they go there, they will find miracles. They go because of the [evangelical churches'] propaganda.

Father Bernardo, the Portuguese-born priest who led one of the Brazilian Catholic groups I visited, expressed similar sentiments. He noted that migrants converted to evangelical Christianity for instrumental reasons, approaching religion as if they were in a "supermarket." Migrants, he asserted, chose the religion they thought would most immediately satiate their appetites and needs.[17] He acknowledged that migrants more easily met friends and received financial assistance or job information in evangelical churches, which tended to be smaller and more personalized.

Imelda, a devout Catholic who lived in Baltimore, noted how her enduring Catholic devotion had disadvantaged her in finding work. She explained, "Most people become evangelical, you know why? Because inside evangelical churches they find work. I was unemployed for a long time because I didn't want to leave my church. If I had left my church and gone to [an evangelical] church, I would have found work more easily." Citing migrant employment networks, financial assistance, and business opportunities, studies of migrant evangelicalism often echoed the criticism I encountered from Catholics and Spiritists: migrants converted primarily for utilitarian purposes, rather than because of inward spiritual motivations.[18]

Despite such vocal and pointed criticism, however, I was surprised to learn that Catholic and Spiritist migrants shared remarkably similar stories of deepening faith in the United States. Such stories cohered to the structure of the evangelical conversion narrative discussed above, and also exemplified the three key evangelical markers I identified, including personal encounter, embodied experience, and religious transformation postmigration. Like evangelical converts, Catholic and Spiritist migrants underscored the entanglement of their spatial and spiritual journeys. Proximity to God corresponded with distance from Brazil, and conversely, distance from God corresponded with proximity to Brazil. Like evangelicals, Catholic and Spiritist migrants associated their growing intimacy with God and cobelievers with the experience of a "dark night of the soul" in a foreign land. As a result, they also encountered heightened and newly sensorial spiritual experience as migrants, including prophecies, dreams, premonitions, and embodied phenomena. Such experiences convinced them of God's intimate presence in their daily lives and God's explicit desire for them to live in the United States.

Catholic Migrants: Toward a More Intimate God

I interviewed Cláudia at the townhouse she shared with her husband in an affluent neighborhood in Montgomery County. Unlike most evangelical migrants I met, who had arrived after 2000, Cláudia had lived in the United States for almost three decades and had arrived with a green card in hand. Her father had acquired a green card in the 1980s, and, according to the laws of the time, was able to confer legal permanent residency on Cláudia and her brother.[19] Despite her legal status, however, Cláudia emphasized that life in the United States had not been easy. Without English fluency, she found most jobs out of reach. The jobs she took—as babysitter, bus driver, and administrative assistant—exposed her to financial and emotional exploitation. Cláudia explained that when people saw where she and her husband currently lived, and learned they owned their townhouse, they assumed they were rich, and always had been. To the contrary, she insisted, they had struggled.

Cláudia was raised Catholic but considered herself to be "nonpracticing" (não-praticante) for most of her life. Since moving to the United States, she became deeply involved in her faith. All of her friends attended the same parish. Cláudia organized Portuguese-language activities for Brazilian Catholics in the area, including the terças, weekly prayer groups, that I attended for several months in the basement of the local church. When I first contacted Father Bernardo about my research, he referred me to Cláudia, whom he considered to be the most involved and knowledgeable person in the group.

As Cláudia reflected on her faith during our conversation, she utilized a structure that had become familiar. Religious conversion—or in this case, religious deepening—corresponded with her migration trajectory. Brazil was a place of sin, her arrival in the United States brought on a dark night of the soul, after which she turned to God and experienced affective transformation. First, Cláudia spoke of her faith in terms of spatial discontinuity. She insisted that her novel seriousness of faith corresponded with moving to the United States. Like many Brazilians, she had regarded her Catholic identity casually in Brazil. She reflected:

> I was always Catholic. My family was always Catholic. But I wasn't practicing. Today, I see many things that I was doing. For example, during Holy Week in Brazil, most people travel, go to the beach, no one worries about church. And I was one of those people. I remember I was traveling by Paulinas, which is a store that sells religious products. They always put on [religious] music, and when I was passing by the door, I heard religious music and thought, "This music is so annoying! Why do they have to play this music?" But, today, I *only* like religious music!

As in Laura's narrative discussed at the outset of the chapter, Cláudia characterized her religious identity in Brazil as shallow and insincere. She had not taken faith seriously, and so considered Holy Week to be an opportunity to travel and go to the beach, rather than commune with God.

Like the evangelical conversion narratives I encountered, Cláudia reported that the foreignness and isolation she encountered in the United States prompted her to search for God in earnest. She was impelled to go to church because "there wasn't much else to do" as a migrant living in the outskirts of Washington, DC, and she felt very alone. When she began to go to church, she enjoyed being with compatriots and native Portuguese speakers. She put it simply: "You feel at home. You can interact with people. You can talk." Such fellow feeling developed into deep Catholic devotion and community involvement. Considering the impact of her immersion into Catholic faith and belonging, Cláudia spoke of affective transformation. "Before, I think I was a more bitter person. Today, I think that my manner of thinking has changed a lot. That my faith will bring me somewhere. That I can achieve things through faith, through religion, through God. I don't know. It's really different. I move differently. I feel differently." Significantly, this affective transformation depended on intimacy with a newly personal and intimate God.

When I asked her about her relationship with God, Cláudia at first insisted she had never felt particularly close to God, neither in Brazil nor in the United States. She wanted to feel such intimacy, and she knew that some of her friends regularly experienced this feeling, but she simply had not. She did not talk to God regularly and had a hard time concentrating during prayer, where, she confessed, her mind wandered. She considered God to be a benign but somewhat distant "protector," and described God as the "base of everything" and "what gives you force to continue, to not give up your dreams." Her comments reflected the traditional Catholic portrait of God as "the Father"—a remote, stern, and powerful first mover. Such comments invoked a stark contrast to evangelical descriptions of God, which emphasized proximity and intimacy with words like "my friend," "my guide," "my companion."

In the next breath, however, Cláudia mentioned her novel encounters with the Holy Spirit while in the United States, sensations that reflected embodied experience. She explained, "When I go to retreats (*retiros*), and we start talking about the Holy Spirit, I get a premonition (*eu pressinto*), and I feel shivers, as if He is moving me. I have a lot of affinity (*afinidade*), a lot of intimacy (*intimidade*) with the Holy Spirit." Several Catholic migrants I interviewed shared similar stories of embodied spirituality and intimate encounters with divinity, be it God (the Father, the Son, or Holy Spirit), or the Virgin Mary.

Tati, another active member of the Catholic prayer group, separated her need for social connection from her need for intimacy with God. She told me that she did not attend *terça* or Mass to make friends. Instead, she went to feel God's presence, experience peace, and find comfort. Like Cláudia, she identified as Catholic in Brazil but had never practiced regularly since childhood. Once in the United States with her husband and two children, however, she found herself searching for God with novel urgency. As a truck driver, Tati's husband traveled for months at a time, leaving her feeling lonely and overwhelmed as the sole caretaker of two teenage children. While she had almost completed her law degree in Brazil—her dream, she told me—she had only found work cleaning homes in the United States. Deep feelings of disappointment and resentment aggravated her home life. Reaching a point of acute despair, Tati contemplated returning to Brazil alone and abandoning her family. Such intrusive feelings drove her back to the Catholic Church in search of relief.

Through frequent participation in Mass, retreats, and the weekly prayer group, Tati forged a meaningful personal relationship with God. Concerning her prayer life, Tati commented, "Throughout the day, I have a conversation with God as if he was my father. It's conversation from father to daughter, daughter to father. It's extremely personal (*bem pessoal*)." Reflecting on the significance of this relationship, Tati remarked, "For me, the most important thing that happened here [in the United States] was this closeness [to God] (*aproximação*). Sometimes God takes us far away in order to see the necessity of Him in our lives." As in evangelical conversion narratives, Tati analyzed her migration, and its significance, in religious and affective terms. In order to fully experience God, she had to travel "far away" from friends, family, and achieve- ments. She had to experience crisis and doubt in order to viscerally sense the "necessity of Him," and forge such "closeness." After turning to faith, Tati newly discovered personal and familial *tranquilidade*.

Similar to evangelical migrants, Tati asserted that God brought her to the United States to forge closeness with Him, and in turn, transform her most significant interpersonal relationships. While Tati privileged closeness with God over closeness with co-congregants, she recognized that human relation- ships facilitated access to the divine. When Cláudia cancelled prayer meetings owing to inclement weather or scheduling conflicts, Tati explained, she felt a deep loss, recognizing that her faith community facilitated her sensation of God's presence. She reflected on this fact at a poorly attended meeting one day in March, lamenting the absence of other congregants since God intended humans to pray together and to be in union (*união*).

As an institution, the US Catholic Church had alienated many migrants through failing to provide an individualistic, attentive, and migrant-oriented affective therapeutics. Despite *decepção* (disappointment) in the church itself, however, Catholic migrants reported familiar narratives concerning the causes and consequences of their turn, or return, to God. Like evangelicals, they had weathered disappointment, loneliness, and distress as migrants in the United States. Like evangelicals, they yearned for a more proximate God and religious community to embrace them. As indicated in Tati's and Cláudia's comments above, Brazilian Catholics, like evangelicals, yearned for God more deeply, and experienced God more intensely, as a result of migrant distress. They too felt God enter their bodies, and imagined divinity as an intimate and loving parent. Such divine proximity reoriented their daily experience as migrants.

The Catholic parish these women belonged to, however, did not foster such orientations in migrants. I never heard the priest account for migrants' presence in the United States by referring to "God's plan," or encourage mi- grants to feel divinity in their bodies, or imagine God as loving parent and confidant. Instead, the practicing Catholics I interviewed found Mass to be stiff, inaccessible, and uninspiring. While they longed for the Catholic Charismatic Renewal (CCR) in their own parish, and spoke enthusiastically about experiences at CCR retreats in nearby cities, Father Bernardo remained generally opposed to embracing the movement locally.[20] Rather than being institutionally nurtured, the Catholic women I interviewed suggested that their novel orientations to an intimate divinity and embodied spiritual experience emerged from distinct forms of migrant distress in the United

States. Like evangelical migrants, these women invoked interwoven logics of spatial and spiritual discontinuity to account for their turn toward highly personalized, sensorial faith.

Spiritist Migrants: The Search for Answers

Spiritists also reported an increased religious drive once in the United States. Unlike the explicit "search for God" among evangelical and Catholic migrants, however, Spiritist migrants described an intensified "search for answers" upon arriving in the United States. In mobilizing such language, Spiritists similarly presented their novel religious drive and commitments as emerging from migrant experiences of uncertainty, doubt, dislocation, and loneliness. Like their evangelical peers, Spiritists echoed the double logic of spiritual and spatial discontinuities. In their narratives, migrant distress in the United States stimulated the desire for proximity to the divine, and furthermore, embodied religious experience. Spiritists also represented such religious experience as fundamental to their subsequent affective transformation, namely, the ability to maintain equanimity in the face of adversity in the United States.

Vera, a devoted Spiritist practitioner introduced in the previous chapter, told me during our interview at her local Spiritist center, "I always had this search for something that would give me my answers, but you know, I never had real answers. I was just struggling." Vera had come to Maryland as an exchange student twenty years earlier, and soon after, met her future husband, Tiago, another student from Brazil. While Vera's language ability, stable work as a translator, and legal status ensured that her transition to the United States was relatively smooth, her husband struggled. Without English fluency, he couldn't find work, and felt isolated. He desperately wanted to return to Brazil and spiraled into a deep depression that threatened their new marriage and young family. Spiritism provided them both with lasting relief. Vera recounted Tiago's reaction to his first meeting: "He came back and he was crying. He was so happy because, he said, 'You know, they prayed with me, and I felt better. And there was support.'"

Elza, a woman in her early fifties, also framed her novel interest in Spiritism as a quest for "answers." I interviewed Elza in her small condominium outside of Baltimore, where she lived with her husband, Tim, a veteran fifteen years her senior. Prior to moving to the United States in 2008 to marry Tim, whom she had met online, Elza had little knowledge of Spiritism. Raised by Italian immigrants in the southern Brazilian state of Paraná, Elza grew up in a rural and deeply Catholic community. As an adult, she lived nearby in Mato Grosso do Sul, where she continued to, in her words, "go to church, like this is my obligation, I need to go to church." Yet, she had always felt dissatisfied, noting, "It didn't answer my questions." Such questions often revolved around unsettling and frightening supernatural phenomena that Elza had encountered throughout her life. As a child, she had premonitory nightmares, seeing accidents while asleep days before they occurred. During stressful periods of transition, like graduating from college, she saw "spots of light." After each of these occurrences, her mother urged her to pray regularly and attend church.

Elza recalled a resurgence and intensification of disturbing supernatural phenomena after migrating. Faced with her own unemployment and her husband's disability, and living far from family, Elza again began seeing "spots." Instead of benign spots of light, she began to see more sinister spots—of blood. The spots appeared on her body, clothing, and around her apartment. These instances became increasingly disturbing, motivating Elza to seek help. She described one particularly unsettling incident:

> I was in a pub and I was just drinking a beer, a Bud Light. It's [usually] very clear, but my blouse here was all black [patting the front of her shirt]. I showed it to our waitress, and she took me to the bathroom, and we got baking soda, and carbonated water, and she cleaned it up. . . . The beer is not dark, and that stain was very dark. If I had spilled beer on my chest, I would have noticed it right away.

Elza reported that "things like that started happening" frequently in 2010, when she and Tim considered returning to Brazil as a last resort.

One night, in the midst of this turmoil, Elza saw an apparition of her deceased grandfather. Frightened by the vision, where her grandfather appeared "next to [her] bed, close to [her] legs and arms, and [with] something in his arms . . . like [he was] conducting," she sought counsel from Vera, her coworker and friend. Elza explained, "So, I said, you know what, it's time to go to the Spiritists and see if they can help me understand these things. And everything cleared up, and I mean . . . I felt so good there. Well, I decided, this is the place that I want to go. [The Catholic] Church has nothing to do with this. It does not answer my questions . . . but Spiritism does." The Spiritists provided an alternative and hopeful interpretation of her grandfather's appearance. Rather than confirm her own sense of foreboding at the stress-induced hallucination, her Spiritist teachers explained that her grandfather appeared to offer reassurance. Elza recounted the Spiritist interpretation she had learned, and how it subsequently bore out: "The spirits of your relatives are always watching [over you]. [My grandfather] came over here to tell us something, and everything went fine. I got a job two months later after I lost my job, and he [my husband] got retirement [benefits] and everything went fine."

While the language of Elza's spiritual quest was distinct from Catholic or evangelical narratives, the themes and structure she articulated remained strikingly similar. Faced with financial uncertainty, family separation, and social isolation as a migrant in the United States, Elza became increasingly distressed and newly oriented toward the spiritual realm. While she had considered herself to be nominally Catholic in Brazil, she insisted that the religion had never "answered her questions," and she prayed and attended church out of familial obligation rather than personal conviction. Like Catholic and evangelical conversion narratives examined above, Elza's account of intensified faith hinged upon a vivid dark night of the soul provoked by the multiple dislocations of migrant experience, in this case, the apparition of "spots" and "ghosts." Plunged into financial uncertainty and living far from family, Elza experienced affective distress in the form of hallucinations and nightmares. Rather than seek medical or psychological help, Elza looked toward divine intimacy and religious community for comfort and guidance.

Like Elza and Vera, most Spiritists I met had left the Catholic Church upon migrating to the United States owing to their intensified search for answers. While the Catholic Church, they insisted, had left their most deeply held questions unaddressed, Spiritism provided "scientific," "philosophic," and "religious" answers to everyday experiences. Faced with loneliness, downward social mobility, family separation, and marginalization, migrants experienced a surge of questions regarding meaning, purpose, and future prospects: why suffer, for what purpose, and for how long?

Spiritism directly addressed such questions, teaching migrants that adversity was not random, nor was it punishment from a vengeful God. Instead, as I outline at length in the previous chapter, Spiritists understood adversity to be divinely ordained for each individual to learn personalized lessons for future incarnations. Earthly life existed as a "learning school" whereupon each incarnation provided opportunities to overcome negativity, selfishness, and greed, and in its place, cultivate the affective ideals of contentment, gratitude, and peace. In keeping with such expansive notions of divine design, Spiritism legitimized spiritual experience, including dreams, prophecies, and visions. Rather than consider these phenomena to be diabolic, or symptomatic of mental disturbance, spiritual experiences amounted to communication with the "higher minds," an array of enlightened beings who had "graduated" from Earth and served as spiritual guides in perpetuity.

Spiritist theology, and the comprehensive "answers" it outlined, provided reassurance and satisfaction to migrants, especially in light of the novel challenges they faced. Reflecting on the appeal of Spiritism's powerful explanatory model, Elza remarked, "Those things that you don't understand, they always explain." Divine knowledge, in turn, supplanted migrant feelings of anxiety, uncertainty, and upset with sensations of tranquility and ease. Gabriela, a young woman introduced in chapter 2 who attended the center with Vera and Elza, similarly described her sense of affective relief emerging from her encounter with Spiritism. Despite the very real challenges of a tumultuous marriage and unexpected pregnancy, Gabriela asserted her novel ability to maintain equanimity:

> Spiritism [creates] a change that a lot of other people can see. The way you show . . . other people want to know more about it, because it's a change in *you*. You're a lot more, I don't know how to explain this . . . it's more calm, it's more honest, it's more truthful. Things that, you know, you thought before, were right or feelings like, I don't know, envy, pride, and those things, are not on the table anymore.

Gabriela's, Vera's, and Elza's insistence that their novel Spiritist faith, encountered and assumed in the United States, had tamed their baser affects resembled typical evangelical narratives charging the same. While migration had provoked anxiety, fear, resentment, and uncertainty, Spiritists, like evangelicals, asserted that faith had granted them calm, contentment, peace, and understanding.

Spiritist migrants also cited heightened intimacy with an explicitly Christocentric and monotheistic God providing them strength to endure migrant distress. Despite belief in a panoply of "higher spirits," Spiritists' articulation of divine intimacy centered on either God, the Father, or Jesus as the "governor" of earthly experience. Juanéli, who had become Spiritist two decades earlier in Brazil, reflected on how her faith had intensified as an undocumented migrant in the United States. Echoing evangelical tropes of divine election, she asserted God's divine plan in bringing her to the US, sharing, "If I'm here, it's because there is a reason. So, I feel secure. Even though I don't have my documents, I feel secure." In her daily life, this "security" and feeling of "protection" manifested in God's active presence. While cleaning wealthy people's homes and handling their precious objects, Juanéli sensed God there with her, working in her body: "when I bump something . . . it's like I feel that He helped my reflex, you know what I mean? To be faster and to catch and grab hold of it [before it breaks]."

Such embodied perceptions of constant help and security from the divine realm, she charged, enabled her to survive, and ultimately leave her drug-addicted and occasionally violent husband of six years. Realizing her life was in danger one night, Juanéli recounted, she fled from her home with nothing. Without money, she slept on the street and in her car until she saved enough to formally move out. Despite this ordeal, she reported never feeling afraid, recalling, "I felt assured that nothing would happen to me. I had strength; I wasn't afraid of anything. I always knew that something was protecting me. I never felt anyone would get me on the street."

Emboldened by belief in a personal and proximate God, Juanéli asserted confidence and trust in her life in the United States. In her narrations of increasing faith, moments of crisis constituted opportunities to grow closer to God. Like evangelicals, she explained God as a constant, daily, and beloved companion. Strikingly, she also repeated the frequent evangelical distinction between formal, rote, Catholic prayer (*rezar*) and intimate, extemporaneous, evangelical prayer (*falar com Deus*). Juanéli explained, "I pray (*rezo*), but really I talk (*falo*) to God like I'm talking to you. Despite having a multiplicity of spirits, my guardian angel, the spirits that protect me, always my thoughts go to God, to Jesus."

Juanéli's comments reflected the Spiritist teaching that, despite the variety of "higher minds" operating in the cosmos, the Christian God, and His son, Jesus, governed the universe. Migrants reported growing closeness with this Christian, biblical, and monotheistic divinity as a result of their migration experiences. Further aligning their tradition with mainstream Christianity, Spiritists also claimed that Allan Kardec's writings and mediumship practices helped illuminate, rather than supplant, the Bible. In fact, several Spiritists claimed that they understood the Bible more intimately than when they were Catholics. Elza, for instance, reported a conversation she had with her Catholic mother, who had grown uncomfortable with her daughter's new affiliation and pleaded with her to stop practicing Spiritism. Elza repeated her calm but resolved response: "I said, 'Mom, I learn about God and Jesus, as you learn in the Catholic Church. And I learn *more* than that. Not only about Jesus, but about the Bible. Everything that you can learn in church, I can learn, and I learn more.'"

The Evangelization of God

In describing the role of faith in migration, Brazilian migrants across denominations asserted the central role of intimate and embodied experience of God. Despite differing institutional approaches and theologies, the individual migrants I met asserted strikingly similar accounts of increased religious longing and resulting devotion while in the United States. Such accounts approximated the conversion narratives I came to expect from evangelicals. Similarly, Catholics and Spiritists explicitly linked their migratory journeys with increasing religious commitment, deepening relationship with God, and sensorial experience of the divine.

Despite comparatively better socioeconomic resources, such as education, legal status, and job security, Catholic and Spiritist migrants, like their evangelical counterparts, reported transformative "dark nights of the soul" while living as migrants in the United States. Their resources, I learned, did not wholly insulate them from migrant distress. Instead, they too reflected on the lasting affective imprint of migrant experience in the US. They had encountered heightened loneliness, depression, anxiety, and generalized despair. In the case of several interviewees, such stress triggered disturbing spiritual phenomena such as hallucinations and nightmares.

While Catholic and Spiritist migrants openly criticized evangelical Christianity, and were suspicious of evangelical conversion among migrants as opportunistic, their own accountings of increased faith in the United States reflected deeply evangelical tropes of overlapping spatial and spiritual discontinuities. In contrast to their faith-based lives in the US, they described their religious identities in Brazil as casual or obligatory. In their telling, leaving Brazil and becoming migrants in the United States triggered affective distress, and in turn, a novel commitment to and reliance on God.

The yearning for God, however, was not shapeless. Instead, it aimed at a deeply personal and evangelical-inflected divinity, who, through attentive love and felt companionship, promised to alleviate the particular maladies of migrant distress, including loneliness, worry, and despair. Like evangelicals, Catholics and Spiritists drew on increased intimacy with God to assert rightful and divine belonging in their new land. Despite practicing within traditions that professed divergent understandings of God,[21] Catholics and Spiritists conjured this divinity as a consoling, ever-present companion. Not only did this intimate God provide psychic comfort in the form of deeply satisfying answers, but He also offered sensorial peace. As a result, Catholic and Spiritist migrants, like their evangelical counterparts, felt held *nas mãos de Deus*, in the hands of God.

The striking similarity of conversion narratives among evangelical and nonevangelical migrants alike suggests the evangelization of God and religious experience among migrant populations. The experience of migration itself, such convergence underscores, shapes the kind of religious longing individuals feel, and the kind of divinity toward which they strive. Out of common experiences of dislocation, isolation, and marginalization, migrants across denominations desire and draw close to a consoling and intimate divinity that literally "holds them" in body and mind. Feeling "held" amounts to accessing resounding and affirmative answers to migrants' deepest existential anxieties: Do I belong here? Am I secure? Why do I suffer? The turn to an evangelical conception of God, therefore, is affective in nature, as it emerges from the affective distress of migrant experience itself.

The evangelization of God and religious experience among migrants further sheds light on the rapid success of evangelical churches among such communities. Beyond deliberately articulating and effectively assuaging migrant distress through affective therapeutics, such churches deliver exactly the kind of God for which migrants yearn. The conjoined experiences of isolation, alienation, rupture, and marginalization configure a specific form of divine longing. The object of such longing can be addressed daily; perceived in body and mind; considered friend, consoler, companion, and guide; and best accessed through frequent and socially embedded encounters. This God combats the profound loneliness and marginalization migrants feel. Through divine partnership, this God imbues them with confidence. Evangelical churches not only best articulated the forms of distress migrants experienced but provided regular access to the exact divinity for which they longed.

Conclusion

When Affective Therapeutics Fail

MIGRANT FAITH AND RESILIENCE IN UNCERTAIN TIMES

EVANGELICAL CHURCHES effectively articulated, managed, and alleviated migrant-related distress. Through therapeutics aimed at psychic and bodily healing, churches transformed the affective imprint of migrant distress into positive religious devotion. Beyond simply helping migrants feel better, evangelical faith and belonging altered how migrants acted daily, emboldening them to proactively pursue concrete goods that would improve their lives. Evangelical narratives of divine election and love allowed migrants to assert rightful belonging in a society that increasingly rejected them, and to assert their moral imperative to stay and endure. An antidote to loneliness, anxiety, and feeling stuck, evangelical belonging allowed migrants to forge intimacy with God and a dense "family in Christ."

Yet, if evangelical belonging made migrants feel better and enabled them to experience themselves as potent and rightful actors in US society, why did some migrants, like Neusa and Rubém, ultimately leave? Despite their committed religious practice, they struggled to fully reconcile themselves to their lives in the United States. Despite professed healing and transformation, they, like so many others, continued to experience the very forms of distress that first primed them for intense religious longing upon arrival as new migrants: isolation, exploitation, family separation, and precarity.

The persistence of migrant distress also led some migrants to leave their congregations or organized churches altogether. Migrants left when the opportunity to make more money elsewhere or live near relatives arose. Migrants also left because of bitter personal conflicts. Some migrants I met experienced migrant evangelical churches not as communities of care (see chapter 3), but rather as communities of harm. Instead of experiencing churches as the hospitals they purported to be, some migrants felt profoundly injured at the hands of churches. In these cases, affective therapeutics not only failed to deliver relief from migrant distress but exacerbated suffering.

In the final pages of the book, I examine these multiple forms of the apparent failure of evangelical affective therapeutics. Doing so, however, paradoxically reveals the resilience, flexibility, and tenacity of migrant evangelical faith. While migrants at times broke with church, local community, and even the United States owing to the persistence of distress, they espoused steadfast personal faith, and furthermore, drew on such faith to cope with growing uncertainty in both the United States and Brazil.

Vignettes of Failure

During one of our many visits, Neusa showed me pictures of the beach home she and Rubém were building in their home state of Santa Catarina, Brazil. She smiled while pointing out the pristine white walls and impressive size of the new construction. It was almost done, she explained, with notes of both pride and hesitation. From the time we had first met, Neusa had given me frequent updates on the house and its state of completion. Such updates often led to discussions of her and her husband Rubém's plans for return and her own ambivalence. Rubém wanted to leave immediately. They had been working too hard, and, at the age of fifty-three, he wanted to retire in Brazil. He was eager to stop grueling construction work, and instead fill his days with visits to the beach, and time spent with his aging parents and eldest child, Vanessa.

While she was also desperate to see Vanessa, Neusa could not imagine indefinitely leaving her two sons, their families, and her beloved church. Neusa's talk of return became more pronounced over time. In August 2014, Neusa shared that she and Rubém had decided to *really* leave. When my fieldwork ended a few weeks later, I doubted whether they would really go.

A few months later, Neusa and I exchanged Christmas and New Year's greetings over Facebook. She still posted photos of her family on outings in Washington, DC, on vacation in Myrtle Beach, and dressed for church. It seemed that she and Rubém had extended their stay indefinitely, as they had every year since they arrived in 2000. But then, in spring 2015, Neusa posted a series of very different content: household furniture for sale, goodbye messages to her friends, and photos from her and Rubém's church send-off. Soon after, Neusa shared photos of her reunion with her parents, daughter, and granddaughter in Santa Catarina, and of holding hands with Rubém on a sunny Brazilian beach. They had left.

———

On one of my final Sunday evenings at church, Priscila, usually vibrant and loquacious, appeared downcast and sullen. Priscila had befriended me earlier in the year when she learned that I was pursuing my doctorate. Since our first meeting, every time we met, she inquired about the American university system and potential scholarship opportunities. Priscila enumerated three goals: to learn English, to pass the US nursing exam, and to be admitted to a US university. Although she spoke perfect English, she had failed the nursing exam and had no money to apply to university programs. Despite these challenges, she was not ready to give up.

During our last encounter, however, Priscila's mood had darkened. She had no plans to retake the nursing exam and wanted to return to Brazil. "Everyone's dying," she said. In the last two weeks alone, Priscila had learned that her uncle had been fatally hit by a bus and a close friend had suffered a fatal heart attack. "If I feel so much pain with my uncle, and my friend, imagine if it was my mom or dad." Ultimately, she concluded, it wasn't worth sacrificing for a dream that continually eluded her. And so, she left.

———

Bruna, who had arrived two years earlier to join her husband in Maryland, expressed deep upset at her congregation. During one afternoon at her house, she became irate. She was currently unemployed and had asked the *irmãs* for assistance. While women promised to help her, they never followed through. She had asked women to lend her their car so she could take the Maryland driving test, and no one replied. Most injurious of all, Juliana, the pastor's wife, had publicly criticized online dating, knowing that Bruna had met her husband on Skype. After detailing these injuries, Bruna concluded that the church was full of "impostors" who cared solely about money and status.

Throughout research, I spoke with many individuals who had changed churches following similar personal upset. In each of these cases, migrants noted their deep *decepção* (disappointment) at the hands of the church and its members. Rather than embodying the *hospital*, these communities of care had become communities of harm for the individuals it had cast out. When I visited Bruna at the end of 2014, she had broken with the church, writing a letter of complaint to Pastor Jeferson, to which, in her telling, he never responded. Outside of the church's reliable structure of multiple meetings and social events per week, and without work or family nearby, Bruna rarely left the small annex where she and her husband lived.

The Resilience of Migrant Faith

Despite the persistent disappointments and injuries migrants weathered both within and beyond the church, their personal faith remained surprisingly steadfast. Rather than lose faith due to continued marginalization, separation from family, or disappointment at church, the evangelical migrants I met drew upon their faith, and the affective therapeutics it afforded, to cope with ongoing risk and uncertainty.

While conversion narratives ended with assertions of triumphant healing, it was clear that migrant distress was ongoing and indefinite. Evangelical healing, in its very conception, however, responded to this reality. Healing did not constitute a single, lasting outcome, but instead a practiced disposition toward adversity that insisted upon theological commitments to "God's time" and "the happiness of believers." Like the unending work of drawing close to God and ushering in God's Kingdom on Earth, healing depended upon migrant believers' continued ability to reinterpret and reexperience their suffering, not to conclusively end it. Failures of the kind described above like returning to Brazil, "breaking" with one's church, and persistent migrant distress provided rich opportunities for incessant evangelical reinterpretation and ongoing efforts to return to one's *primeiro amor*, first love, for God.

When I last visited Bruna following her *parada* (pause from the church), she insisted that her intimacy with God had only grown. Evidence of Bruna's commitment was strewn about her home: an open Bible densely highlighted and littered with Post-it notes, evangelical Brazilian TV playing in the background, Sunday school study guides on the couch. While she had declined joining Juliana's book group, she read the same assigned text, Joyce Meyer's *Battlefield of the Mind*, and effusively detailed its impact on her faith. Bruna explicitly refuted my assumption that she felt increased loneliness or loss without church. Instead, she insisted on improved well-being on account of greater proximity to God. Bruna explained that she had felt aggravated and disappointed at the various slights she experienced from Pastor Jeferson, his wife, and several members of the congregation. Her relationship with God had begun to suffer. God helped her understand that the church was filled with uncaring people who said "I love you" to your face, but then rejected you. Free from human *confusão* (drama), she told me, she felt calm and able to focus on *coisas de Deus* (things of God) rather than *coisas de Homem* (things of Man). Bruna's renewed commitment to sincere personal faith, she asserted, had ushered in concrete blessings. After three failed attempts to secure her driver's license, on the fourth try, she left the test *nas mãos de Deus*. With only God as her translator, she had passed.

While evangelical affective therapeutics failed Bruna institutionally, its discursive and practiced-based teachings continued to define how Bruna related to her own interior landscape and migrant experience. Rather than bemoan the loss of church and community, she interpreted her *parada* through the comprehensive cosmology she had studied in the church's pews. She continued to act upon the world through the spiritual disciplines she had learned, namely, prayer and discernment. When confronted by adversity, like multiple failures of the Maryland driver's test, she called upon faith to bolster her confidence.

Neusa and Rubém, as well as Priscila, mobilized such evangelical narrativity, asserting that God had determined it was time for them to return to Brazil. Back in Santa Catarina, Neusa and Rubém assumed active roles in the evangelical church their daughter began attending in their absence. On Facebook, Neusa shared clips of her daughter leading worship in her church in Brazil, as well as her sons, Felipe and Frederico, leading worship in a new Brazilian congregation in Maryland. Armed with affective therapeutics and the expansive interpretive power it afforded, migrants understood such breaks to be mandated by God and part of His broader plan for their lives.

Persistent Faith amid Uncertainty

In November 2019, I reached out to several of the women I knew best during fieldwork, hoping to learn how their lives had changed in the politically tumultuous five years since we had last talked. At the time of my initial phase of research in 2013–14, many of the young people I met had newly married. Many of these migrants and their friends, siblings, and spouses had just applied for legal status through President Obama's DACA program, which aimed to improve opportunities for undocumented migrants who had arrived in the United States as children. This program, as well as the Obama administration's keen interest in providing a pathway to citizenship for this group of "Dreamers," encouraged hopefulness and optimism among the migrants I knew. Such political measures corroborated migrants' evangelical interpretation that God had chosen them to live in the United States and would facilitate their endeavor to stay.

While younger migrants planned for futures in the United States, older migrants, including many parents of these young adults, vocalized dreams of return. After decades of hard work, migrants in their forties and fifties wagered that they had earned enough money to support comfortable retirements in Brazil. Many migrants finally made concrete plans to leave, like Neusa and Rúbem.

At the time they made their decision in the summer of 2014, Brazil's economy had begun to slow, but its stunning collapse, and adjoining social, political, and environmental upheaval, had not yet commenced. The country appeared insulated from the 2008 housing crisis, and its political and economic stability seemed to be intact. These projections encouraged migrants who had toiled for years in low-wage work to feel confident about their return. The former president, Dilma Rousseff, had not yet been impeached; her predecessor and mentor, Luiz Inácio Lula da Silva, had not yet been imprisoned nor released; the Workers' Party (Partido dos Trabalhadores) had not yet incurred popular wrath for the twin scandals of Lava Jato and Mensalão; the far right-wing politician, Jair Bolsonaro, had not yet won the presidency; and apocalyptic images of Brazil's Amazon burning or public health-care collapse in the face of Covid-19 had not yet flooded newspapers around the world.[1]

In 2014, the United States also looked starkly different. Trump had not yet won the presidency. He and his administration had not yet brought an explicitly anti-immigrant agenda to the forefront of mainstream politics, abruptly foreclosing avenues of relief, mobility, and security for undocumented migrants. The Supreme Court, with a new conservative majority, had not yet upheld several parts of Trump's agenda, including the approval of $2.6 billion for securing the southern border, the "public charge" law for all existing and potential migrants, and an ever-expanding "Muslim ban."

With such dramatic shifts in both the United States and Brazil, the context in which the Brazilian migrants I knew lived and worked had transformed. From afar, I imagined that such changes would impinge upon migrants' sense of security and hopefulness *nas mãos de Deus*. With their home country rapidly deteriorating, and their host country newly persecuting them, how could migrants remain optimistic about their futures in either country? And yet, amazingly, I learned, they did, even in the most trying circumstances. The women I spoke with at the end of 2019 expressed dogged optimism in their lives in the United States, informed by evangelical faith and belonging. The uncertainty of the present moment seemed only to strengthen their commitment to, and reliance upon, their evangelical faith.

As an outward marker of such optimism, all three women I spoke with were pregnant or had recently welcomed a new baby into their families at the time of our interview. Luana, Neusa and Rubém's daughter-in-law, was seven-months pregnant with her third daughter, Neusa and Rubém's fifth US-born grandchild. Luana sent responses to my questions over text message in the fleeting moments between caring for her two older children, ages eight and three, and working full-time as an administrator for a Brazilian-owned real estate firm. Diana, who had arrived from São Paulo in 2013 and intended to return the following year, had married Anderson, a prominent *obreiro* from her church in 2015, welcomed her first child in 2018, and was pregnant with her second child. We communicated over WhatsApp while she also juggled the competing demands of administrative work and her eighteen-month-old daughter. Paula was thirty-seven-weeks pregnant with her second baby and scheduled for an induction two weeks later. We spoke on the phone before she went to pick up her five-year-old daughter from kindergarten at a public school near her home.

At the time of our conversations, both Paula and Luana had recently lost critical family support and reliable child-care providers. Luana's in-laws, Neusa and Rubém, and Paula's mother, Maria, all returned to Brazil between 2015 and 2016. Paula and her family had moved twice within the last year, first from Maryland to Connecticut, and then from Connecticut to North Carolina, in pursuit of better construction opportunities for her husband.

Despite the very real challenges they faced in 2019, all three women framed intensified distress within broader narratives of evangelical hopefulness. While Paula had initially felt "angry with God," "stuck" and like she had to "begin all over again" upon finding out she was unexpectedly pregnant in 2018, she emphasized her current feeling of peace, gratitude, and contentment. Despite her and her family's year spent living in her sister-in-law's cold and dilapidated basement in Connecticut, which she deemed "the worst place in America," she quickly moved on to describing her new well-appointed home in North Carolina. They had moved a few months earlier, attracted by the sun and proximity to beaches, and now lived in an affordable, updated apartment close to her daughter's school.

Luana also emphasized the "blessings" that she and her family had received in the past several years. Her husband, Frederico, who had received a final deportation order when he entered the country at the age of nine in 2003, received temporary legal status in 2016 through DACA. With this new legal visibility and the permission to work it conferred, Frederico was hired as a superintendent for a local construction company. His increased income enabled the family to purchase their first home in Montgomery County.

Despite her emphasis on these "blessings," however, Luana also expressed persistent uncertainty, fear, and anxiety on account of her husband's unresolved legal status. Soon after taking office in 2017, President Trump announced plans to rescind the renewable two-year protections afforded to "Dreamers" like Frederico, his brother Felipe, and his sister-in-law, Viviane, under DACA. As a result, they were all plunged into an anxiety-ridden "waiting period." While Luana had gained citizenship soon after arriving in the United States at the age of three, conferred by her father, she found her family's unity under constant threat. Luana revealed anger and disbelief regarding the impossible choice confronting them if DACA were to be permanently rescinded:[2] indefinite separation from her husband or indefinite exile from her home in the United States. Of such painful deliberations, Luana wrote:

> Frederico and I have been married for 9 years, we will soon have 3 U.S. Citizen daughters, we pay our taxes, we own a home, contribute to our community and have very large and real expenses; I can't imagine the government one day deciding to remove my husband from us. He's our main provider and soon may be our sole provider as we're trying to decide if I can stay home with our girls. It's very, very tough and scary. I can't even imagine. This is our home, we grew up here. It's not fair for someone to think that they can just send him back to Brazil. What will be of us here without him? And if we go with him, what kind of life can we lead in a country we never studied in, without any kind of college degree?

While President Biden has promised to overhaul immigration, including a pathway to citizenship for DACA recipients and all 11 million undocumented migrants in the US, it remains to be seen whether such legislation will pass a bitterly divided Congress. It is also unclear whether or not Trump's anti-immigrant agenda, broadly embraced by the Republican Party, will be championed by future administrations.[3] What is certain, however, is how Trump's muscular tactics, ascendant for four years and defended widely, have impacted the affective landscape of migrants and their loved ones. Migrants daily confront evidence of a more belligerent, menacing, and determined opposition to their presence in the United States.

Between 2017 and 2020, the Trump administration made their anti-immigrant agenda clear with measures aimed at increased deportation and border enforcement, and foreclosing legal pathways to migration. Despite legal challenges and injunctions in lower courts, the conservative-leaning Supreme Court, led by Trump appointees, upheld several consequential elements of Trump's platform, delivering clear victories to his administration, and bolstering his popularity.[4] Together, these measures and their legal mandate intensified vulnerability among migrants, what Nicholas De Genova terms "deportability," the feeling of being subject to removal at any moment.[5] As Luana's comments affirm, feelings of insecurity permeated migrants' daily lives, forcing them to imagine violent separations from their loved ones and abrupt endings to their present lifeworlds. It is unsurprising that such realities harm the physical and bodily health of migrants, leading to increased rates of substance abuse, anxiety, and depression among migrants.[6]

The women I spoke with expressed little anger at Trump himself and did not identify him as the source of their heightened anxiety. Instead, their views confirmed what I had witnessed unfold on social media during Trump's campaign and eventual election in 2016. Many of the evangelical migrants I knew either actively supported him or amusedly tolerated him. Like most white, conservative evangelicals in the US, migrant evangelicals celebrated his lip service to conservative social values, and his promise to align the Supreme Court with such values. Most did not take offense at his aggressive anti-immigrant policies or rhetoric and suggested that he ought to be "more careful" with his words.

Paula, for example, suggested that people were too hard on him. "He's not a very bad man," she explained. "If you stop and think about it, all American presidents have thrown people out of the country who cause problems. Drinking, drunk driving, for example, these people should be eliminated from here (*seriam eliminadas por aqui*)." Diana agreed. She explained, "In truth, I don't think President Trump is wrong about everything he says. I agree with parts. For example, when he says that Americans should have more opportunities and privileges than illegal immigrants, I think he's fulfilling his duty to defend the people of his country." Diana diminished the risk that Trump posed to people like her. Despite initial fears, Diana shrugged and noted, "[our fear] passed, and no one was deported, or at least, no one I know."

Perhaps these women's reluctance to condemn Trump stemmed from their broader suspicion of all politicians, and their sense that no government, neither American nor Brazilian, could dramatically improve their daily lives. Migrants had watched successive US administrations promise and then fail to implement comprehensive immigration reform. They witnessed the public unraveling of Obama's ambitious executive orders and Trump's stunning reversals. And, they professed little faith in Brazil and its government, which, during the time of my research and writing between 2013 and 2021, plummeted catastrophically from among the world's most promising economies to a country defined by political corruption and economic and environmental devastation.

Despite political cynicism and heightened risk, however, each of the women I spoke with asserted a doggedly hopeful vision of their family's future in the United States. Paula told me that she maintained the "American dream" (sonho americano) to one day buy her own house, have her children educated in American universities, and become regularized. She looked forward to her kindergartener's eighteenth birthday, when, she joked, perhaps her child would then be able to sponsor her parents' regularization. Diana and Luana also expressed staunchly optimistic visions of their futures, wholly rooted in the United States. Both women looked forward to taking care of their children full-time as their husbands found increasing success in the workforce, and imagined increasing security, certainty, stability, and mobility for themselves and their families.

Such optimism flowed from the strength of these women's evangelical commitments despite the many transitions they had endured and the novel risks they faced. In both Connecticut and North Carolina, Paula and her husband set out to identify a Brazilian evangelical church immediately upon arrival. While they had not yet become members at the church that had opened nearby, they attended regularly as visitors, and relied on congregants' generosity. As Paula awaited her second child's arrival, women from church brought her meals, and the pastor routinely checked on her. Although less involved than she had been in her previous church, Paula insisted that her "personal faith" remained at the very center of her life.

While still living in Montgomery County, Luana also had left the Brazilian church in which I first met her. Frederico, her husband, and Felipe, her brother-in-law, had determined they had "done all they could" for their Brazilian congregation and wanted a new opportunity for growth. They began attending a diverse nondenominational church housed in the same building where their eldest child attended Christian primary school. Soon, the pastor asked the brothers to spearhead a Brazilian ministry, with Felipe, Neusa's eldest son, serving as pastor, and Frederico, her youngest, serving as praise director. Luana explained that "God put us right back in the thick of things." She noted that faith had become more fundamental to her life in recent years. As she coped with the regular stress of parenthood, the loss of Frederico's parents to Brazil, and intense fears regarding Frederico's migration status, her relationship to God buoyed her. Luana described the importance of faith amid uncertainty:

> I don't know how I could handle everything if it wasn't for our faith and support from our church community. I was diagnosed with ADHD as a teen and later on with anxiety and depression. If it wasn't for my faith, I don't know how I could get up in the morning. There is just so much that medication and therapy can't do if you don't have something within you pushing you forward.

Diana, who was the only one of the three women who still attended the same church where I first met her in 2013, reported her own increasing faith and involvement since our first conversations. When we first met, Diana had arrived in the United States only months earlier, overwhelmed by feeling stuck and alone. In chapter 3, I described witnessing her transformation from *visita* to *irmã*, where she gradually entered Pastor Jeferson's inner circle. From her account, she remained dedicated to this congregation, serving as one of the leaders of the women's ministry. When I asked about the content of her frequent conversations with God, she responded, "Beyond thanking Him for everything he has done in my life, requesting forgiveness for my failures, I talk to Him (*falo com Ele*) about everything that's important to me, everything that I need, everything that afflicts me, everything that makes me sad . . . *tudo*."

Evangelical Therapeutics in the United States

You take risks every time you leave the church.

—MATTEO, 45, SEVENTH-DAY ADVENTIST

Like the estimated 25,000 undocumented migrants in the nation's capital, the migrants I knew outside of Washington, DC, lived in close proximity to the world's most powerful government, often cleaning the homes, watching the children, or tending the gardens of the city's and country's elite.[7] Proximity to power made them acutely aware of their own vulnerability. Matters of family, health, housing, education, travel, and employment remained dictated by their "illegality" in the eyes of the American government. In Matteo's words, every time migrants left their home or church, they assumed "great risks."

Such physical insecurity, as I detail in the preceding chapters, was compounded by intense loneliness and feelings of being stuck. Most migrants watched from afar while loved ones in Brazil faced sickness or grew old. They weighed the impossible decision of living in the United States with some of their children or returning to Brazil to be with others. They endured low wages, long hours, and often lonely work in profoundly isolating conditions. Without US credentials, English-language fluency, or legal work permits, their degrees, skills, and achievements were rendered meaningless. They lived in the midst of suburban sprawl, driving vast distances to get to work or church or to return home. They endured life in a "cold" culture, both socially and physically, longing for the *calor humano*, human warmth, of Brazil. Even those migrants who eventually attained legal status noted that these circumstances continued to shape their lives in the United States.

Together, these factors led to loneliness, isolation, anxiety, and depression. These specific forms of distress produced novel and intensified religious longings among migrants, leading them to reach for a more personal God and engaged religious community to ease their suffering. While the Catholic Church and Spiritist centers also aimed to console and reassure migrants, evangelical churches most effectively addressed migrant distress through affective therapeutics. In stark contrast to the Catholic Church, and in greater specificity than Spiritist centers, evangelical churches provided congregants with practical strategies for felt transformation. Importantly, these churches also valorized Brazilian identity and Portuguese language, not only encouraging adherents to pray in their native tongue, but implying the theological imperative of doing so.

Through affective therapeutics, evangelical churches redirected migrants' gaze from the external world, and the havoc it wreaked on their lives, both inward and upward. By generating committed participation in evangelical fellowship, churches combatted migrants' isolation. Through fostering daily intimacy with cobelievers, clergy, and most importantly, God, churches taught believers to feel securely held *nas mãos de Deus*. By instructing migrants to become "vessels" for the Holy Spirit, clergy encouraged migrants to sublimate their feelings of powerlessness into experiences of evangelical-inflected joy, liberation, and potentiality. And, by emphasizing a different temporality defined by "God's time" and "God's plan," evangelical churches imbued migrant experience with divine purpose. Migrants interpreted their presence in the United States as divinely orchestrated, thus refuting their illegality and marginality in the eyes of the law.

This story of therapeutic evangelical faith among migrants, and its efficacy, unfolds against the ongoing contraction of social support for vulnerable populations throughout Western liberal democracies. In both the United States and across Europe, governments both implicitly and explicitly have called upon citizens to heal themselves and to heal others by appealing to an increasingly affective register—feelings of injustice, responsibility, and outrage. In doing so, governments increasingly shirk the responsibility for suffering subjects onto an affectively ripe citizenry.[8]

In the United States, this tendency has become infused with a distinctly Christian political discourse, that of "compassionate conservatism," which charges capitalism, private philanthropy, and faith-based charities with the alleviation of suffering. Proponents of this ideology assert that an "army of the faithful" best meets the needs of the poor and vulnerable. Compassionate conservatism has been formalized through state contracts with explicitly faith-based organizations. Christian organizations currently run state-funded programs in addiction recovery, prison education, and sex education.[9] In addition to this more formalized structure, compassionate conservatism calls upon individual Christians to broadly engage in personal missions of social uplift.

In this context, the twenty-first century has witnessed evangelical organizations increasingly emerge as first responders to human suffering. In the wake of disasters like Hurricane Katrina (2005), churches provide resources, energy, and resolve where the government remains either absent or ineffective.[10] In the face of everyday poverty, overwhelmingly white and middle-class believers, like those in Knoxville, Tennessee, immerse themselves in aid work in inner cities.[11] Besides bringing boots on the ground, these workers bring their distinctly evangelical message. As a result, Vincanne Adams documents, victims of Hurricane Katrina interpreted their post-Hurricane predicament according to evangelical tropes. She writes, "In the stories people told about their return and struggle to rebuild, we can see how what was considered a betrayal by the government was transformed into a *spiritual sense of purpose* through faith-based volunteers."[12]

How do migrants, particularly undocumented migrants, fit into this expansive picture of individual and state-sanctioned evangelical relief and discursive dissemination? To what extent do migrants view themselves as part of US evangelical churches' broader effort to impart explicitly Christian healing and recovery on a struggling nation? While the migrant believers I met expressed desires to help others through social outreach, they infrequently acted on these "moral ambitions" beyond their own community.[13] Instead, they presented themselves and their inner worlds as the primary terrain for evangelical healing.

While it is beyond the scope of this project, future research should consider the relationship between diverse and disparate communities united by evangelical therapeutics. How do predominantly white and conservative US evangelicals, like those who canvas the inner city in Knoxville and serve as first responders in New Orleans, evaluate fervent evangelical belief among predominantly undocumented migrant communities? Would they recognize their Christian beliefs and practices, and invite them into their homes as cobelievers and "family" in Christ, or would they castigate them for breaking American law and living in the United States "illegally"? Do these migrants qualify as "needy Others" to whom engaged evangelicals reach out to "heal" equipped with their healing message of salvation in Christ? On parallel trajectories, evangelical therapeutics wins devoted adherents among two opposing constituencies: US citizens and undocumented migrants. It is clear, however, that growth among migrants will continue to outpace that of white US-born citizens.

As migrants confronted the daily frustrations and injustices of life in the US, they looked to God and faith to help them and their loved ones cope. Evangelical belonging, theology, and the therapeutics it afforded provided migrants' lives with interpretive coherence, converting their suffering into an intelligible, meaningful sense of purpose. The refusal of the US government to recognize or adequately care for migrants leaves a growing vacuum to be filled. Promoting themselves as hospitals, with an intimate God and Christian community as their universal curative, evangelical churches step willingly into this void.

1. Self-Authored Migration and Religion Survey Data According to Affiliation

TABLE 1.1. Gender (N = 49)

Affiliation	Men	Women
Pentecostal	4	7
Baptist		7
Adventist	6	6
*Total Evangelicals	10	20
Spiritist	1	6
Catholic	3	5
Other		4
Total	**14**	**35**

TABLE 1.2. Age (N = 47)

Affiliation	20–30	31–40	41–50	51–60	61–66
Pentecostal	3	3	1	3	
Baptist	1	2	2	2	
Adventist	1	5	3	2	1
*Total Evangelicals	5	10	6	7	1
Spiritist	1	1	1	3	1
Catholic	1		2	1	3
Other	1		2		1
Total	**8**	**11**	**11**	**11**	**6**

TABLE 1.3. Year of Arrival in the U.S. (N = 48)

Affiliation	Before 1980	1980–1985	1986–1990	1991–1995	1996–2000	2001–2005	2006–2010	After 2010
Pentecostal			1		3	5	1	1
Baptist			1			5		1
Adventist		2		2	2	4		2
*Total Evangelicals		2	2	2	5	14	1	4
Spiritist			1	1		3	2	
Catholic	1		1	1	2	1	1	
Other					2	1	1	
Total	**1**	**2**	**4**	**4**	**9**	**19**	**5**	**4**

TABLE 1.4. Region of Origin (Brazil) (N = 49)

Affiliation	South	Southeast	Northeast	North	Central-West
Pentecostal	5	4	2		
Baptist	1	2	2	1	1
Adventist	2	9	1		
*Total Evangelicals	8	15	5	1	1
Spiritist		4	1	2	
Catholic	3	4	1		
Other	1	2		1	
Total	**12**	**25**	**7**	**4**	**1**

By region, respondents emigrated from the following states: South—Paraná, Santa Catarina, and Rio Grande do Sul; Southeast—Minas Gerais, São Paulo, Rio de Janeiro, and Espírito Santo; Northeast—Bahia, Paraíba, and Maranhão; North—Pará; Central-West—Goiás.

2. Interview Participants' Data by Affiliation

I did not explicitly ask interviewees to state their gender or age as in the survey, but recorded this data based on information shared during the interview.

TABLE 2.1. Gender (N = 78)

Affiliation	Men	Women
Pentecostal	7	15
Baptist	4	11
Adventist	7	7
*Total Evangelicals	18	33
Spiritist	1	9
Catholic	2	12
Other/Expert	2	1
Total	**23**	**55**

TABLE 2.2. Age (N = 78)

Affiliation	20–30	31–40	41–50	51 and above
Pentecostal	5	9	5	3
Baptist	1	9	4	1
Adventist	3	5	2	4
*Total Evangelicals	9	23	11	8
Spiritist		1	5	4
Catholic		4	7	3
Other/Expert			2	1
Total	**9**	**28**	**25**	**16**

TABLE 2.3. Year of Arrival in the U.S. (N = 76)

Affiliation	Before 1980	1980– 1985	1986– 1990	1991– 1995	1996– 2000	2001– 2005	2006– 2010	After 2010
Pentecostal		1			1	14	3	3
Baptist				1	3	6	3	1
Adventist		1		2	1	3	2	5
*Total Evangelicals		2		3	5	23	8	9
Spiritist	1		2		4	3		
Catholic		1	1	1	2	6	1	1
Other/Expert		1			1			1
Total	**1**	**4**	**3**	**4**	**12**	**32**	**9**	**11**

TABLE 2.4. Region of Origin (Brazil) (N = 78)

Affiliation	South	Southeast	Northeast	North	Central-West
Pentecostal	12	7	3		
Baptist		10	1	1	3
Adventist	1	9	1		3
*Total Evangelicals	13	26	5	1	6
Spiritist	1	7	1		1
Catholic	3	11			
Other/Expert	1	1			1
Total	**18**	**45**	**6**	**1**	**8**

By region, interviewees emigrated from the following states: South—Paraná, Santa Catarina, and Rio Grande do Sul; Southeast—Minas Gerais, São Paulo, Rio de Janeiro, and Espírito Santo; Northeast—Bahia, Paraíba, Maranhão, and Alagoas; North—Pará; Central-West—Goiás, Mato Grosso do Sul, and Federal District.

NOTES

Introduction

1. I provide English translations of biblical passages from the New International Version (NIV). Brazilian migrants most commonly used the Bíblia de Estudo Pentecostal, one of the most widely circulated Bibles in Brazilian Portuguese.

2. The three studies cited here are published on the Pew Forum's website, pewforum.org: "In U.S., Decline of Christianity Continues at Rapid Pace"; "America's Changing Religious Landscape"; "U.S. Religious Landscape Survey."

3. Max Weber hypothesized that industrialization, modernization, and rationalization would ultimately lead to the complete "disenchantment" of the world, making religion obsolete. See Weber, *The Protestant Work Ethic and the Spirit of Capitalism.*

4. While I use the term "immigrant" in this section in reference to the Pew Forum's findings, and in sections where I discuss other scholarly research that explicitly considers "immigrants," in most of the book, I deliberately use the word "migrant." By doing so, I point to the continued liminality of Brazilians who live in the United States. Brazilians rejected the unidirectional label "immigrant," preferring the word "tourist," even if they had been in the United States for decades. Their plans for the future generally remained open-ended, and often included return to Brazil.

5. US researchers gathered data from what they called "authorized immigrants" and "legal permanent residents" in another Pew Forum study, "The Religious Affiliation of U.S. Immigrants." As for the nation's now 11 million undocumented migrants, researchers simply reported the predominant Christianity and intense religiosity of this group, estimating that over 83 percent of undocumented migrants identified as Christian.

6. Of the estimated 11 million "unauthorized" immigrants living in the United States, the Department of Homeland Security's Office of Immigration Statistics found that the four largest sending countries were Mexico (55 percent), El Salvador (6 percent), Guatemala (5 percent), and Honduras (4 percent). See B. Baker, "Population Estimates Illegal Alien Population Residing in the United States."

7. Many of the churches serving migrant populations, like the one where Rubém preached, were distinct from the megachurches often associated with predominantly white, suburban, and affluent evangelical Christianity in America, such as those documented by recent ethnographies, including Harding's *The Book of Jerry Falwell*; Elisha's *Moral Ambition*; and Luhrmann's *When God Talks Back*. Instead of owning and operating their own church complex, these more

modest congregations frequently rented space from other groups and maintained much smaller populations.

8. Several social scientists have documented the explosive growth of evangelical and charismatic Christianity among undocumented Latin American populations in general, and particularly among Brazilians. See Althoff, "Religious Identities of Latin American Immigrants in Chicago"; Rodrigues, *Jesus in Sacred Gotham*; Mariz, "Missão religiosa e migração"; Martes, *New Immigrants, New Land*; Williams, Steigenga, and Vásquez, *A Place to Be*. In one study, scholars surmised that more than 60,000 Latin American migrants converted to Pentecostal or charismatic Christianity every year. See Vásquez, "Pentecostalism, Collective Identity, and Transnationalism among Salvadorans and Peruvians in the U.S.," 617.

9. See the Pew Forum's demographic findings on evangelical Protestants from its Religious Landscape Survey (2014), entitled "Religion in America: U.S. Religious Data, Demographics and Statistics."

10. Early accounts of Latin American evangelicalism tended to focus on conversion and uplift among predominantly poor and marginalized populations. These accounts suggested that evangelical promises of material improvement and reward largely motivated conversion among the destitute or disempowered. See, for example, Burdick's *Looking for God in Brazil* and *Blessed Anastácia*; Chesnut's *Born Again in Brazil* and *Competitive Spirits*; Mariz's *Coping with Poverty*; and Lehmann's *Struggle for the Spirit*.

11. Researchers often describe Brazilians, despite their majority undocumented status in the US, as a "middle-class" migrant population due to their having comparatively better socioeconomic resources than other Latin American migrant populations, including higher educational attainment and financial resources upon arriving in the US. See Margolis, *Little Brazil*; Martes, *New Immigrants, New Land*; Blizzard and Batalova, "Brazilian Immigrants in the United States."

12. Scholars estimate that 70 percent of Brazilian migrants in the United States are undocumented. See Margolis, *Little Brazil*; Margolis, *An Invisible Minority*; Margolis, *Goodbye, Brazil*, 373. While I refrained from asking interviewees to disclose their status, and therefore cannot officially confirm this statistic, most migrants I spoke with shared their statuses anecdotally. My research confirms the general portrait of Brazilians in the United States as a majority undocumented population. Like other undocumented groups in Greater Washington, DC, deemed a new migrant "gateway," Brazilians most often lived in sprawling suburbs far outside of the expensive city center. For the suburbanization of new migrant gateways, see Brick, Jones-Correra, and Singer, "Local Goes National."

13. For a comprehensive discussion of chosenness as it relates to national identity, see Smith's *Chosen Peoples*. Among those asserting chosenness claims, the Puritans famously understood themselves to be divinely elected by God, and the "New World" to be their Promised Land. Baer and Singer identify chosenness narratives as integral to several prominent Black religious and cultural organizations in the United States, such as the Nation of Islam, the Moorish Science Temple, and the African Hebrew Israelites, in their essay "Toward a Typology of Black Sectarianism." Each group, they argue, professes "messianic-nationalism," a theology that asserts the divine election of African and Black American people as God's chosen, and promotes the idea of cultural and territorial self-determination in a messianic age. Several studies consider such assertions of chosenness among Black Americans with regard to Judaism. See, for example, Chireau and Deutsch, *Black Zion*; Dorman, *Chosen People*; and Landing, *Black Judaism*.

14. The "economic miracle" referred to the period of profound economic growth under the military regime, led by General Médici (1969–1974) and his economic minister, Delfim Neto. During this period, the government cited economic growth at 10 percent. Following the collapse of the military regime (1964–1985), the first elected president, José Sarney, contributed to runaway inflation by printing money and investing in oil abroad. See Skidmore, *Brazil*, 153–87. Several accounts detail how the subsequent economic crisis triggered the first significant wave of Brazilian migration to US destinations, including Washington, DC. See Marcus, "Brazilian Immigration to the U.S. and the Geographical Imagination"; Margolis, *Little Brazil*; Goza, "Brazilian Immigration to North America"; and Singer, "Metropolitan Washington."

15. Tremura records this broad population estimate of Brazilian migrants in her dissertation studying "pink collar" workers in Washington, DC, "Transnational Migrant Brazilian Women in 'Pink Collar Jobs' in the Greater Washington D.C. Area," 67. During the time of research and analysis, I found no other formal assessment of the Brazilian migrant population in the region.

16. K. O'Neill, "Beyond Broken," 1103.

17. R. Williams, "Structures of Feeling."

18. My understanding of affect emerges from the work of critical theorists who view intimate feelings and sensations as deeply political, and understand particular feeling states as endemic to late capitalism. I have been particularly influenced by Berlant's *Cruel Optimism*; Cvetkovich's *Depression*; and Ahmed's *The Promise of Happiness*. General accounts theorizing affect have also shaped my understanding. These writings include Butler's *Giving an Account of Oneself*; Mazzarella's "Affect: What Is It Good For?"; and Massumi's "The Autonomy of Affect." These works find inspiration in Foucault's notion of "governmentality" in *Society Must Be Defended* and in Rose's notion of "governing the soul" in *Governing the Soul*. Both accounts detail how power penetrates the individual person, shaping personal feeling, want, aspiration, and desire.

19. Vincanne Adams provides a succinct description of neoliberalism and market-driven governance in her study of New Orleans's residents struggling to rebuild five years after Hurricane Katrina. Considering the ongoing failure of federal and state institutions to meaningfully address suffering owing to their penetration by for-profit logics, Adams writes, "Emerging out of a half-century commitment to neoliberal policies that favor and advance market-based solutions for our most pressing economic and social problems, we see now a steady transformation of public-sector institutions into market-based consortia, wherein fiscal, for-profit transactions become the means by which access to federal resources, even for things like disaster relief, is determined." See *Markets of Sorrow, Labors of Faith*, 5.

20. Berlant, *Cruel Optimism*.

21. Cvetkovich, *Depression*, 17.

22. Scholars have documented related dimensions of stuckness throughout the globe. Anne Allison's *Precarious Japan* describes the "anguish of everyday life" for contingent workers in Japan. Economic decline and familial dissolution have led to growing poverty, instability, violence, and withdrawal. For growing numbers of Japanese, precariousness becomes an "existential state" (9). Bruce O'Neill documents the overwhelming sense of boredom that grips new homeless men and women in Romania who have been excluded, or "cast aside," from the global economic order in his article "Cast Aside" and his book *The Space of Boredom*. Without consistent work, and displaced to squatter camps, these men and women "describe endless days without work and speak of feeling stuck in place" (*The Space of Boredom*, 3). Like stuckness, boredom

and precariousness result from exclusion, not only from the social and economic order, but from the imagined future promised by capitalist and neoliberal logics. In his essay "Time and the Migrant Other," Ruben Andersson considers how these logics and their production of bureaucratic and open-ended "waiting" specifically constrain and confine migrants. According to Andersson, temporality is "weaponized" against migrant others.

23. Ahmed, *The Promise of Happiness*, 118.

24. As Donovan Schaefer aptly notes, contemporary writings on affect developed according to "a dual genealogy," what he calls the "Spinozistic/Deleuzian" tradition informed by Baruch Spinoza and Gilles Deleuze, and the "phenomenological" tradition, viewing the body, subjective experience, and embodiment as the primary site of knowledge production. See *Religious Affects*, 24. Scholars of the first tradition define affect in the more restrictive sense, viewing it as "prediscursive," according to K. O'Neill in "Beyond Broken," 1102; or "preconscious," according to Massumi in "The Autonomy of Affect," 98. In this framing, preconscious, preverbal affect differs absolutely from emotion, which is instead defined as socially recognized and culturally patterned, like anger and joy. The "autonomy" of affect lies in "its escape from structures of capture and control" (Massumi in Schaefer, *Religious Affects*, 26).

25. For a comprehensive overview of the critique of affect studies, see Ruth Leys's essay, "The Turn to Affect."

26. The study of emotion remained central to US anthropology throughout the first half of the twentieth century, given disciplinary prominence by the "culture and personality school." Prominent scholars like Ruth Benedict and Margaret Mead infused their work with psychological discourse, inquiring into ideal and anomalous "types" of popular culture. See, for example, Benedict's *The Chrysanthemum and the Sword*; Benedict's *Patterns of Culture*; and Mead's *Growing Up in New Guinea*. Later scholars theorized emotion as culturally embedded and shaped. See, for example, Rosaldo, "Grief and a Headhunter's Rage"; Geertz, *The Interpretation of Cultures*; Lutz and White, "The Anthropology of Emotions"; Boellstorff and Lindquist, "Bodies of Emotion." Ethnographers also documented patterns of expression in diverse cultural traditions. See, for example, Abu-Lughod, *Veiled Sentiments*; Lutz, *Unnatural Emotions*; Briggs, *Never in Anger*; Scheper-Hughes, *Death without Weeping*; Cassaniti, *Living Buddhism*. Related subfields of anthropology have considered emotion with regard to mental illness and suffering cross-culturally. See Kleinman, *Patients and Healers in the Context of Culture*; Kleinman and Good, *Culture and Depression*; Crapanzano, *Tuhami*. Anthropologists of emotion also aim to provide accounts of life "as lived." See, for example, Jackson, *The Palm at the End of the Mind*; Desjarlais and Throop, "Phenomenological Approaches in Anthropology."

27. For a review of contemporary emotion research in the field of anthropology, see Beatty, "Current Emotion Research in Anthropology."

28. This study contributes to scholarship on the "public feelings" of the twenty-first century. These works include theorization of "loneliness," "depression," "abandonment," "precarity," "boredom," "cruel optimism," and "happiness" as public feelings of late capitalism. For prominent works in this literature, see Cobb, "Lonely"; Cvetkovich, *Depression*; Povinelli, *Economies of Abandonment*; Allison, *Precarious Japan*; B. O'Neill, *The Space of Boredom*; Berlant, *Cruel Optimism*; Ahmed, *The Promise of Happiness*.

29. In contrast to the relatively thin research on migrant interiority or migrants' affective lives in the US, migrants' external lives (including employment, religious and civic participation, education, and domestic life) have been exhaustively studied since the First Chicago School's

inception in the 1920s. These early sociological accounts of US migrants, and the large body of work they have since inspired, remain primarily descriptive, documenting the "ethnic enclaves" of migrants in urban centers like Chicago, San Diego, and New York. See, for example, Park and Burgess, *The City*; Chavez, *Shadowed Lives*; Margolis, *Little Brazil*.

30. The field of ethnopsychology employs traditional psychological testing, such as the Diagnostic and Statistical Manual (DSM), to quantify and categorize migrants' elevated risks of suffering, including depression, anxiety, and "acculturation stress." See Breslau et al., "Migration from Mexico to the United States and Subsequent Risk for Depressive and Anxiety Disorders"; Cruz, "Poor Mental Health"; Plascencia et al., "Undocumented and Uninsured Part 3."

31. In addition to the ethnographic accounts I reference in the notes below, Alba, Raboteau, and DeWind explore the therapeutic benefit migrants have derived from religion throughout US history in their edited volume, *Immigration and Religion in America*.

32. Sarat, *Fire in the Canyon*.

33. Suh, *Being Buddhist in a Christian World*.

34. Chen, "A Self of One's Own"; Chen, *Getting Saved in America*.

35. Olupona and Gemignani, *African Immigrant Religions in America*.

36. Several ethnographies suggest that migrant religion in the US promotes inclusion and incorporation, allowing migrants to become more "American" through their religious identity. See, for example, Park, "'Born Again'"; Chen, *Getting Saved in America*; Olupona and Gemignani, *African Immigrant Religions in America*.

37. Scholars of migrant religion in Europe often evaluate Islam, the predominant religion of migrants, as a barrier to European assimilation and inclusion. See Foner and Alba, "Immigrant Religion in the U.S. and Western Europe"; Sniderman and Hagendoorn, *When Ways of Life Collide*; Rogozen-Soltar, *Spain Unmoored*.

38. Concerned with the intimacy of daily life, existential anthropology and the anthropology of social suffering aim to document the feeling and texture of the everyday, informed by American phenomenologists and pragmatists, such as William James and John Dewey. See, for example, Jackson, *The Palm at the End of the Mind*; Biehl, *Vita*; Biehl, *Will to Live*; Kleinman, *What Really Matters*; Kleinman, Das, and Lock, *Social Suffering*; Garcia, *The Pastoral Clinic*.

39. Kleinman, *What Really Matters*.

40. Kleinman, Das, and Lock, "Introduction," ix.

41. Robbins, "Beyond the Suffering Subject," 458.

42. For comprehensive accounts of the emergence of the anthropology of Christianity as a subdiscipline, and the role of Christianity in anthropology prior to the 1990s, see Cannell's edited volume *The Anthropology of Christianity*; Robbins's review article "The Globalization of Pentecostal and Charismatic Christianity"; Robbins's monograph *Becoming Sinners*; and Bialecki, Haynes, and Robbins's article "The Anthropology of Christianity."

43. Harding, "Representing Fundamentalism."

44. Christian practice and identity now constitute an important and growing subfield within the anthropology of religion, attracting robust ethnographic attention. While currently in what Joel Robbins deems its "middle-age," the field remains ripe for further contributions. See Robbins's introduction to the special issue of *Current Anthropology* dedicated to the subject, "The Anthropology of Christianity: Unity, Diversity, New Directions." Earlier work in the subdiscipline remained preoccupied with the emergence of Christian subjectivity in colonial and postcolonial contexts, and largely focused on the reasons and consequences for conversions of

non-European populations. See, for example, Comaroff and Comaroff, *Of Revolution and Revelation*; Engelke, *A Problem of Presence*; Keane, *Christian Moderns*; Keller, *The Road to Clarity*; B. Meyer, *Translating the Devil*; Robbins, *Becoming Sinners*. While such questions remain important, more recent work broadens the field's concern by evaluating and documenting the multiplicity of global Christian experience including in the United States and Europe, where "missionary encounter" joins many other focuses. See, for example, Bialecki, *Diagram for Fire*; Bialecki, "Between Stewardship and Sacrifice"; Bielo, *Words upon the Word*; Bielo, *Emerging Evangelicals*; Luhrmann, "Metakinesis"; Luhrmann, *When God Talks Back*; Humphrey, "Schism, Event, and Revolution"; Hann, "The Heart of the Matter"; Engelke, *God's Agents*. In addition to asking why people reject their old systems of belief, these studies consider how Christians make themselves anew through religious practice and experience. Toward this end, ethnographers have studied Christian materiality and language practices. See Harding, *The Book of Jerry Falwell*; Schieffelin, "Christianizing Language and the Dis-Placement of Culture in Bosavi, Papua New Guinea." Researchers also study the content and consequence of spiritual disciplines. See Luhrmann, *When God Talks Back*; Csordas, *The Sacred Self*; Luhrmann, "Metakinesis"; Luhrmann, *How God Becomes Real*. Scholars have also considered Christianity to be a political and moral resource in diverse contexts. See K. O'Neill, *City of God*; K. O'Neill, *Secure the Soul*; Sarat, *Fire in the Canyon*; Ikeuchi, *Jesus Loves Japan*. Rather than approaching conversion as a singular rupture, researchers recognize conversion as a varied and dynamic process requiring active and continued spiritual labor. Additionally, by putting anthropology in conversation with theology in the emerging field of theologically engaged anthropology, scholars have worked to develop new theoretical concepts through which to observe and analyze Christian life. For these contributions, see Robbins, *Theology and the Anthropology of Christian Life*; Lemons, *Theologically Engaged Anthropology*.

45. Lester in Richlin, "The Affective Therapeutics of Migrant Faith," 384.

46. For classic articulations of the hermeneutics of suspicion regarding religion in nineteenth- and twentieth-century social theory, see Durkheim's *The Elementary Forms of Religious Life*; Weber's *The Protestant Work Ethic and the Spirit of Capitalism*; Marx's *Critique of Hegel's "Philosophy of Right"*; and Freud's *The Future of an Illusion*.

47. Turner, *The Ritual Process*.

48. Geertz, "Religion as a Cultural System."

49. Douglas, *Purity and Danger*.

50. Tambiah, "A Performative Approach to Ritual."

51. Asad, *Genealogies of Religion*.

52. Scholars have considered how evangelical churches exploit marginalized populations and reinforce existing hierarchies, thus furthering structural oppression according to race, class, gender, and immigration status. For examples of this literature, see Elisha, *Moral Ambition*; Alves, "Immigrant Regime of Production"; Poloma and Hood, *Blood and Fire*.

Chapter 1

1. The Brazilian consulate of Washington, DC, represented not only Washington, DC, Maryland, and Virginia, but also Ohio, West Virginia, Kentucky, Delaware, and North Carolina. At the time of our conversation, Nelson had been stationed at the consulate for over three years and anticipated serving another two before returning to Brasília, the capital of Brazil.

2. Operação Lava Jato exposed wide-ranging and institutionalized corruption throughout Brazilian and Latin American politics. The investigation probe, run between 2014 and 2017, was overseen by Brazil's independent judiciary, led by Sérgio Moro, in the southern city of Curitiba. It exposed a pervasive and longstanding kickback scheme between politicians and Brazilian construction and energy companies, including Petrobras, the national oil company. The investigation led to the imprisonment of former president Lula da Silva, the impeachment of former president Dilma Rousseff, and the downfall of her successor, former president Michel Temer, as well as the indictment of hundreds of top officials, and the recovery of billions of dollars. After the leaking of private messages among the investigators, the probe itself has come under intense scrutiny for corruption. For comprehensive reporting, see Londoño and Casado, "With a Second President in Jail, Brazil's Carwash Probe Lives On."

3. At the height of its growth in 2010, the Brazilian economy grew by 7.5 percent. See Margolis, *Goodbye, Brazil*, 221. By 2014, when I was conducting fieldwork, the economy had effectively stagnated, with growth at a mere .1 percent. Hit particularly hard by the Covid-19 pandemic, growth reached negative 4.5 percent in 2020. At the time of writing, annual growth is projected at 2.5 percent. See economic projections by the World Bank.

4. The explosion of evangelical and charismatic churches catering to Latin American migrants in general, and Brazilian migrants in particular, has been well documented. Such studies have observed the outsized presence of Brazilian evangelical churches among migrants in Boston and New York. See Martes, *New Immigrants, New Land*; Margolis, *Goodbye, Brazil*; Rodrigues, *Jesus in Sacred Gotham*. Scholars have investigated Brazilian diasporic communities in the UK, Japan, and Australia. See Sheringham, *Transnational Religious Spaces*; Ikeuchi, "From Slaves to Agents"; Ikeuchi, *Jesus Loves Japan*; Rocha, "Two Faces of God"; Rocha, "God Is in Control." Scholars have also documented the prominence of evangelical belonging and practice among Latin American migrants. See Vásquez, "Pentecostalism, Collective Identity, and Transnationalism among Salvadorans and Peruvians in the U.S."; Williams, Steigenga, and Vásquez, *A Place to Be*; Sarat, *Fire in the Canyon*.

5. Brazil had special status as Portugal's largest and most economically productive territory throughout the colonial period (1500–1822). In the wake of the Napoleonic Wars, the Portuguese court relocated to Brazil, making Rio de Janeiro the administrative center of its empire. Thomas Skidmore emphasizes the "unprecedented" nature of this spatial shift, writing, "Never before had a European monarch even set foot in a New World colony, much less settled in one as a seat of power." See Skidmore, *Brazil*, 42.

6. As Brazil espoused regional "exceptionalism," drew close to the United States, and rejected ties to "Latin America," so too did Spanish American nations reject Brazil. In his conception of América Latina, for instance, Simón Bolivar understood Spanish republics to be intimately tied by common ancestry, consciousness, language, culture, and interest. Given Brazil's Lusophone inheritance, imperial and monarchical policies, US and European affinities, and defense of slavery, the nation fell outside of this conception. See Bethell, "Brazil and 'Latin America,'" 459–63.

7. Bethell, 455–56.

8. Bethell, 470, quotes the work of the Brazilian intellectual Eduardo Pardo. The translation is my own.

9. Informed by European fascism and corporatism, Vargas consolidated centralized, authoritarian power in the Estado Novo (New State) by relying on secret police, detention camps,

military support, and censorship to eradicate dissent. Similar to fascist regimes in Italy and Germany, such efforts were bolstered by the assertion of a strong, coherent, and distinctive national culture. See Skidmore, *Brazil*, 116–19.

10. Skidmore describes Vargas's political manipulation of popular culture for the purpose of "making Brazil look good in the international context," 119.

11. Brazilian sociologist Gilberto Freyre advanced the now deeply contested idea that Brazil's race relations remained "cordial," especially when compared to race relations in the United States, in his well-known work, *Casa-Grande e Senzala*. He considered the mixture of African, European, and Indigenous ancestry to be one of Brazil's greatest assets.

12. The United States, and its overt racism, has served as a constant foil for Brazilian claims of comparatively harmonious, equitable, and just racial relations. See Hanchard, *Orpheus and Power*, 43.

13. Several books detail the collapse of military rule in Brazil, the tumultuous transition to civilian government, and the resulting economic crisis and readjustment under President Fernando Collor's Plano Real. See, for example, Skidmore, *Brazil*; Green, *We Cannot Remain Silent*; Margolis, *Little Brazil*; Margolis, *An Invisible Minority*; Margolis, *Goodbye, Brazil*. Scholars of Brazilian migration describe how this economic collapse galvanized Brazil's first sustained period of out-migration. For English-language work on Brazilian out-migration, see, for example, Margolis, *Little Brazil*; Goza, "Brazilian Immigration to North America"; Martes, *New Immigrants, New Land*.

14. Like the United States, Brazil frequently celebrates its ethnic diversity, and portrays itself as a nation of immigrants. As early as the seventeenth century, the first Portuguese settlers encouraged the Portuguese crown to bring Africans to Brazil in large numbers because they were seen to be a more malleable labor force than Indigenous peoples. See Skidmore, *Brazil*, 29–40. After the abolition of slavery in the late nineteenth century, the government actively recruited European and Asian migrants as "free" wage laborers to replace enslaved Africans. See Skidmore, 74–83. As a result of these national efforts, entire communities of Italians, Germans, Japanese, and Lebanese emerged throughout the Brazilian countryside and within cities. For a comprehensive history of immigration in Brazil, see Lesser, *Immigration, Ethnicity and National Identity in Brazil*.

15. Scholars suggest that Brazilians' racial identity significantly alters in the United States. While migrants tend to consider themselves to be "white" premigration, many identify as "mixed" or "other" once in the United States and confronted with the "one drop" rule of racial classification. For discussions of racial identity among Brazilian migrants, see Martes, "Neither Hispanic, nor Black"; Joseph, *Race on the Move*. One of Martes's interviewees gives voice to this shift in identity, saying, "Here, I became even blacker, I'm a Brazilian Black," 237. While I did not inquire into racial identifications, anecdotally, most Brazilians I interviewed emphasized their European ancestry and noted how they often "passed" as white Americans owing to their fair complexion.

16. Established Brazilian communities have been well-studied by both Brazilian and American social scientists, who have published detailed profiles of the migrant populations in the Northeast, including studies of Boston and New York. For detailed ethnographies of these communities, see Martes, *New Immigrants, New Land*; Margolis, *Little Brazil*; Margolis, *An Invisible Minority*. For a consideration of second-generation experience among Brazilian

migrants, see Sales, *Brazilians Away from Home*. For analysis of the impact of migration on Brazilian gender roles, see DeBiaggi, *Changing Gender Roles*.

17. For a synthesis of the new patterns of settlement among Brazilians in the United States, see chapter 5, "Doing America," in Margolis, *Goodbye, Brazil*.

18. After 2008, more migrants returned to Brazil from the United States than at any other period in history, reflecting the economic losses Brazilian migrants, like all migrants, sustained in the face of the 2008 US economic crisis. According to the Brazilian census, 52,000 migrants returned to Brazil from the United States alone. The American Community Survey corroborates these figures, in its findings that the Brazilian population in the United States declined by 8 percent between 2009 and 2011; in Massachusetts, a hub of Brazilian migration in the US, that decline was 22 percent. See Margolis, *Goodbye, Brazil*, 206. For more detailed accounts of causes and consequences of return migration to Brazil, see Margolis, 208–13; Siqueira, "Emigrants from the Micro-Region of Governador Valadares in the USA" and *Sonhos, sucesso e frustrações na emigração de retorno*.

19. See the Migration Policy Institute's report on increased Brazilian migration to the United States in Blizzard and Batalova, "Brazilian Immigrants in the United States."

20. Due to the difficulty counting a majority undocumented population, scholars consider the official figure of Brazilian migrants given by the US Census Bureau through its American Community Survey to be a gross underestimate. See Margolis, *Goodbye, Brazil*, 5–7. Importantly, the Covid-19 pandemic generated new waves of Brazilian migration to the US between 2020 and 2022 as individuals fled the collapse of their health-care infrastructure and economy. Because of the foreclosure of legal channels of migration under Title 42, the "public health rule," Brazilian migrants attempted unauthorized border crossings through Mexico at unprecedented rates. More than 46,000 Brazilians were detained at the US-Mexico border between October 2020 and August 2021, compared with 18,000 in 2019 and 284 in 2009. See T. Phillips, "A Nurse's Journey to Treating Covid in Brazil to Death in the US Desert."

21. Existing literature commonly describes Brazilian migrants as exceptional when compared to other Latin American migrant populations. See, for example, Margolis's influential ethnography on Brazilian migration in New York City and subsequent titles: *Little Brazil*; *An Invisible Minority*; *Goodbye, Brazil*. These works describe Brazilians as "sojourners" rather than "settlers," and a particularly "disunited" ethnic group in New York City. Further, Martes describes the racial and ethnic exceptionalism of Brazilians in her essay "Neither Hispanic, nor Black."

22. For accounts of Brazilian migrants' socioeconomic exceptionalism as compared to Latin American migrants, see Margolis, *Little Brazil*; Margolis, *An Invisible Minority*; Margolis, *Goodbye, Brazil*; Goza, "Brazilian Immigration to North America."

23. Following September 11, 2001, and the intensification of border security, greater numbers of Brazilians found their tourist visa applications denied. This was especially true for Brazilians from the cities of Governador Valadares (Minas Gerais) and Criciúma (Santa Catarina), which became infamous for sending large numbers of migrants to the United States without documents. While some crossed the Mexican border, many Brazilians I met in Greater Washington, DC, traveled to the United States on European passports, documents they had acquired through German or Italian ancestry. Such documents privileged Brazilians with European ancestry, for they obviated the need for a tourist visa to gain legal entry to the United States.

24. Margolis, *Little Brazil*, 258–75.

25. See Birman and Leite's aptly titled essay, "Whatever Happened to the Largest Catholic Country in the World?"

26. In 1549, Dom João III sent the first Jesuit mission to Brazil, later deemed "The Land of the Holy Cross" owing to the mission's success. In this initial effort at colonization, the Jesuits proved enormously useful to the crown. The Jesuits forcefully converted and "pacified" Indigenous people by organizing them in Jesuit-controlled villages, called *aldeias*. The Jesuits also established the standard form of Tupi, thereby facilitating communication between native peoples and the crown. The order also inaugurated missions throughout the interior, providing nascent infrastructure to the Amazon Basin region. See Skidmore, *Brazil*, 17. For an in-depth discussion of the role of the Catholic Church in twentieth-century Brazilian politics, especially in the face of rapid Protestant growth and ascendancy, see Helgen, *Religious Conflict in Brazil*.

27. As in the United States, evangelical Christianity has become deeply politicized in Brazil since the 1980s, culminating in the rise of Jair Bolsonaro, and the *bloco evangélico* that helped elect him. See Encarnación, "Amid Crisis in Brazil, the Evangelical Bloc Emerges as a Political Power"; Polimédio, "The Rise of the Brazilian Evangelicals." Despite being nominally Catholic, Bolsonaro has fostered a close alliance with evangelicals, naming pastors to head critical federal bureaus, such as the National Indian Foundation and the Ministry for Human Rights, Family, and Women; see Londoño and Casado, "Will an Ex-Missionary Shield Brazil's Tribes from Outsiders?" and "Brazil under Bolsonaro Has Message for Teenagers."

28. Several studies explore Brazilian evangelicalism as a global phenomenon. Such works include ethnographic accounts of Brazilian evangelicalism among Brazilian migrants in Japan and England; see, for example, Ikeuchi, "From Slaves to Agents" and *Jesus Loves Japan*; Sheringham, *Transnational Religious Spaces*. Scholars also detail how Brazilian evangelicalism influences Latin American Christianity outside of Brazil. See, for instance, K. O'Neill, *Secure the Soul*. Several edited volumes theorize Brazilian evangelicalism as a transnational force throughout the Brazilian diaspora and beyond. See Oro, Corten, and Dozon, *Igreja Universal do Reino de Deus*; Oosterbaan, Kamp, and Bahia, *Global Trajectories of Brazilian Religion*; Rocha and Vásquez, *The Diaspora of Brazilian Religions*.

29. Protestant churches first appeared in Brazil in the early nineteenth century, at the same time European migrants entered the country en masse. Beginning in the early 1800s, European migrants established Anglican (1808) and Lutheran (1824) congregations. Later, North American missionaries established other "historic" Protestant churches, such as Presbyterian (1859) and Methodist (1867). These churches remained popular through the first half of the twentieth century, especially among Brazilians of European descent. See Freston, "Neo-Pentecostalism in Brazil"; E. Kramer, "Spectacle and the Staging of Power in Brazilian Neo-Pentecostalism." By the 1980s, however, these churches no longer represented Protestant or "evangelical" experience in Brazil. Instead, the vast majority of Protestants belonged to Pentecostal and Neo-Pentecostal charismatic churches. By 2010, 13 percent of the Brazilian population identified as Pentecostal or Neo-Pentecostal, according to the Pew Forum's study on Brazilian religion. Comprising more than two-thirds of the Protestant population as a whole (42 percent of the total population), these believers numbered over 24 million, compared to 7 million "mainline" Protestants. See Pew Research Center, "Brazil's Changing Religious Landscape."

30. Paul Freston suggests that Edir Macedo's Igreja Universal do Reino de Deus, founded in 1977, embodies the archetype of "third wave" Pentecostal expansion in Brazil. See his

comprehensive essay on the subject, "Neo-Pentecostalism in Brazil." Scholars often deem third-wave churches to be Neo-Pentecostal to distinguish them from traditional Pentecostal denominations such as Assembly of God or Foursquare. Third-wave churches like Macedo's IURD continue to reach new demographics, like young people and the well-off, through extensive media engagement. The IURD's empire includes television, internet and radio stations, multiple newspapers and magazines, and enormous "temples" that provide multiple daily services for thousands of dedicated *crentes*. See Freston, 145–53. As the most visible and lucrative Brazilian Neo-Pentecostal church domestically and internationally, the IURD has attracted substantial scholarly attention. See, for example, the edited volume by Oro, Corten, and Dozon, *Igreja Universal do Reino de Deus*.

31. "Reverse mission" refers to the reversal of the traditional direction of missionary activity. Rather than white European and North American missionaries evangelizing the Global South, missionaries from the Global South increasingly evangelize populations in North America and Europe. See Freston, "Reverse Mission."

32. For more on the relationship between Brazilian tourism and Brazilian religion, see the volume edited by Oosterbaan, Kamp, and Bahia, *Global Trajectories of Brazilian Religion*; and Rocha's ethnography, *John of God*.

33. For a comprehensive report on Washington, DC's transformation into a migrant gateway in the postwar period, see Singer, "Metropolitan Washington."

34. On the US Census Bureau's 2016 findings regarding the growth of Washington, DC's foreign-born population, see Tatian et al., "State of Immigrants in the District of Columbia," 2. Of this population, roughly 40 percent originated from Latin America, with the largest populations from El Salvador (14 percent), Mexico (4 percent), Guatemala (3.2 percent), and Peru (3.2 percent). Other large migrant populations originated from India (6.4 percent), Korea (4.9 percent), Ethiopia (3 percent), and Sub-Saharan Africa (Nigeria—1.6 percent, Ghana—1.4 percent, Cameroon—1.4 percent). As of 2012, Brazil ranked thirtieth of 193 origin countries, with an estimated .7 percent of the foreign-born population. See Singer, "Metropolitan Washington," 15–16. Later estimates show that Brazilians accounted for 1.2 percent of the foreign-born population in Washington, DC. See Migration Policy Institute, "State Demographics Data—DC." Census data on Brazilian migrant populations remains necessarily constrained, however, due to its inability to account for undocumented migrants, and due to the growth of migrant populations in Maryland and Virginia suburbs of Washington, DC. Consequently, these numbers most likely represent gross underestimates.

35. For earlier studies of Washington, DC's migrant populations and their particular histories and residential patterns, see, for example, Repak's *Waiting on Washington* on Salvadorans; and Cary's edited volume *Urban Odyssey* regarding Native Americans, Black Americans, Irish, Jews, and Latinos, among other populations. While these accounts largely document migrants living in ethnic enclaves in the city center, contemporary reports document the growing suburbanization of migrant populations in Greater Washington, DC. For findings and analysis, see Singer, "Metropolitan Washington," 7.

36. Until the first half of the twentieth century, Washington, DC, attracted few foreign-born residents other than diplomats. The area's industrial sector remained virtually nonexistent throughout the early twentieth century, making Washington, DC, a small "southern town" when compared to its neighboring East Coast cities. See Brick, Jones-Correra, and Singer, "Local

Goes National," 5. In 1900, for example, the foreign-born population of Washington, DC, as counted by the US Census Bureau was merely 7 percent, while Boston's was 35 percent, New York's 37 percent, and Philadelphia's 23 percent. See Singer, "Metropolitan Washington," 2. Notably, the region was home to a growing number of Black Americans, who first settled in DC after escaping slavery, and then moved there in large numbers following the Civil War. See Repak, *Waiting on Washington*, 52; Cary, *Urban Odyssey*, xxi.

37. Through syncretic cosmologies and practices, Brazilians often incorporated devotion to Indigenous spirits and African *orixás* with Catholic saints to form fluid and flexible religious identities under the banner of Catholicism. See Birman and Leite, "Whatever Happened to the Largest Catholic Country in the World?," 273.

38. See data from the following Pew Forum studies: "Religion in Latin America"; "Brazil's Changing Religious Landscape."

39. In examining evangelical experience, as well as religious experience more generally among Brazilians, scholars have attended primarily to the broadly pragmatic function such faith has played. For considerations of how participation in evangelical, versus Catholic or Afro-Brazilian religious groups, fosters socioeconomic betterment, see Burdick, *Looking for God in Brazil*; Burdick, *Blessed Anastácia*; Chesnut, *Born Again in Brazil*; Chesnut, *Competitive Spirits*; Drogus, *Women, Religion, and Social Change in Brazil's Popular Church*; E. Kramer, "Spectacle and the Staging of Power in Brazilian Neo-Pentecostalism." For discussions of how evangelical belonging impacts political mobilization, see Stoll, *Is Latin America Turning Protestant?*; Martin, *Pentecostalism*; Lehmann, *Struggle for the Spirit*; Burdick, *Looking for God in Brazil*; Burdick, *Blessed Anastácia*; Drogus, *Women, Religion, and Social Change in Brazil's Popular Church*. Regarding the comparative healing benefits of different religious traditions, see Chesnut, *Born Again in Brazil*; Lehmann, *Struggle for the Spirit*; Seligman, "The Unmaking and Making of Self"; Seligman, *Possessing Spirits and Healing Selves*; Van de Port, *Ecstatic Encounters*. And, regarding religious belonging's impact on self-esteem for marginalized populations, see Burdick, "What Is the Color of the Holy Spirit?"; Johnson, *Secrets, Gossip and Gods*; Seligman, "The Unmaking and Making of Self"; Seligman, *Possessing Spirits and Healing Selves*; Lehmann, *Struggle for the Spirit*. In such studies, scholars document the real-world benefits that belonging confers on Brazilians who are overwhelmingly poor, marginalized, and of Afro-Brazilian descent. Frequently, scholars consider religious identity as "a search for solutions and meaning within a range of alternatives," as indicated by E. Kramer in "Spectacle and the Staging of Power in Brazilian Neo-Pentecostalism," 96; and a rational deliberation of the "mercado dos bens da salvação" (market of salvation "goods") as Van de Port describes in *Ecstatic Encounters*, 174.

40. See Margolis, *Goodbye, Brazil*, 77; Tremura, "Transnational Migrant Brazilian Women in 'Pink Collar Jobs' in the Greater Washington D.C. Area," 67.

41. See the Migration Policy Institute's report: Blizzard and Batalova, "Brazilian Immigrants in the United States."

42. While most of the churches reflected a similar geographic spread, one had a congregation originating almost exclusively in a city well known for manufacturing as well as for migration: Criciúma, Santa Catarina. By the end of the 1990s, almost 26,000 Criciúma residents lived in the United States, making the city rival Governador Valadares (nicknamed Governador "Valdollares" for its heavy reliance on migrant remittances) as a point of departure for Brazilian migrants

headed to the United States and Europe. See Assis, "De Criciúma para o mundo"; Aparecida dos Santos, "O caso dos migrantes da cidade de Criciúma Brasil para os Estados Unidos."

43. See Blizzard and Batalova, "Brazilian Immigrants in the United States."

44. Prince William County, for instance, passed one of the most restrictive policies in the nation, mandating local police to check immigrant status at traffic stops and to work with federal authorities in detaining and deporting undocumented immigrants. See Singer, "Metropolitan Washington," 23. On November 5, 2019, however, an increasingly foreign-born electorate in Northern Virginia helped elect Democratic majorities in both houses of the General Assembly for the first time since 1993. See Tavernise and Gebeloff, "How Voters Turned Virginia from Deep Red to Solid Blue."

45. See Martes, *New Immigrants, New Land*; Margolis, *Goodbye, Brazil*; Rodrigues, *Jesus in Sacred Gotham*. While research indicates the predominance of evangelical Christianity among Brazilians in the US, scholarship conversely documents the predominance of Catholicism in Brazil. For data on religious affiliation in Brazil, see the Pew Research Center, "Brazil's Changing Religious Landscape." For data on the religious affiliation of migrants in the US, see the Pew Research Center, "The Religious Affiliation of U.S. Immigrants."

46. In order to protect the identity of these congregations, and their undocumented congregants, I discuss each church in general terms. I have deliberately withheld identifying details, such as specific name, location, organizational history, and descriptions of the physical church.

47. Scholars highlight the increasingly transnational character of evangelical churches, noting that migrants continue to participate in home congregations while abroad. For instance, many Brazilians in the Boston area still tithed in their home church. See Levitt, *God Needs No Passport*, 132–33. Although North American pastors first introduced Brazilians to Protestantism, Brazilian missionaries now travel to the United States to support and grow their diasporic congregations. See Martes, *New Immigrants, New Land*, 69, 80; Mariz, "Missão religiosa e migração." Many of these US–based congregations maintain frequent contact with sister churches in Brazil, facilitating conferences, pastor trainings, and joint ministries. Scholars suggest that these churches' connections to Brazil may constitute part of evangelical Christianity's allure for migrants. In her account of evangelical experience among Brazilian migrants in Boston, for instance, Martes notes that evangelical churches employ Brazilian pastors who come from backgrounds similar to migrants'. See Martes, *New Immigrants, New Land*, 80. Marcus suggests that Brazilian evangelical churches explicitly encourage migration by first exposing Brazilians to American values of entrepreneurialism and individualism in Brazil, and then fostering employment opportunities once individuals reach the United States. See his articles "Brazilian Immigration to the U.S. and the Geographical Imagination" and "Convenient Liaisons." Churches, according to Marcus, become "convenient liaisons" in the transmigrant circuit. Recent volumes explicitly analyze evangelical churches as transnational institutions. See, for example, Sheringham, *Transnational Religious Spaces*; Rocha and Vásquez, *The Diaspora of Brazilian Religions*; Oosterbaan, Kamp, and Bahia, *Global Trajectories of Brazilian Religion*.

48. See Tanya Luhrmann's description of the defining markers of US evangelical experience among predominantly white and middle-class Americans in *When God Talks Back*. In addition to listing their commitments to being born again, biblical inerrancy, and evangelization, Luhrmann writes, "These evangelicals have sought out and cultivated concrete experiences of God's realness," xv.

214 NOTES TO CHAPTER 1

49. Bialecki, "After the Denominozoic," 194.

50. Scholars generally agree that wildly popular US evangelical movements originating in California, such as the Vineyard Church and Calvary Church, have profoundly impacted US and global Christianity in terms of style, format, and theology. See Luhrmann, *When God Talks Back*; Bialecki, *Diagram for Fire*; Miller, *Reinventing American Protestantism*. Flory considers three main elements that have impacted US Christianity and evangelicalism more generally: (1) adapting church to culture; (2) informal dress and attire; and (3) California "soul." See "How California's Megachurches Changed Christian Culture."

51. See McCann, *The Throes of Democracy*, 122.

52. For further reading on Pentecostalism in Brazil, see Martin, *Pentecostalism*; Freston, "Neo-Pentecostalism in Brazil"; Chesnut, *Born Again in Brazil*; Chesnut, *Competitive Spirits*; Lehmann, *Struggle for the Spirit*; Ireland, *Kingdoms Come*; Burdick, *Looking for God in Brazil*; Burdick, *Blessed Anastácia*; Burdick, "What Is the Color of the Holy Spirit?"; Oro, Corten, and Dozon, *Igreja Universal do Reino de Deus*; Oro and Semán, "Pentecostalism in the Southern Cone Countries."

The Assembly of God (Assembleia de Deus), introduced by two Swedish missionaries in 1902 in the Northeast of Brazil, remains among the oldest and most conservative Pentecostal denominations in Brazil. It had particular success due to foreign missionaries' willingness to transfer leadership to local Brazilians. See Stoll, *Is Latin America Turning Protestant?*, 107–10. Historically, the denomination prohibited members from drinking, smoking, playing soccer, and attending movies. Women were prohibited from cutting their hair and wearing makeup or jewelry. In recent years, however, these restrictions have loosened, particularly among migrant populations in the United States. In 2010, 12.3 million Brazilians belonged to the Assembleia de Deus. See De Andrade, "Censo 2010 aponta migração de fiéis da Universal do Reino de Deus para outras igrejas evangélicas."

As with the Methodist and Presbyterian churches, North American missionaries established the first Baptist church in Brazil in the late nineteenth century. See Stoll, *Is Latin America Turning Protestant?*; Martin, *Pentecostalism*; Weaver, "Confederate Immigrants and Evangelical Churches in Brazil." David Martin cites the group's decentralized structure, emphasis on evangelism and participation, and conservative theological principles as responsible for Baptism's success in Brazil, as compared to Presbyterianism and Methodism. Brazilian Baptism, according to Martin, remained an important precursor to the Pentecostal and Charismatic boom. See his writings on the topic in *Pentecostalism*, 62–64. In 1907, the National Convention of Brazilian Baptists (Convenção Nacional de Batistas Brasileiras) was founded, giving Brazilians authority over the church structure in Brazil. Multiple Baptist organizations exist in Brazil, including both traditional and "renewalist" churches that mimic Pentecostalism. In 2010, Brazil had a population of 3.7 million Baptists. Between 2000 and 2010, the number of Baptists grew by 17 percent. See Instituto Paracleto, "Entre os pentecostais, os batistas e adventistas cresceram no Brasil."

The SDA Church emerged out of the Millerite movement in America in the middle of the nineteenth century. After the "Great Disappointment" of 1844, when the Millerite belief in the imminent Second Coming of Christ failed to pass, the SDA Church was founded with a new interpretation of the book of Daniel and its prophetic message. For the general history of Seventh-day Adventism, see Bull and Lockhart, *Seeking a Sanctuary*. American missionaries established the first SDA congregations in Brazil in the 1890s. The movement especially took hold in Santa Catarina among German immigrants. In 1902, the Brazilian association of the SDA Church was formally organized. See "Centro de Pesquisas Ellen G. White." For more on the history of the SDA Church in Brazil and Latin America, see Greenleaf, *A Land of Hope*. The SDA Church maintains congregations in 208 countries, with its largest membership base in Brazil. In addition to churches, the SDA congregations run wide-ranging and well-resourced medical and educational facilities. In 2010, the country maintained a population of 1.5 million Adventists. Between 2000 and 2010, the Adventist church grew by 29 percent. See Instituto Paracleto, "Entre os pentecostais, os batistas e adventistas cresceram no Brasil."

53. While the local priest and the multicultural director emphasized the smallness of the Brazilian communities in their dioceses, especially when compared to other migrant groups, neither could estimate the number of Brazilians in their charge. Instead, both referred to the difficulty in counting migrant populations, and the tendency for migrant adherents to resist formal church registration.

54. For an overview of the history of Spiritism in Brazil, see Warren, "Spiritism in Brazil"; Hess, "The Many Rooms of Spiritism in Brazil."

55. See Burdick, *Blessed Anastácia*; Hess, "The Many Rooms of Spiritism in Brazil"; Lehmann, *Struggle for the Spirit*; Warren, "Spiritism in Brazil."

56. The names I give the Spiritist centers, the Center of Healing and Peace and the Washington Kardecistas, are pseudonyms.

57. This corresponds with an investigation of class-based religious preference among Brazilian migrants in Sydney, Australia, where the researcher found Spiritism to be popular among the Brazilian international elite. See Rocha, "Two Faces of God."

58. Several ethnographies explore the embeddedness of evangelicalism among Brazilian migrant populations. See, for example, Martes, *New Immigrants, New Land*; Margolis, *Goodbye, Brazil*; Mariz, "Missão religiosa e migração"; Freston, "The Religious Field among Brazilians in the United States"; Ikeuchi, *Jesus Loves Japan*; Rocha and Vásquez, *The Diaspora of Brazilian Religions*; Williams, Steigenga, and Vásquez, *A Place to Be*; Oosterbaan, "Spiritual Attunement"; Sheringham, *Transnational Religious Spaces*.

59. Margolis, *Little Brazil*, 211–19.

60. Fortuny et al., "Brazilian and Mexican Women."

61. Margolis, *Goodbye, Brazil*.

62. Vásquez, "Beyond Homo Anomicus," 33–35. Other scholars, however, have questioned these positive assessments, instead foregrounding the negative impact of evangelical belonging among migrants. Churches, according to some studies, may exacerbate divisions, engage in exploitative labor practices, and promote individual gain over collective uplift. See Alves, "Immigrant Regime of Production"; Martes, *New Immigrants, New Land*, 89, 150–55.

63. See Althoff, "Religious Identities of Latin American Immigrants in Chicago"; Mariz, "Missão religiosa e migração"; Martes, *New Immigrants, New Land*; Williams, Steigenga, and Vásquez, *A Place to Be*.

Chapter 2

1. K. Stewart, *Ordinary Affects*, 94, 97–98.

2. Researchers have documented a particularly high stigma surrounding psychic distress and emotional suffering among Latin American populations both in the United States and in Latin

America. See Plascencia et al., "Undocumented and Uninsured Part 3"; Cruz, "Poor Mental Health." This finding suggests that many migrants might diminish the psychic suffering they report, or withhold it altogether.

3. While my research focuses on the experience of undocumented migrants, I also draw from conversations and interviews with individuals who eventually obtained work permits and green cards (legal permanent residence), through employee sponsorship, amnesty, or marriage. For many of these migrants, the stresses of daily life, including low-wage work, family separation, English-language difficulty, and marginalization, continued long after the receipt of formal legal status.

4. Pew Research Center, "A Nation of Immigrants."

5. On the prevalence of mixed-status families in the United States, which includes approximately 9 million people nationwide, see Schueths and Lawston, *Living Together, Living Apart.* The edited volume's introduction considers the grave impact of punitive immigration measures, including aggressive deportation and removal practices, not only on undocumented migrants but on their family members, many of whom maintain permanent residence or citizenship status. See pp. 5–8.

6. See "U.S. Immigration and Customs Enforcement Fiscal Year 2019 Enforcement and Removal Operations Report," 19.

7. The Trump administration invoked Title 42 in March 2020 to quickly seal US borders at the onset of the Covid-19 pandemic. While the measure reduced formal encounters at the border by half in fiscal year 2020, investigative reporting revealed how the measure led migrants to attempt more dangerous and deadly crossings. See Dias and Calderon, "The Obscure Public Health Law That Trump Wielded against Migrants Is Still Ruining Lives." For reporting on the ongoing crisis at the southern border, and continued invocation of Title 42 under the Biden administration, see Sullivan and Jordan, "Illegal Border Crossings, Driven by Pandemic and Natural Disasters, Soar to Record High"; "It's Time to End the Pandemic Emergency at the Border."

8. See reporting on the failure of comprehensive immigration reform under the Obama administration, for example, Shear and Preston, "Dealt Setback, Obama Puts Off Immigrant Plan"; Downes, "Another Setback for Immigration Action."

9. It is unlikely that the US Citizenship Act of 2021, as introduced in Congress in March 2021, will pass both the House and the Senate, given the Republican Party's large minorities in both houses, and the party's general embrace of Trump's sweeping anti-immigrant platforms. See Shear, "Biden's Immigration Plan Would Offer Path to Citizenship for Millions."

10. On au pair programs, see Hess and Puckhaber, "'Big Sisters' Are Better Domestic Servants?!" On migrant domestic workers in the United States, see M. Romero, *Maid in the U.S.A.* On the feminization of the migrant labor force, see, for example, Sassen, *The Mobility of Labor and Capital*; Sassen, *Globalization and Its Discontents*; Ehrenreich and Hochschild, *Global Woman*; Rodríguez, "The 'Hidden Side' of the New Economy."

11. The 2005–9 American Community Survey published the following findings regarding the demographic profile of domestic workers in the United States: 95 percent were women, 46 percent were foreign-born, 35 percent were not US citizens. In the fourteen metropolitan regions of the United States, the concentration of foreign-born women in the domestic services was even more pronounced: 76 percent foreign-born, 56 percent without citizenship status. The ACS did not survey document status among those who identified as foreign-born. Burnham

and Theodore did inquire into document status in their comprehensive report on the domestic services in the United States and found that 47 percent of respondents did not have documents; see Burnham and Theodore, *Home Economics*. Globally, women care workers account for a growing proportion of migrants, often finding employment in the most intimate, low-wage, and hidden sphere of economic activity—the home. For examples of this growing literature, see Sassen, *The Mobility of Labor and Capital*; Sassen, *Globalization and Its Discontents*; Rodríguez, "The 'Hidden Side' of the New Economy"; Romero, Preston, and Giles, *When Care Work Goes Global*; Yarris, *Care across Generations*; Leinaweaver, *Adoptive Migration*.

12. Hochschild, *The Managed Heart*, 148.

13. Muehlebach, *The Moral Neoliberal*, 226.

14. Rodríguez, "The 'Hidden Side' of the New Economy," 71.

15. Rodríguez, 71.

16. For more context on Central American migrant flows from El Salvador and Guatemala to the United States, see Repak's ethnographic account, *Waiting on Washington*.

17. Margolis, *Little Brazil*, 141.

18. At the time of writing, ambivalence about return to Brazil has only intensified, as migrants watch their country flounder economically and politically. The promise of growth has halted dramatically over the last several years with the revelation of extreme government corruption and mismanagement of funds. The last president, Dilma Rousseff, was impeached for her role in financial mismanagement and her party's acceptance of graft. See Jacobs, "Brazil's Lower House of Congress Votes for Impeachment of Dilma Rousseff"; Romero and Sreeharsha, "Dilma Rousseff Targeted in Brazil by Lawmakers Facing Scandals of Their Own." The once national hero and champion of ordinary Brazilians, Lula da Silva, was imprisoned in a stunning fall from grace, only to be released two years later. See D. Phillips, "Brazil's Former President Lula Walks Free from Prison after Supreme Court Ruling." The current and much embattled president, Jair Bolsonaro, reversed much of the country's progressive social and environmental legislation, and has flaunted international conventions. Bolsonaro's casual approach to the Covid-19 pandemic, including discouraging quarantine, social distancing, and mask use, and slow vaccine rollout mired in scandal, only exacerbated Brazil's instability and public health catastrophe. See Londoño, "As Brazil Faces Record Covid-19 Deaths, a Variant-Fueled Surge and Lagging Vaccinations, Bolsonaro Disparages Masks"; Londoño and Milhorance, "Brazil Vaccine Scandal Imperils Bolsonaro as Protests Spread." Bolsonaro's gross mishandling of the pandemic has drawn widespread ire among Brazilians, culminating in a damning investigative report compiled by Brazilian lawmakers that blames Bolsonaro for most of the country's 600,000 pandemic deaths. The report, authored by an eleven-member Senate panel, recommends that Bolsonaro should face criminal charges of "crimes against humanity." See Nicas, "Brazilian Leader Accused of Crimes against Humanity in Pandemic Response."

19. Markowitz, "Leaving Babylon to Come Home to Israel," 183.

20. Caldeira, *City of Walls*.

21. Caldeira, 19.

22. To question #31—"Do you intend to return to Brazil?"—21 percent responded "yes," 43 percent "maybe," and 36 percent "no."

23. Owing to heavy import taxes levied on foreign products in Brazil, many consumer goods such as foreign cars, electronics, and appliances remain out of reach for relatively well-off middle-class Brazilians. Upon coming to the United States, Brazilians experienced shock and

delight at their newfound purchasing power. I heard many migrants exclaim at being able to buy iPhones, iPads, and computers with their earnings.

24. Information sheet circulated by the Brazilian consulate at the open meeting with the Brazilian community (Reunião aberta com a comunidade brasileira), March 31, 2014, Washington, DC.

25. Sueli Siqueira's interview was published in *AcheiUSA*'s article on return migrants. See Franco, "Governador Valadares, a América presente em cada canto de uma cidade brasileira."

26. Several prominent ethnographies describe mutual distrust and ambivalence as pervasive among Brazilian migrants in the United States. See, for example, Margolis, *Little Brazil*; Margolis, *An Invisible Minority*; Martes, *New Immigrants, New Land*. Regarding the Brazilian population in New York City, Margolis documents migrants' sense that they are "the most disunited ethnic group in the city"; see *Little Brazil*, 200. Martes observes a similar trend in Boston. Scholarship has long analyzed international migrant experience as broadly "ambivalent" owing to the discrepancy between migrants' imagined dreams and lived experiences. See Boccagni and Kivisto, "Introduction."

27. Massumi, "The Autonomy of Affect," 88.

28. Mazzarella, "Affect," 293.

29. Mazzarella, 291.

30. Cvetkovich, *Depression*.

31. Scholars have documented the proliferation of specific public feelings in the twenty-first century. On loneliness, see Cacioppo and Patrick, *Loneliness*. On depression, see Cvetkovich, *Depression*. On boredom, see B. O'Neill, *The Space of Boredom* and "Cast Aside." On isolation, see Malkki, *The Need to Help*; Putnam, *Bowling Alone*. On precariousness, see Allison, *Precarious Japan*. Such feelings, these researchers reveal, are endemic to late capitalism and market-driven governance that prioritizes the free market above alleviating human suffering. Market logics increasingly extend to philanthropy and faith-based work, leading to a lucrative but ineffective for-profit disaster relief industry. See Adams, *Markets of Sorrow, Labors of Faith*.

32. Breslau et al., "Migration from Mexico to the United States and Subsequent Risk for Depressive and Anxiety Disorders," 430.

33. Potochnick and Perreira, "Depression and Anxiety among First-Generation Immigrant Latino Youth," 472.

34. Plascencia et al., "Undocumented and Uninsured Part 3," 2–3.

35. In the Pentecostal church's formulation, the Devil and his demonic agents tempt human beings to indulge in sinful behavior, such as drinking, drugs, and premarital sex. In order to overcome these demons, humans must experience liberation *(libertação)* through fervent prayer, study, and embodied experience of God.

Chapter 3

1. Ahmed, *The Promise of Happiness*, 138.

2. I use "He," "Him," and "His" to refer to God in keeping with my interviewees' understanding of divinity as decidedly masculine and monotheistic. When speaking about God (as Father), Jesus (as Son), or the Holy Spirit, migrant believers exclusively used masculine words and labels, including *Ele* (Him), *o Senhor* (the Lord), *o Pai* (the Father), *o Filho* (the Son), *o Reino* (the King).

3. See chapters 5 and 6 for discussions of migrants' competing perceptions of Catholicism and evangelical Christianity.

4. Believers and clergy members alike made a distinction between embracing everyone in their congregations and condoning what they understood to be "sinful" behavior. Evangelicals, for instance, argued for the inclusion of LGBTQ-identifying people in church, but asserted they needed to be healed of sinful behaviors that transgressed God's law. The implication was that communion with God would instill heteronormative sexual desires, or at least prevent congregants from acting on same-sex sexual desires.

5. During official congregational meetings, migrant evangelical churches collected *dízimos* (tithes) and *ofertas* (offerings). Tithes, technically 10 percent of one's income donated to the church, were viewed as obligatory and fulfilled a believer's personal covenant with God. Offerings were voluntary and reflected the "heart" of the believer in that particular moment. The collected funds supported the daily functioning of the local church, including rent, social events, teaching material, clergy salary, weekly refreshments. These funds also supported the agendas of the larger US-based and transnational church networks to which local churches belonged.

6. Selection of survey answers to question #40, "When you pray, how do you see God?"

7. The churches' "personal responsibility" rhetoric recalls broader discourses identified with neoliberalism that convert social problems into personal pathologies, particularly amid the continued erosion of the welfare state. See, for example, Cvetkovich, *Depression*; Muehlebach, *The Moral Neoliberal*; Garcia, *The Pastoral Clinic*; Adams, *Markets of Sorrow, Labors of Faith*.

8. Cvetkovich, *Depression*, 4.

9. Foucault, *Society Must Be Defended*.

10. Rose, *Governing the Soul*, 11.

11. Rose, 231.

12. My discussion of the origins of evangelical Christianity in the US, and the central role personal conversion, free will, and feeling played in the movement beginning in the nineteenth century, relies on two foundational accounts: FitzGerald, *The Evangelicals*, and Marsden, *Fundamentalism and American Culture*.

13. FitzGerald, *The Evangelicals*, 26.

14. FitzGerald, 34–35, 88.

15. Marsden, *Fundamentalism and American Culture*, 77.

16. Marsden, 78.

17. Marsden, 100.

18. FitzGerald, *The Evangelicals*, 89–90.

19. See Marsden's comprehensive account of the infamous Scopes trial in *Fundamentalism and American Culture*, 185–86, 194. During the trial, William Jennings Bryan prosecuted the State of Tennessee's case against a high school biology teacher, John T. Scopes, for teaching evolution in public school. Clarence Darrow, a famous defense attorney, defended Scopes. In the face of growing scientific consensus about human evolution, Bryan's attempt to defend biblical literalism met with scorn and ridicule, setting the stage for the redefinition of evangelicalism in the US.

20. On the rise of expressive Christianity within US evangelicalism, see FitzGerald, *The Evangelicals*, 169; Marsden, *Fundamentalism and American Culture*, 232–36, 255.

21. For global contexts, see Lehmann, *Struggle for the Spirit*; Martin, *Pentecostalism*; Engelke, *A Problem of Presence*; Smilde, *Reason to Believe*; Roberts, *To Be Cared For*; K. O'Neill, *City of*

God; K. O'Neill, *Secure the Soul*; Sheringham, *Transnational Religious Spaces*; Ikeuchi, *Jesus Loves Japan*; Cox, *Fire from Heaven*. In the US context, see, for example, Luhrmann, "Metakinesis"; Luhrmann, *When God Talks Back*; Luhrmann, *How God Becomes Real*; Bialecki, *Diagram for Fire*; Bielo, *Words upon the Word*; Bielo, *Emerging Evangelicals*; Miller, *Reinventing American Protestantism*; Poloma and Hood, *Blood and Fire*. These studies highlight the therapeutic effect of evangelical and charismatic Christianity, which center upon personal healing, transformation, and uplift, and often encourage spiritual disciplines that lead to significant behavioral modifications.

22. Marsden, *Fundamentalism and American Culture*, 205.

23. *Testemunho*, meaning "testimony," refers to an adherent's conversion narrative as well as stories of God's presence and activity in daily life. Congregants delivered *testemunhos* during formal meetings and informal services to bolster the faith of others and to demonstrate God's constant involvement in their lives. In chapter 4, I consider testimony to be a key spiritual discipline among migrant adherents.

24. "Whoever does not love does not know God, because God is love" (1 John 4:8 NIV).

25. Rose, *Governing the Soul*, 250.

26. Rose, 232.

27. Rose, 242.

28. Rose, 258.

29. Rose argues that psychotherapeutics moved therapy from the biomedical to the educational realm. As such, experts considered life to be a "skill" attained by patients through behavior and emotion modification. He writes, "Therapy is no attempt to enforce conformity but apparently part of a profoundly emancipatory project of learning to be a self," 242.

30. Ahmed, *The Promise of Happiness*, 158.

31. Ahmed, 11.

32. "The science of happiness could be described as performative: by finding happiness in certain places, it generates those places as being good, as being what should be promoted as goods," Ahmed, 6.

33. Ahmed, 5–8.

34. Ahmed writes of the circular logic inherent in such happiness discourses: "The very 'thing' we aim to achieve is the 'thing' that will get us there . . . to feel better is to *get better*," 9.

35. In 1986, President Reagan signed into law the first sweeping amnesty bill, the Immigration Reform and Control Act, providing a pathway to legalization for undocumented immigrants who had entered the country before 1982. While the bill provided provisions for tightening the Mexican border, it also secured amnesty for 3 million previously undocumented people. See Repak, *Waiting on Washington*, 17–20. President Obama initiated two immigration reform programs during his administration. In 2012, he implemented Deferred Action for Childhood Arrivals (DACA), enabling undocumented immigrants who had entered the country before their sixteenth birthday, and prior to 2007, to obtain renewable two-year work permits, thus qualifying for in-state tuition. In 2014, Obama announced Deferred Action for Parents of Americans (DAPA), an extension of DACA to parents of US citizens and permanent residents who had resided in the United States since 2010. During the remainder of Obama's term, and the beginning of the Trump administration, however, the executive orders were mired in litigation, and ultimately discontinued. In December 2020, a federal judge in Brooklyn ordered the

government to fully reinstate the program, including accepting new applications from an anticipated 300,000 eligible young people. In July 2021, however, a federal judge in Houston deemed the program unlawful, and disallowed the approval of new applications after the decision date of July 16, 2021. While the Biden administration is expected to appeal the decision, the fate of DACA recipients and their parents, as well as all undocumented migrants across the country, still depends on a lasting legislative solution. While the Biden administration introduced far-reaching legislation to Congress, termed the US Citizenship Act of 2021, at the time of writing, it faces strong opposition from the Republican Party. See Dickerson and Shear, "Judge Orders Government to Fully Reinstate DACA Program," and M. Jordan, "Judge Rules DACA Is Unlawful and Suspends Applications."

36. For example, Maryland's prominent and expansive nongovernmental organization CASA de Maryland works to empower low-income immigrant communities through sponsoring frequent events aimed at supporting undocumented workers. These year-round events occur in the same neighborhoods in Montgomery County in which I conducted fieldwork. The organization offers legal and health-care counsel, connects workers to employment opportunities, and hosts job training programs. As indicated in its name, the organization targets Spanish-speaking migrant communities. See the website for CASA de Maryland.

37. Joyce Meyer remains one of the best-selling Christian authors in North America and throughout the United States, with frequent book tours, conferences, and television appearances worldwide. Because the Portuguese texts were sold out when I joined the group, I used an English copy of the text. All quotations are from the English edition.

38. J. Meyer, *The Battlefield of the Mind*, 39.

39. J. Meyer, 43.

40. J. Meyer, 44.

41. "Africa" figured prominently in the imaginary of the Brazilian migrant evangelicals with whom I spent time. During interviews, several individuals told me that God called them to be missionaries in Africa. One woman even began to cry as she described the work she felt called to do, "hugging African children who had nothing." During worship services, pastors frequently encouraged this orientation by telling congregants of the miracles taking place in Africa among people they described as "hungry for Jesus" despite what they broadly characterized as destitution. "Africa" and "Africans" in this overly reductionist and inherently racist narrative that rehearses the imperialist portrayal of Africa as a "dark" and "primitive" continent remained devoid of any specificity and instead served as a foil for Brazilian migrant believers to minimize their own difficulties and assert their relative position of wealth as Christian believers in the United States. For writings on the genealogy of Africa as a land of "darkness," see, for example, Brantlinger, *Rule of Darkness*.

42. "American Idol Contestant's Heartbreaking Song."

43. "The acts of the flesh are obvious: sexual immorality, impurity and debauchery; idolatry and witchcraft; hatred, discord, jealousy, fits of rage, selfish ambition, dissensions, factions and envy; drunkenness, orgies and the like. I warn you as I did before, that those who live like this will not inherit the kingdom of God." Galatians 5:19–21 NIV.

44. In Boyer's classic essay on the topic, he considers "mana-terms" of "traditional" religious systems to be the paradigmatic example of empty concepts, which exist as the repository of

otherwise unexplainable events and ideas. He further considers the complex set of rules that ultimately determine the use and mastery of empty concepts. See "The 'Empty Concepts' of Traditional Thinking."

45. The practice of speaking in tongues, also known as glossolalia, originates from the first Pentecostal preachers' application of Acts 2 to modern-day Christianity. In the passage, the Holy Spirit overpowers Jesus's disciples and speaks through them about God's glory in strange and otherwise undecipherable languages. Charles Parnham, a Kansas minister preaching in the late nineteenth century, asserted the relevance of this spiritual gift to contemporary times. William Seymour, a Black preacher and student of Parnham's, publicized speaking in tongues through the wildly popular Azusa Street revival in Los Angeles in 1906. See Luhrmann, *When God Talks Back*, 24–26, 334n.29–31. For general histories of Pentecostalism, see Cox, *Fire from Heaven*; Miller, *Reinventing American Protestantism*; Martin, *Pentecostalism*.

46. Garcia, *The Pastoral Clinic*, 68, 181.

47. Garcia, 182.

48. Garcia, 182.

49. Gilroy, *Postcolonial Melancholia*.

50. Gilroy, xv, 119.

51. Scholars of affect and public feeling, including those who write about the contemporary happiness turn, often reveal the deleterious consequences of happiness discourse, which incentivizes and lauds certain feelings and dispositions (upbeat, positive, happy), while discrediting and demeaning others (depressed, melancholic, negative). See Cvetkovich, *Depression*. Frequently, individuals from marginalized groups, like women, people of color, and migrants, are particularly demeaned for expressing feelings that depart from "happiness culture" (see, for instance, the entrenched tropes of the feminist "killjoy," the "angry Black woman," and the "melancholic" migrant). For such discussions, see Ahmed, *The Promise of Happiness*; Ahmed and Bonis, "Feminist Killjoys (and Other Willful Subjects)." Invoking Rose's writings on "governmentality of the soul" and Foucault's understanding of "biopower," these writings underscore how power, politics, and brute force penetrate and discipline the most intimate sphere of human experience, that of private feeling. As such, happiness discourse often reinforces oppression, hierarchy, and silencing, especially among the most disempowered members of society. See Rose, *Governing the Soul*; Foucault, *Society Must Be Defended*.

52. On the profitability of happiness discourse, see Davies, *The Happiness Industry*.

53. On the use and etymology of this phrase, see D. Stewart, "The Hermeneutics of Suspicion."

54. Rather than agitating for meaningful and just inclusion, Ahmed writes, happy migrants learn to strive for citizenship as the ultimate happy object. See *The Promise of Happiness*, 130–33.

55. Mattingly, *The Paradox of Hope*, 6.

Chapter 4

1. Several scholars have reflected on anthropology's enduring discomfort and "disciplinary nervousness" with Christianity. While ethnographers have frequently engaged with Christianity as "secondary phenomena" and "almost against their will," sustained engagement with the

particularities of Christian experience only began in earnest at the start of the twenty-first century. See, for example, Cannell, *The Anthropology of Christianity*; Robbins, "The Globalization of Pentecostal and Charismatic Christianity"; Robbins, "Anthropology and Theology"; Robbins, "The Anthropology of Christianity"; Coleman and Hackett, *The Anthropology of Global Pentecostalism and Evangelicalism*.

2. Robbins, "Beyond the Suffering Subject."

3. Marx, *Critique of Hegel's "Philosophy of Right."*

4. Lester in Richlin, "The Affective Therapeutics of Migrant Faith," 384.

5. Lester posits that religious vocation, or accepting one's calling from God, involves a therapeutic reconstitution of "self," especially for the Mexican women she considers in her monograph *Jesus in Our Wombs*. For novitiates, religious training conferred "authentic femininity" on women, which existed as a "third way" between the upwardly mobile career woman and the traditional homemaker that conventional Mexican gender norms prescribed.

6. In her work on the Mosque movement among Egyptian women, Saba Mahmood writes of the tendency to equate religious submission, especially among women, with an absence of agency. See Mahmood's essay "Feminist Theory and the Egyptian Islamic Revival" and her monograph on the subject, *Politics of Piety*.

7. Prominent historical and ethnographic studies in the field of Latin American Christianity examine the extent to which "Protestantization" or "evangelization" of the traditionally Catholic region serves to empower or further dispossess historically marginalized populations. See, for example, Stoll, *Is Latin America Turning Protestant?*; Bastian, "The Metamorphosis of Latin American Protestant Groups"; K. O'Neill, *City of God*; Vásquez, "Pentecostalism, Collective Identity, and Transnationalism among Salvadorans and Peruvians in the U.S."

8. Many ethnographic accounts on the subject of Latin American Christianity suggest that religious belonging and experience promote self-valorization. In turn, self-valorization generates broader political consciousness. See, for instance, Burdick's account of evangelical Christianity among Black Brazilians in *Blessed Anastácia* and "What Is the Color of the Holy Spirit?" For an analysis of religion's impact on women's self-esteem and political consciousness, see Drogus's monograph *Women, Religion, and Social Change in Brazil's Popular Church*. For discussions of self-respect and uplift among evangelical men in Venezuela, see Smilde, *Reason to Believe*.

9. For a summary of this scholarly debate, see Vásquez, "Pentecostalism, Collective Identity, and Transnationalism among Salvadorans and Peruvians in the U.S."

10. For ethnographic accounts of evangelical Christianity's emancipatory effects on marginalized populations across Latin America, see, for example, Burdick's analysis of Black Brazilian Pentecostal experience in his writings, *Blessed Anastácia*, "What Is the Color of the Holy Spirit?," and *Looking for God in Brazil*, as well as Mariz's study of Pentecostalism among Brazil's poor in *Coping with Poverty*. Also see Vásquez's study of transnational Salvadoran evangelicalism in "Pentecostalism, Collective Identity, and Transnationalism among Salvadorans and Peruvians in the U.S." For evangelical Christianity's ossifying effect, see Vásquez's succinct synopsis in the same article, which largely summarizes Bastian's work "The Metamorphosis of Latin American Protestant Groups."

11. John Locke's writings on the agency of individuals and their natural rights remain the touchstone of political liberalism. These discussions are contained in his *Two Treatises of*

Government (1689). John Stuart Mill expanded on Locke's initial statement in *On Liberty* (1859). For contemporary debates concerning the legitimacy and tenability of political liberalism, especially in regard to multiculturalism, see, for example, Rawls, *Political Liberalism*; Appiah, *The Ethics of Identity*; Taylor, "The Politics of Recognition"; Kymlicka, *Multicultural Citizenship*.

12. In this chapter, I find inspiration in Mahmood's writings in *Politics of Piety*. Like the Mosque movement, which emphasized increasing religious orthodoxy among women, the forms of evangelical Christianity I witnessed among migrants emphasized docility and submission to church and God. Despite its emergence out of the West, and its operation in the United States, the form of evangelical Christianity I observed appeared similar to the Muslim practices, self-understandings, and theological orientations of Mahmood's subjects.

13. Mahmood, "Feminist Theory and the Egyptian Islamic Revival," 208.

14. Mahmood, 210.

15. For an overview of the debate between intellectualism and materialism in the anthropology of religion, see Joel Robbins's comprehensive account in *Becoming Sinners*, 84–87.

16. For debates on sincerity within Christianity, see Webb Keane's comprehensive account in his monograph *Christian Moderns* and his article "Sincerity, 'Modernity,' and the Protestants." For debates on sincerity in the Brazilian context, see Clara Mafra's essay, "Santidade e sinceridade na formação da pessoa cristã."

17. In the Seventh-day Adventist and Baptist congregations, prayer generally remained quiet and contemplative. During the period of *oração* within each worship service, adherents often stood or kneeled with eyes closed, and gently nodded to the pastor's words or prompts. In the Pentecostal congregation, prayer was more active and much louder. Adherents pumped their fists, stomped their feet, let out yells, and swayed or jumped in response to the pastor and their experience of the Holy Spirit.

18. Evangelicals frequently contrasted the activity of evangelical prayer (*orar*) with Catholic prayer (*rezar*). According to the prevailing evangelical critique, Catholic prayer, based upon a set liturgy, required rote memorization and little feeling. In contrast, evangelical prayer depended upon spontaneously opening one's heart to God.

19. Pastor Jeferson's emphasis on loudness during prayer recalls Bruno Reinhardt's essay "Soaking in Tapes." Reinhardt reflects on the auditory impartation of grace among evangelicals in Ghana. By "soaking in tapes," Ghanaian evangelicals zealously listened to recorded sermons and absorbed their power, including the "touch" of their prophetic leader. Reinhardt identifies soaking in tapes as a "method of impartation that transposes laying on hands into a new sensorial realm." In this way, he writes, voice "replaces [the pastor's] hands as the material channel for an interpersonal flow of grace," 316. Among Brazilian migrants, praying loudly also indicated a "new sensorial realm" of the "interpersonal flow of grace." While individuals prayed loudly over one another, they also prayed loudly to God. In doing so, they compelled God to hear their prayers.

20. Anthropological studies of evangelical Christianity increasingly understand prayer to be an important form of action. This action extends from the ritual and religious realm into the worldly and secular realm. For example, Kevin O'Neill considers in his book, *City of God,* how Christian prayer efforts to "save" Guatemala reconstitute the meaning of national citizenship. In *When God Talks Back,* Tanya Luhrmann considers how prayer practices among American evangelicals dramatically alter an individual's sense perception and enable intimacy with God. Across religions, Luhrmann argues, recurrent and dedicated ritual, including prayer, makes

divinity real, felt, intimate, and consequential for believers across traditions; see *How God Be-comes Real*. Like Lévi-Strauss's analysis of Cuna birth incantations and the "efficacy of symbols," scholars increasingly recognize the far-reaching physiological and psychological impacts of prayer activity; see Lévi-Strauss, "The Effectiveness of Symbols." Not only do believers under-stand prayer to be significantly impacting their felt and lived realities by communicating with God, but observers increasingly confirm prayer's far-reaching consequences as well.

21. In her study of predominantly white and middle-class congregants of Vineyard Church, one of the most prominent evangelical nondenominational churches in the United States, Luhrmann considers prayer to be one of many spiritual disciplines that believers repeatedly "train," and aim to master, for the purpose of making God real, felt, and present. See *When God Talks Back*, 195.

22. Selection of survey responses to question #39, "When you pray, how do you know when God is present?"

23. "Crying in the presence of God" is one of six emotional practices that Luhrmann identi-fies as essential skills Vineyard congregants learn to experience proximity to God. Like psycho-therapy, she argues, these practices enable congregants to experience intense emotion in a safe setting. The generation of these deep feeling states enables internal transformation that becomes identified with the activity of God in one's life. I also witnessed in the churches I attended the other five practices Luhrmann identifies: "seeing from God's perspective," "practicing 'love, peace, and joy,'" "God the therapist," "reworking 'God the father,'" and "emotional cascades." *When God Talks Back*, 113–16.

24. As Luhrmann notes in *When God Talks Back*, when charismatic churches introduced the possibility for believers to directly experience God and God's miracles, they also introduced the possibility of charlatanism, p. 70. Like Vineyard congregants, pp. 47–60, Brazilian evangelicals also described experiencing God directly through prayer, prophecy, events, scripture, and dreams. For each of these experiences, however, believers were instructed to pray for discern-ment in order to correctly attribute and interpret the experience.

25. This is also in keeping with Luhrmann's findings regarding white American evangelicals in *When God Talks Back*, 64–65.

26. According to Maura, the management office at Appletree Condominiums, where many congregants from her church lived, required only a tax identification number rather than a social security number for a contract, making it an obvious choice for undocumented migrants of all nationalities.

27. Often interviewees considered their conversations with me to constitute *um testemunho*, a testimony of God's great and transformative power. Speaking about their lives to a nonbeliever presented an opportunity to testify.

28. Stephen, *We Are the Face of Oaxaca*, 2–3.

29. See scholarship on the role of religious and political testimony in mobilizing US social movements, especially among Black and migrant communities. On the role of testimony in Black churches and theology, see, for example, Warnock, *The Divided Mind of the Black Church*; and Pattillo-McCoy, "Church Culture as a Strategy of Action in the Black Community." On the role of secular testimony in decrying anti-Black racism more generally, see C. Jordan, "Bearing Witness to Testimonies of Antiblackness"; Schreiber, "Repressed Memory, Testimony, and Agency in Toni Morrison's *Home*." On the mobilization of testimony among Mexican migrant

communities, see, for example, Stephen, *We Are the Face of Oaxaca*; and Watt, *Farm Workers and the Churches*.

30. Stephen, *We Are the Face of Oaxaca*, 11.

31. Stephen, 34–35.

32. Migrant communities in Greater Washington, DC, frequently rented church space from other established congregations owing to high real estate costs in the area. The Pentecostal church where I spent most time, for instance, rented space from a predominantly Black Baptist congregation. Other congregations also rented the space, including a Spanish-speaking and a Korean-speaking congregation. This made meeting times somewhat unconventional. Rather than holding Sunday morning worship, the Brazilian church met on Sunday nights and three other weeknights from 8 p.m. to midnight.

33. Mattia Fumanti also suggests that migrants assert their political belonging through faith in his study of Ghanaian Methodists in London, "Virtuous Citizenship." Despite remaining formally without documents, Ghanaian migrants performed their belonging to the British polity as "virtuous citizens" through their faith. Much of Fumanti's claim centers around the historical relationship Ghanaian Methodists have to the Methodist Church and the British Empire as former colonial subjects. Here, I consider the relationship Brazilian migrants had to the United States—a polity to which they have no historical or legal claim. Yet, like Ghanaian Methodists, Brazilian evangelicals proclaimed their immense contribution to their host society. Not only did Brazilian migrants, like Ghanaians, contend that their host society depended on their manual labor and domestic services; they also asserted their spiritual contribution. Fumanti articulates this sentiment well, writing, "Just as industries such as the service sector, health, and caring were dependent on migrant labor, so too churches also needed the presence of migrants for their survival, growth and consolidation," 28.

34. Many migrants repeated this information to me. They told me that for every year they overstayed their tourist visa, the US government would make them wait another ten years to reapply for an official tourist visa. This collective wisdom corresponds with the US official policy, documented in the US Immigration and Nationality Act (1965) and amended in the 1990s. The policy imposes on migrants who enter the US without legal documents, or overstay their visas, "time bars" of three to ten years, depending on the period of unlawful presence. See Bray, "Consequences of Unlawful Presence in the U.S." In the event of a one-year period of "unlawful presence," migrants can be permanently inadmissible. See Bray, "The Permanent Bar to Immigration for Certain Repeat Violators."

35. *Visitas* designated individuals who attended church without accepting Jesus or becoming tithing members of the Pentecostal congregation.

36. Ephesians 6:13–17 NIV.

37. On national citizenship as the happy object par excellence for migrants, see Ahmed, *The Promise of Happiness*, 130–33. On evangelical forms of hope as passive and apathetic waiting, see two heavily cited articles on the subject: Guyer, "Prophecy and the Near Future," and Crapanzano, "Reflections on Hope as a Category of Social and Psychological Analysis."

38. Ethnographic studies of religion document how spiritual practices fundamentally alter subjective experience. For studies on how prayer shapes the mind, sense perception, and belief, see Luhrmann, "Metakinesis"; Luhrmann, *When God Talks Back*; Luhrmann, *How God Becomes Real*. For studies on how spiritual disciplines shape individual and collective identity, see Haeri,

"The Private Performance of Salat Prayers"; Bielo, *Words upon the Word*. For investigations on spiritual disciplines and gender identity and expression, see Lester, *Jesus in Our Wombs*. For spiritual disciplines and physical somatic healing, see Csordas, *The Sacred Self*. For how spiritual disciplines impact individual and collective morals, ethics, and identity, see Robbins, *Becoming Sinners*; and Ikeuchi, *Jesus Loves Japan*. In this body of work, scholars demonstrate how frequent engagement in socially embedded spiritual disciplines like prayer recitation, ecstatic worship, group Bible study, and healing rituals profoundly change how individuals perceive themselves and their world.

39. Anthropological studies of subjectivity frequently study personhood and the construction of self in relation to power, politics, domination, and suffering. See Biehl, Good, and Kleinman, *Subjectivity*. Much of this literature adopts Foucauldian frameworks of "biopower," "technologies of power," and "governmentality," which document the insidiousness of power, and how violence, oppression, and domination enter the body and mind and shape our most personal desires and thoughts. This literature is further influenced by Nikolas Rose's consideration of "therapeutics," regarding how "experts" manipulate individual capacities and desires. Alternative approaches modify this understanding of subjectivity with a psychological model of emotion as socially and culturally embedded. See Luhrmann, "Subjectivity."

40. This perspective is not new. Rather, it revives the long-held argument within the anthropology of religion that religion's efficacy lies precisely in these kinds of socially embedded subjective transformations. See, for example, classic anthropological writings on religion, including Turner, *The Ritual Process*; Geertz, "Religion as a Cultural System"; Lévi-Strauss, "The Effectiveness of Symbols."

Chapter 5

1. Eleven out of 49 survey respondents indicated that they had left Catholicism after migrating to the United States. This figure includes 3 Baptists, 3 Pentecostals, 2 Spiritists, and 3 "Other affiliated." During formal interviews, 17 out of 78 Brazilian migrants shared that they had formally left Catholicism after moving to the United States. By denomination, this includes 6 Baptists, 5 Pentecostals, 4 Spiritists, and 2 "Other affiliated." It is important to note that almost all of the Adventists I interviewed and surveyed, except for two, identified as Adventist from birth. I found the same to be true for many Pentecostals I interviewed. Yet, as indicated in chapter 1, a significant number of these migrants had experienced a period of distancing (*afastamento*) prior to migration and cited migrant experience in the United States as motivating their religious intensification and/or reconversion.

2. Several previous studies have compared the Catholic Church's and evangelical churches' relationship to Brazilian migrant populations. In contrast to my findings, Sheringham suggests that the Catholic Church generates greater support among Brazilians in London by producing an enclave of Brazilian identity, language, and culture. Evangelical churches in London, she writes, remain more "multicultural," and less tied to Brazilian culture and identity. See *Transnational Religious Spaces*, 84. In Washington, DC, and the US more generally, I found the opposite to be true. Whereas the Catholic Church emphasized multiculturalism, evangelical churches remained enclaves of Brazilian identity, led exclusively by Brazilian-born pastors. My findings support Freston's conclusions suggesting that Brazilians leave the Catholic Church in diaspora

in favor of evangelical churches' "theology of the undocumented"; see his essay "The Religious Field among Brazilians in the United States," 264–66. Freston further suggests that evangelical churches succeed among migrants owing to their "non-territorial" nature, thus enabling organizational flexibility and local autonomy, as opposed to the hierarchical and centralized structure of the Catholic Church, 261–63. In her comparative study of the Catholic Church and evangelical churches among Brazilians in Boston, Martes suggests that migrants' engagement with the Catholic Church results in a "culture clash" and profound alienation, while evangelical churches assuage homesickness through Brazilian culture and community. See her discussion in *New Immigrants, New Land*, 84.

3. According to popular mythology, fishermen discovered a statue of the Virgin Mary in 1717 during a severe fish shortage in the Paraíba River Valley, located in the state of São Paulo. Following their discovery, the fishermen's boats filled with fish, inciting fervent Marian devotion. The statue was thereafter known as Nossa Senhora de Aparecida (Our Lady of Aparecida) and deemed the patron saint of Brazil. The most celebrated feast day among Brazilian Catholics occurs on October 12, in Nossa Senhora de Aparecida's honor. See Brittanica Escola's web entry, "Nossa Senhora Aparecida." Several ethnographic studies analyze popular Catholicism in Brazil, including Marian devotion. See, for example, Burdick, *Looking for God in Brazil*; Burdick, *Blessed Anastácia*; Drogus, *Women, Religion, and Social Change in Brazil's Popular Church*.

4. Several studies have confirmed Brazilian migrants' discomfort and frustration with racial binaries in the United States. See Falconi and Mazzotti's edited volume *The Other Latinos*. In contrast to the entrenched Black/white dichotomy in the United States based on legacies of racial classification based on hypodescent, in Brazil, the racial spectrum includes multiple classifications between "Black" (*negro*) and "white" (*branco*), such as *pardo* and *moreno*, both terms referring to mixed African, European, and Indigenous heritage. The Brazilian census allows individuals to "write in" their own racial classifications, resulting in over two hundred recognized racial categories. See Joseph, *Race on the Move*, 37. Anecdotally, many Brazilians shared that they had never thought about racial categorizations until they moved to the United States, where others described them as "Black" or "white." Several scholars note that the US Census's question on race presents Brazilians with this quandary most concretely: not African American, White/Non-Hispanic, or Hispanic, Brazilians often opt to leave this question blank, or write in their self-designation. For further discussions, see Joseph, *Race on the Move*; Martes, "Neither Hispanic, nor Black."

5. At one point during the Mass, Bishop Loverde called for an increase of "vocations" (young people entering the religious life) from multicultural groups and not just the "Anglo" community.

6. In reference to his own lexicon in *Blessed Anastácia*, I utilize Burdick's terminology, "Afro-Brazilian," while discussing his findings. In recent years, other terminology has gained prominence, including "Black Brazilian" (*negro brasileiro* in Portuguese), or "Brazilian of African descent" in English. It is important to note that growing numbers of Brazilians embrace Black identity, self-identifying as *negro* on the census. Scholars suggest that this shifting pattern of self-identification stems from the prominence of the Black civil rights and consciousness movement, Movimento Negro, as well as growing representation and celebration of Black Brazilians throughout all segments of society. For these findings, see Jesus and Hoffman, "De norte a sul, de leste a oeste."

7. Burdick, *Blessed Anastácia*, 94.

8. Frazer, *The Golden Bough*.

9. Tylor, "Animism."

10. Said, *Orientalism*.

11. The culture and personality school, championed by Ruth Benedict and Margaret Mead, considered "cultures" to be contiguous with national territorial boundaries. See Benedict, *The Chrysanthemum and the Sword*, and Mead, *Growing Up in New Guinea*. Clifford Geertz's "interpretive model" of culture, defining culture as shared meanings and symbols that must be "read" by ethnographers, has also drawn criticism. For Geertz's approach, see *The Interpretation of Cultures*. For a critique, see Talal Asad's famous argument that the interpretivist and symbolic approach imbued the Western ethnographer with the "power to create meaning"; *Genealogies of Religion*, 194.

12. In 1887, the bishop of Piacenza, Italy, John Baptist Scalabrini, launched the mission in the United States to expressly serve migrants in their transition to the US. The order was founded in the period of massive emigration of European migrants to the United States. As stated on their website, the order currently works in thirty-two countries, ministering to refugees and migrants. For more information, see their web page, "Scalabrinians: Missionaries of St. Charles."

13. Brazilian Catholics celebrate Nossa Senhora de Aparecida, Brazil's patron saint, on October 12, and venerate St. John the Baptist, St. Anthony, and St. Peter during the month of June, in celebrations called Festas Juninas.

14. Given the small number of Spiritist centers in the Greater Washington region, and to protect the privacy of study participants, I have chosen to withhold information regarding geographical location of centers and instead identify centers according to pseudonyms (Center of Healing and Peace, Washington Kardecistas).

15. It is important to note that the therapeutics I discuss in relation to Spiritism remains quite distinct from the therapeutics of other Brazilian religions such as Candomblé or Umbanda. In the latter groups, spirit possession stimulates healing, according to some researchers, through reconstituting the self. See Seligman, "The Unmaking and Making of Self"; Seligman, *Possessing Spirits and Healing Selves*. Spiritists do not practice spirit possession, and very strongly reject any kinship with religions that do employ such practices. Instead, trained experts, called mediums, converse with spirits, and provide "spiritual counseling" to adherents based on these exchanges. I suggest that Spiritist therapeutics, like evangelical therapeutics, depends upon the production of good feeling and positive frames of interpretation through faith practices.

16. Because scant, if any, research on Spiritism among Brazilians in the United States exists, I was unable to find concrete numbers concerning migrant "conversion" to the movement. I reached the conclusion of Spiritist growth in the United States ethnographically, through interviews, surveys, and informal conversations. My impression was corroborated during interviews with three presidents of area centers. Each president remarked on migrants' novel "openness" and "emotional need" for Spiritism in the United States. In order to confirm such impressionistic findings, however, long-term study of Spiritism in the United States is needed.

17. While Spiritism defines itself as a Christian movement promoting "Christ consciousness," most mainstream Christians would vehemently oppose the inclusion of the movement as Christian. Instead of following the Bible, Spiritists adhere to principles outlined in texts written and "psycho-graphed," received through mediumship, by Allan Kardec, including, most

notably, *The Gospel According to Spiritism*. The volume presents a reinterpretation of the New Testament based on Spiritist principles. Another volume, based on Kardec's telepathic conversations with "the highest minds" in the Spirit realm, provides advice for daily living. See Kardec, *The Spirits' Book*. Among other significant divergences from mainstream Christianity, Spiritists reject the existence of Heaven and Hell, insist on the centrality of reincarnation, and believe that each individual is born with a "spirit mentor" who assists them throughout multiple incarnations.

18. The event was held in celebration of the 150th anniversary of the release of Kardec's *The Gospel According to Spiritism*. Attendees received a free copy of the text.

19. I was often struck by Spiritists' representation of their beliefs as fundamentally Christian. During interviews, individuals told me that their families had embraced their beliefs because, they stressed, "it's the same God." Spiritists represented Jesus as the "governor" of Earth, and therefore, the most elevated spirit. Spiritist teachings originated in the four Gospels, making frequent references to New Testament biblical stories during lectures common. However, Spiritists reinterpret these texts through Kardec's *The Gospel According to Spiritism*.

20. Ahmed, *The Promise of Happiness*, 8–9.

21. Vera's comments, equating Baltimore, a city that maintains a Black majority population, with "poverty" and "ignorance," rehearses well-worn racist tropes in the United States. Former president Donald Trump gained infamy in 2019 for broadcasting similar language in his attack against former congressman Elijah Cummings, calling Baltimore "disgusting, rat- and rodent-infested," and "very dangerous." See coverage in P. Baker, "Trump Assails Elijah Cummings, Calling His Congressional District a Rat-Infested 'Mess.'"

22. Spiritists believe that each human being is born with a "spirit mentor," an "elevated mind" who guides them through multiple lives toward enlightenment.

23. While Regina and several other Spiritists told me about the workshop, "Spiritist Therapy for the Immigrant," during the time of my research, it was no longer offered regularly. Therefore, I was never able to attend. Because she planned to publish her findings about migration and Spiritism in a Spiritist publication, Regina explained that she did not feel comfortable sharing her data, slides, or survey prior to publication.

Chapter 6

1. Scholars of Christianity, and evangelical Christianity in particular, have long understood conversion stories to cohere to a standard narrative arc. These stories often relate to being "lost" prior to encounter, and through communing with God, attaining spiritual awakening, evidenced through health, joy, and blessing. See descriptions of specific narrative tropes in Lehmann, *Struggle for the Spirit*; Chesnut, *Competitive Spirits*; Chesnut, *Born Again in Brazil*; Harding, *The Book of Jerry Falwell*; Stromberg, *Language and Self-Transformation*; Rambo, *Understanding Religious Conversion*.

2. Migrants' conversion narratives generally cohered with the "stage model" of conversion delineated by Lewis Rambo, progressing through seven narrative elements: (1) context, (2) crisis, (3) quest, (4) encounter, (5) interaction, (6) commitment, and (7) consequences. See Rambo, *Understanding Religious Conversion*, 16–18. In my discussion, I condense these elements into three stages of conversion: sinfulness, encounter, and rebirth. For migrants, these

stages mapped onto specific geographies where sinfulness was associated with premigration experience in Brazil, and encounter and rebirth associated with postmigration experience in the United States.

3. Anthropologists of Christianity understand "discontinuity" to be a defining characteristic of evangelical conversion, especially among non-Western and nonwhite populations where conversion constitutes a significant "break" with traditional customs, rituals, and beliefs. For writings on discontinuity, see, for example, Matthew Engelke's writings on apostolic Christianity in Zimbabwe, "Discontinuity and the Discourse of Conversion"; *A Problem of Presence*. Also see Birgit Meyer's ethnographic account of Pentecostalism in Ghana, *Translating the Devil*.

4. Several ethnographic accounts document the intensification of evangelical experience and conversion among individuals postmigration. On Brazilians in Japan, see Ikeuchi, *Jesus Loves Japan*. On Brazilians, Jamaicans, and Ghanaians in the UK, see Sheringham, *Transnational Religious Spaces*; Toulis, *Believing Identity*; Fumanti, "Virtuous Citizenship." On Koreans and Salvadorans in the US, see Park, "'Born Again'"; Chen, *Getting Saved in America*; Williams, Steigenga, and Vásquez, *A Place to Be*.

5. Ikeuchi, *Jesus Loves Japan*, 79.

6. Ikeuchi, 84.

7. Fumanti, "Virtuous Citizenship."

8. Ikeuchi, *Jesus Loves Japan*, 185.

9. Regarding the centrality of rejecting ancestral tradition, custom, and ritual in Ghanaian Pentecostalism, see B. Meyer's essay "Make a Complete Break with the Past." Regarding the making of moral sense of traumatic occurrences through "emplotment" and "narrativity," see Cheryl Mattingly's *Healing Dramas and Clinical Plots*.

10. Mattingly, *Healing Dramas and Clinical Plots*, 29.

11. Stromberg, *Language and Self-Transformation*, 4.

12. Rambo, *Understanding Religious Conversion*, xii.

13. Despite their insistence on radical "born-again" conversion, migrant evangelical churches also tacitly acknowledged the incompleteness of conversion. Pastors warned their congregants to defend against "tepid" faith and what one congregant called "the slow fade"—the gradual falling away from God. Pastors admonished congregants to actively work to feel God present in their daily lives. This was the work of returning to one's *primeiro amor*, first love, for God. The premise of affective therapeutics acknowledged the requirement of frequent and repeated engagement with discursive practices, spiritual disciplines, and Christian fellowship as an antidote to the "slow fade" of casual faith, and as a way to bolster *primeiro amor*.

14. St. John of the Cross, a Spanish friar, first used the phrase "dark night of the soul" in a sixteenth-century religious poem to describe a lonely spiritual crisis that ultimately led to deepening faith. Scholars of religion have long used the phrase to describe the profound spiritual crisis that precedes religious awakening. See, for example, William James's well-known account, originally published in 1902, *The Varieties of Religious Experience*. For relevance in the fields of anthropology and psychological anthropology, see Gananath Obeyesekere's reflections in his books, *The Awakened Ones*, *The Work of Culture*, and *Medusa's Hair*.

15. While clergy insisted upon their congregation's and denomination's special favor in God's eyes, most evangelical migrants I met repeatedly diminished the importance of their congregation's denominational affiliation. Instead, they insisted upon a clear demarcation

between those who truly "followed Jesus" and those who did not. Such rhetorical oppositions reflected Brazil's religious binary between Catholics (*católicos*) and evangelicals (*evangélicos* or *crentes*). Most fundamental to my research, evangelical faith and belonging among migrants depended on an understanding of God as an attentive, loving, responsive, and physically felt divinity.

16. The Universal Church of the Kingdom of God (Igreja Universal do Reino de Deus, IURD) and its founder, Edir Macedo, have attracted public scrutiny and scorn for thirty years. For comprehensive discussions of the church, see, for example, S. Romero, "Brazil on Edge as World Cup Exposes Rift"; Birman and Leite, "Whatever Happened to the Largest Catholic Country in the World?"; Reuters, "Brazil to Investigate Evangelical Church's Funds." One of the more well-known scandals in the United States involved Estevam and Sonia Hernandes, prominent Brazilian Pentecostal preachers who were caught smuggling money into the United States, with $9,000 cash hidden in their Bibles. See Rohter, "Brazilian Pentecostal Leaders Caught in a Scandal." More recently, Brazilian Pentecostal preacher and gospel singer Flordelis dos Santos de Souza was suspected of aiding and abetting her husband's murder. See Anderson, "The Murder Scandalizing Brazil's Evangelical Church."

17. Father Bernardo's statement echoed scholarly work comparing the religious landscape in Latin America to a salvation "market." See Chesnut, *Competitive Spirits*.

18. Scholarly writings that reflect on the comparative growth of evangelical Christianity among Brazilian and Latin American migrants often underscore the material benefits migrants derive from conversion. See, for example, Margolis, *Little Brazil*; Martes, *New Immigrants, New Land*; Williams, Steigenga, and Vásquez, *A Place to Be*.

19. Before 1990, Cláudia explained, green card holders (legal permanent residents) could petition to bring their adult children to the United States with the same status.

20. At the close of my fieldwork in September 2014, I learned that the group was planning its first ever retreat, bringing together Brazilian Catholics from the region and hosting a CCR priest from Brazil for the first time.

21. In traditional Catholicism, parishioners do not have firsthand experience of God but must access God through clergy. God the Father is viewed as remote, formal, and all-powerful. In order to bridge this gap, Catholics often pray to Mary or saints as "intercessors" that can bring their everyday concerns to God's attention. In Spiritism, God also remains somewhat aloof, and authorizes the "higher minds" and "spirits" to engage regularly with human beings. Despite these formal tenets, however, Catholic and Spiritist migrants noted they had forged deeply intimate and embodied relationships with God, understood exclusively in Christocentric and monotheistic terms.

Conclusion

1. In 2014, the national progressive party, the Workers' Party, governed Brazil through a series of progressive reforms. Lauded internationally for reducing poverty and inequality in Brazil, these provided cash assistance for the poor through the Bolsa Família program, and also put in place policies protecting affirmative action and green climate initiatives. At the time, the current president, Jair Bolsonaro, was a regionally known congressman in a minority party, whose vitriolic and divisive statements represented Brazilian politics' extreme right wing.

2. Although the Supreme Court ruled against Trump's immediate ending of the DACA program on procedural grounds on June 18, 2020, and the Biden administration fully reinstated the program by executive order on January 21, 2021, the program was ruled unlawful by a federal judge on July 16, 2021. While the Biden administration plans to appeal the decision, long term protection for DACA recipients and their parents depends upon a permanent legislative solution granting a pathway to citizenship. While President Biden's immigration bill, the US Citizenship Act of 2021, includes a permanent pathway to citizenship for DACA recipients and all eligible undocumented migrants in the US, it has not yet been passed. For coverage, see Shear, "Biden's Immigration Plan Would Offer Path to Citizenship for Millions"; Sotomayor, "Biden Will Pledge to Tackle Immigration Overhaul in Address to Congress"; M. Jordan, "Judge Rules DACA Is Unlawful and Suspends Applications."

3. In addition to expanding the "Muslim ban," the Trump administration enhanced the militarization of the US-Mexico border, foreclosing pathways to legal asylum through the "Remain in Mexico" program and its proposed "merit-based" immigration system. Experts also point to the untold damage the Trump presidency wrought on immigration through "an extensive, unpublicized bureaucratic effort to transform immigration through rule changes, adjustment to asylum officers' guidelines, modifications to enforcement norms, and more." While President Biden quickly dismantled many of Trump's most notorious and egregious anti-immigrant efforts on his first day of office by executive order, undoing the Trump administration's widespread, consequential, and pernicious administrative changes will be a much longer endeavor. See the investigative report by Stillman, "The Race to Dismantle Trump's Immigration Policies," and the compilation of anthropological perspectives on *Hot Spots* edited by Almendariz, Brennan, and Oliveira, "The Damage Wrought." Furthermore, in the wake of unprecedented numbers of migrants arriving at the southern border in 2021, the Biden administration retained Title 42, an emergency public health measure utilized by the Trump administration to quickly turn away migrants during a pandemic. Under the policy, the Biden administration presided over 1 million deportations of migrants in 2021 alone. The enduring use of this policy has drawn ire from immigrant rights' activists, and undermined Biden's promise to overhaul migration. For coverage, see Sullivan and Jordan, "Illegal Border Crossings, Driven by Pandemic and Natural Disasters, Soar to Record High"; "It's Time to End the Pandemic Emergency at the Border."

4. Following Trump's impeachment trial in January 2020, he enjoyed a 49 percent approval rating, the highest of his presidency. See "Presidential Approval Ratings—Donald Trump."

5. De Genova, "Migrant 'Illegality' and Deportability in Everyday Life."

6. Large-scale public health and psychological studies have documented the negative bodily and psychic toll migration exacts. Regarding increased rates of substance abuse among migrants, see Borges et al., "The Mexican Migration to the US and Substance Use in Northern Mexico"; Borges et al., "Substance Use and Cumulative Exposure to American Society." Regarding increased rates of anxiety and depression, see Suárez-Orozco, Bang, and Kim, "I Felt Like My Heart Was Staying Behind"; Suárez-Orozco, "Identities under Siege"; Potochnick and Perreira, "Depression and Anxiety among First-Generation Immigrant Latino Youth"; Gulbas et al., "Deportation Experiences and Depression among U.S. Citizen-Children with Undocumented Mexican Parents."

7. In 2016, the American Immigration Council, a DC-based immigration rights advocacy organization, estimated that 25,000 undocumented migrants lived in Washington. This estimate

does not include the number of undocumented migrants living in Greater Washington, DC. See "Immigrants in the District of Columbia."

8. See, for example, scholarship on volunteerism in Europe, including Muehlebach, *The Moral Neoliberal*; Malkki, *The Need to Help*. Additionally, see scholarship on faith-based philanthropy in the United States, including Adams, *Markets of Sorrow, Labors of Faith*; Elisha, *Moral Ambition*; Streensland and Goff, *The New Evangelical Social Engagement*.

9. On the use of faith-based programs in addiction recovery, prison, and sex education, see, for example, F. Kramer, "The Role for Public Funding of Faith-Based Organizations Delivering Behavioral Health Services"; Runions, "Immobile Theologies, Carceral Affects"; Slominski, "How Religion Made Modern Sex Ed."

10. Adams, *Markets of Sorrow, Labors of Faith*.

11. Elisha, *Moral Ambition*.

12. Adams, *Markets of Sorrow, Labors of Faith*, 131.

13. See Elisha, *Moral Ambition*, concerning US evangelical Christians' impulse to engage with suffering "Others" for the purpose of self-edification and the ushering in of God's Kingdom.

BIBLIOGRAPHY

Abu-Lughod, Lila. *Veiled Sentiments: Honor and Poetry in a Bedouin Society.* Berkeley: University of California Press, 1986.

Adams, Vincanne. *Markets of Sorrow, Labors of Faith: New Orleans in the Wake of Katrina.* Durham: Duke University Press, 2013.

Ahmed, Sara. *The Promise of Happiness.* Durham: Duke University Press, 2010.

Ahmed, Sara, and Oristelle Bonis. "Feminist Killjoys (and Other Willful Subjects)." *Cahiers du Genre* 53, no. 2 (2012): 77–98.

Alba, Richard, Albert J. Raboteau, and Josh DeWind, eds. *Immigration and Religion in America: Comparative and Historical Perspectives.* New York: New York University Press, 2009.

Allison, Anne. *Precarious Japan.* Durham: Duke University Press, 2013.

Almendariz, Xitlalli Alvarez, Denise Brennan, and Gabrielle Oliveira. "The Damage Wrought: Immigration before, under, and after Trump." *Hot Spots, Fieldsights,* October 19, 2021. https://culanth.org/fieldsights/series/the-damage-wrought-immigration-before-under-and-after-trump.

Althoff, Andrea. "Religious Identities of Latin American Immigrants in Chicago: Preliminary Findings of Field Research." Religion and Culture Web Forum, 2006. https://www.academia.edu/22811997/Religion_and_Culture_Web_Forum_RELIGIOUS_IDENTITIES_OF_LATIN_AMERICAN_IMMIGRANTS_IN_CHICAGO_PRELIMINARY_FINDINGS_FROM_FIELD_RESEARCH.

Alves, José Cláudio Souza. "Immigrant Regime of Production: The State, Political Mobilization, and Religion and Business Networks among Brazilians in South Florida." In *A Place to Be: Brazilian, Guatemalan, and Mexican Immigrants in Florida's New Destinations,* edited by Philip J. Williams, Timothy J. Steigenga, and Manuel A. Vásquez, 128–50. New Brunswick: Rutgers University Press, 2009.

"American Idol Contestant's Heartbreaking Song." YouTube video, 2011. https://www.youtube.com/watch?v=okPskDrUvAU.

Anderson, John Lee. "The Murder Scandalizing Brazil's Evangelical Church." *New Yorker,* June 7, 2021. https://www.newyorker.com/magazine/2021/06/14/the-murder-scandalizing-brazils-evangelical-church.

Andersson, Ruben. "Time and the Migrant Other: European Border Controls and the Temporal Economics of Illegality." *American Anthropologist* 116, no. 4 (2014): 795–809.

Aparecida dos Santos, Gislene. "O caso dos migrantes da cidade de Criciúma Brasil para os Estados Unidos." *Scripta Nova* 5 (2001). https://raco.cat/index.php/ScriptaNova/article/view/58868.

Appiah, Kwame Anthony. *The Ethics of Identity*. Princeton: Princeton University Press, 1994.

Asad, Talal. *Genealogies of Religion: Discipline and Reasons of Power in Christianity and Islam*. Baltimore: Johns Hopkins University Press, 1993.

Assis, Gláucia de Oliveira. "De Criciúma para o mundo: Gênero, família e migração." *Campos— Revista de Antropologia* 3 (2003): 31–49.

Baer, Hans, and Merrill Singer. "Toward a Typology of Black Sectarianism." *Anthropological Quarterly* 54, no. 1 (1981): 1–14.

Baker, Bryan. "Population Estimates Illegal Alien Population Residing in the United States: January 2015." Office of Immigration Statistics, Homeland Security. December 2018. https://www.dhs.gov/sites/default/files/publications/18_1214_PLCY_pops-est-report.pdf.

Baker, Peter. "Trump Assails Elijah Cummings, Calling His Congressional District a Rat-Infested 'Mess.'" *New York Times*, July 27, 2019. https://www.nytimes.com/2019/07/27/us/politics/trump-elijah-cummings.html.

Bastian, Pierre. "The Metamorphosis of Latin American Protestant Groups: A Sociohistorical Perspective." *Latin American Research Review* 28, no. 2 (1993): 33–61.

Beatty, Andrew. "Current Emotion Research in Anthropology: Reporting the Field." *Emotion Review* 5, no. 4 (2013): 414–22.

Benedict, Ruth. *The Chrysanthemum and the Sword: Patterns of Japanese Culture*. 1946. New York: Mariner Books, 1989.

———. *Patterns of Culture*. 1934. Boston: Houghton Mifflin, 2005.

Berlant, Lauren, ed. *Compassion: The Culture and Politics of an Emotion*. New York: Routledge, 2004.

———. *Cruel Optimism*. Durham: Duke University Press, 2011.

Bethell, Leslie. "Brazil and 'Latin America.'" *Journal of Latin American Studies* 42, no. 3 (2010): 457–85.

Bialecki, Jon. "After the Denominozoic: Evolution, Differentiation and Denominationalism." *Cultural Anthropology* 55, no. S10 (2014): S193–204.

———. "Between Stewardship and Sacrifice: Agency and Economy in a Southern California Charismatic Church." *Journal of the Royal Anthropological Institute* 14, no. 2 (2008): 372–90.

———. *Diagram for Fire: Miracles and Variation in an American Charismatic Movement*. Oakland: University of California Press, 2017.

Bialecki, Jon, Naomi Haynes, and Joel Robbins. "The Anthropology of Christianity." *Religion Compass* 2, no. 6 (2008): 1139–58.

Biehl, João. *Vita: Life in a Zone of Social Abandonment*. Berkeley: University of California Press, 2005.

———. *Will to Live: AIDS Therapies and the Politics of Survival*. Princeton: Princeton University Press, 2007.

Biehl, João, Byron Good, and Arthur Kleinman, eds. *Subjectivity: Ethnographic Investigations*. Berkeley: University of California Press, 2007.

Bielo, James. *Emerging Evangelicals: Faith, Modernity, and the Desire for Authenticity*. New York: New York University Press, 2011.

———. *Words upon the Word: An Ethnography of Group Bible Study*. New York: New York University Press, 2009.

Birman, Patricia, and Márcia Pereira Leite. "Whatever Happened to the Largest Catholic Country in the World?" *Daedalus* 129, no. 2 (2000): 271–90.

Blizzard, Brittany, and Jeanne Batalova. "Brazilian Immigrants in the United States." *Migration Information Source*, August 29, 2019. https://www.migrationpolicy.org/print/16578#.XbdU80VKhYg.

Boccagni, Paolo, and Peter Kivisto. "Introduction: Ambivalence and the Social Processes of Immigrant Inclusion." *International Journal of Comparative Sociology* 60, no. 1–2 (2019): 3–13.

Boellstorff, Tom, and Johan Lindquist. "Bodies of Emotion: Rethinking Culture and Emotion through Southeast Asia." *Ethnos* 69, no. 4 (2004): 437–44.

Borges, Guilherme, Cheryl J. Cherpitel, Ricardo Orozco, Sarah E. Zemore, Lynn Wallisch, Maria-Elena Medina-Mora, and Joshua Breslau. "Substance Use and Cumulative Exposure to American Society: Findings from Both Sides of the US–Mexico Border Region." *American Journal of Public Health* 106, no. 1 (2016): 119–27.

Borges, Guilherme, Maria-Elena Medina-Mora, Ricardo Orozco, Clara Fleiz, Cheryl Cherpitel, and Joshua Breslau. "The Mexican Migration to the US and Substance Use in Northern Mexico." *Addiction* 104, no. 4 (2009): 603–11.

Boyer, Pascal. "The 'Empty Concepts' of Traditional Thinking: A Semantic and Pragmatic Description." *Man* 21, no. 1 (1986): 50–64.

Brantlinger, Patrick. *Rule of Darkness: British Literature and Imperialism, 1830–1914*. Ithaca: Cornell University Press, 2013.

Bray, Ilona. "Consequences of Unlawful Presence in the U.S.: Three-Year and Ten-Year Time Bars." Www.Nolo.Com. n.d. Accessed April 14, 2020. https://www.nolo.com/legal-encyclopedia/free-books/fiance-marriage-visa-book/chapter2-4.html.

———. "The Permanent Bar to Immigration for Certain Repeat Violators." Www.Nolo.Com. n.d. Accessed April 14, 2020. https://www.nolo.com/legal-encyclopedia/the-permanent-bar-immigration-certain-repeat-violators.html.

Breslau, Joshua, Guilherme Borges, Daniel Tancredi, Naomi Saito, Richard Kravitz, Ladson Hinton, William Vega, Maria-Elena Medina-Mora, and Sergio Aguilar-Gaxiola. "Migration from Mexico to the United States and Subsequent Risk for Depressive and Anxiety Disorders: A Cross-National Study." *Archives of General Psychiatry* 68, no. 4 (2011): 428–33.

Brick, Kate, Michael Jones-Correra, and Audrey Singer. "Local Goes National: Challenges and Opportunities for Latino Immigrants in the Nation's Capital. Reports on Latino Immigrant Civic Engagement, No. 2." Washington, DC: Woodrow Wilson International Center for Scholars, 2009.

Briggs, Jean. *Never in Anger: Portrait of an Eskimo Family*. Cambridge: Harvard University Press, 1970.

Brittanica Escola. "Nossa Senhora Aparecida." Accessed November 15, 2021. https://escola.britannica.com.br/artigo/Nossa-Senhora-Aparecida/483071.

Bull, Malcolm, and Keith Lockhart. *Seeking a Sanctuary: Seventh Day Adventism and the American Dream*. 2nd ed. Bloomington: Indiana University Press, 2007.

Burdick, John. *Blessed Anastácia: Women, Race, and Popular Christianity in Brazil*. New York: Routledge, 1998.

———. *Looking for God in Brazil: The Progressive Catholic Church in Urban Brazil's Religious Arena*. Berkeley: University of California Press, 1996.

———. "What Is the Color of the Holy Spirit? Pentecostalism and Black Identity in Brazil." *Latin American Research Review* 34, no. 2 (1999): 109–31.

Burnham, Linda, and Nik Theodore. *Home Economics: The Invisible and Unregulated World of Domestic Work*. New York: National Domestic Workers Alliance, 2012.

Butler, Judith. *Giving an Account of Oneself*. New York: Fordham University Press, 2005.

Cacioppo, John T., and William Patrick. *Loneliness: Human Nature and the Need for Social Connection*. New York: W. W. Norton, 2009.

Caldeira, Teresa. *City of Walls: Crime, Segregation and Citizenship in São Paulo*. Berkeley: University of California Press, 2001.

Cannell, Fenella, ed. *The Anthropology of Christianity*. Durham: Duke University Press, 2006.

Cary, Francine Curro, ed. *Urban Odyssey: Multicultural History of Washington D.C.* Washington, DC: Smithsonian, 1996.

"CASA de Maryland." Accessed February 7, 2020. http://www.wearecasa.org/.

Cassaniti, Julia. *Living Buddhism: Mind, Self and Emotion in a Thai Community*. Ithaca: Cornell University Press, 2015.

"Centro de Pesquisas Ellen G. White." Accessed May 6, 2016. http://centrowhite.org.br.

Chavez, Leo R. *Shadowed Lives: Undocumented Immigrants in American Society*. Fort Worth: Harcourt Brace, 1998.

Chen, Carolyn. *Getting Saved in America: Taiwanese Immigration and Religious Experience*. Princeton: Princeton University Press, 2008.

———. "A Self of One's Own: Taiwanese Immigrant Women and Religious Conversion." *Gender and Society* 19, no. 3 (2005): 336–57.

Chesnut, Andrew. *Born Again in Brazil: The Pentecostal Boom and the Pathogens of Poverty*. New Brunswick: Rutgers University Press, 1997.

———. *Competitive Spirits: Latin America's New Religious Economy*. New York: Oxford University Press, 2003.

Chireau, Yvonne, and Nathaniel Deutsch, eds. *Black Zion: African American Religious Encounters with Judaism*. New York: Oxford University Press, 2000.

Cobb, Michael. "Lonely." *South Atlantic Quarterly* 106, no. 3 (2007): 445–57.

Coleman, Simon, and Rosalind I. J. Hackett, eds. *The Anthropology of Global Pentecostalism and Evangelicalism*. New York: New York University Press, 2015.

Comaroff, Jean, and John Comaroff. *Of Revolution and Revelation*. Vol. 1, *Christianity, Colonialism and Consciousness in South Africa*. Chicago: University of Chicago Press, 1991.

Cox, Harvey. *Fire from Heaven: The Rise of Pentecostal Spirituality and the Reshaping of Religion in the 21st Century*. Cambridge: Da Capo Press, 2001.

Crapanzano, Vincent. "Reflections on Hope as a Category of Social and Psychological Analysis." *Cultural Anthropology* 18, no. 1 (2003): 3–32.

———. *Tuhami: Portrait of a Moroccan*. Chicago: University of Chicago Press, 1980.

Cruz, Antonio. "Poor Mental Health: An Obstacle to Development in Latin America." World Bank. 2015. https://www.worldbank.org/en/news/feature/2015/07/13/bad-mental-health -obstacle-development-latin-america.

Csordas, Thomas. *The Sacred Self: A Cultural Phenomenology of Charismatic Healing*. Berkeley: University of California Press, 1997.

Cvetkovich, Ann. *Depression: A Public Feeling*. Durham: Duke University Press, 2012.

Davies, William. *The Happiness Industry: How the Government and Big Business Sold Us Well-Being.* New York: Verso, 2016.

De Andrade, Hanrikkson. "Censo 2010 aponta migração de fiéis da Universal do Reino de Deus para outras igrejas evangélicas." *UOL,* June 29, 2012. https://noticias.uol.com.br/cotidiano /ultimas-noticias/2012/06/29/censo-2010-aponta-migracao-de-fieis-da-universal-do -reino-de-deus-para-outras-igrejas.htm.

DeBiaggi, Sylvia. *Changing Gender Roles: Brazilian Immigrant Families in the U.S.* New York: LFB Scholarly Publishing, 2002.

De Genova, Nicholas P. "Migrant 'Illegality' and Deportability in Everyday Life." *Annual Review of Anthropology* 31, no. 1 (2002): 419–47.

De León, Jason. *The Land of Open Graves: Living and Dying on the Migrant Trail.* Oakland: University of California Press, 2015.

Desjarlais, Robert, and C. Jason Throop. "Phenomenological Approaches in Anthropology." *Annual Review of Anthropology* 40, no. 1 (2011): 87–102.

Dias, Isabela, and Andrew R. Calderon. "The Obscure Public Health Law Trump Wielded against Migrants Is Still Ruining Lives." *Mother Jones,* May 26, 2021. https://www .motherjones.com/politics/2021/05/title-42-strict-border-enforcement-policies-put -migrants-in-harms-way-title-42-is-no-exception/.

Dickerson, Caitlin, and Michael Shear. "Judge Orders Government to Fully Reinstate DACA Program." *New York Times,* December 5, 2020. https://www.nytimes.com/2020/12/04/us /daca-reinstated.html.

Dorman, Jacob. *Chosen People: The Rise of American Black Israelite Religions.* New York: Oxford University Press, 2013.

Douglas, Mary. *Purity and Danger.* 1966. New York: Routledge Classics, 2002.

Downes, Laurence. "Another Setback for Immigration Action." *New York Times,* November 11, 2015. https://takingnote.blogs.nytimes.com/2015/11/11/another-setback-for-immigration -action/.

Drogus, Carol Ann. *Women, Religion, and Social Change in Brazil's Popular Church.* South Bend: University of Notre Dame Press, 1997.

Durkheim, Émile. *The Elementary Forms of Religious Life.* 1912. Translated by Carol Cosman. Edited by Mark S. Cladis. New York: Oxford University Press, 2008.

Ehrenreich, Barbara, and Arlie Russell Hochschild, eds. *Global Woman: Nannies, Maids, and Sex Workers in the New Economy.* New York: Holt Paperbacks, 2004.

Elisha, Omri. *Moral Ambition: Mobilization and Social Outreach in Evangelical Megachurches.* Berkeley: University of California Press, 2011.

Encarnación, Omar G. "Amid Crisis in Brazil, the Evangelical Bloc Emerges as a Political Power." *Nation,* August 16, 2017. https://www.thenation.com/article/archive/amid-crisis-in-brazil -the-evangelical-bloc-emerges-as-a-political-power/.

Engelke, Matthew. "Discontinuity and the Discourse of Conversion." *Journal of Religion in Africa* 34, no. 1–2 (2004): 82–109.

———. *God's Agents: Biblical Publicity in Contemporary England.* Berkeley: University of California Press, 2013.

———. *A Problem of Presence: Beyond Scripture in an African Church.* Berkeley: University of California Press, 2007.

Falconi, José Luis, and José Antonio Mazzotti, eds. *The Other Latinos: Central and South Americans in the United States*. David Rockefeller Center Series on Latin American Studies. Cambridge: Harvard University Press, 2008.

FitzGerald, Frances. *The Evangelicals: The Struggle to Shape America*. New York: Simon & Schuster, 2017.

Flory, Richard. "How California's Megachurches Changed Christian Culture." The Conversation. January 10, 2018. https://theconversation.com/how-californias-megachurches-changed -christian-culture-77777.

Foner, Nancy, and Richard Alba. "Immigrant Religion in the U.S. and Western Europe: Bridge or Barrier to Inclusion?" *International Migration Review*, 42, no. 2 (2008): 360–92.

Fortuny, Patricia, Loret de Mola, Lúcia Ribeiro, and Mirian Solís Lizama. "Brazilian and Mexican Women: Interacting with God in Florida." In *A Place to Be: Brazilian, Guatemalan, and Mexican Immigrants in Florida's New Destinations*, edited by Philip J. Williams, Timothy J. Steigenga, and Manuel A. Vásquez, 190–208. New Brunswick: Rutgers University Press, 2009.

Foucault, Michel. *Society Must Be Defended: Lectures at the College de France, 1975–6*. Translated by David Macey. London: Picador, 2003.

Franco, Ana Paula. "Governador Valadares, a América presente em cada canto de uma cidade brasileira." *AcheiUSA: The Brazilian Newspaper*, May 17, 2013. https://www.acheiusa.com /Noticia/governador-valadares-a-america-presente-em-cada-canto-de-uma-cidade -brasileira-9805/.

Frazer, James George. *The Golden Bough: A Study in Magic and Religion*. 1890. Oxford: Oxford University Press, 2009.

Freston, Paul. "Neo-Pentecostalism in Brazil: Problems of Definition and the Struggle for Hegemony." *Archives de Sciences Sociales des Religions* 44, no. 105 (1999): 145–62.

———. "The Religious Field among Brazilians in the United States." In *Becoming Brazuca: Brazilian Immigration to the United States*, edited by Clémence Jouët-Pastré and Leticia J. Braga, 255–68. David Rockefeller Center Series on Latin American Studies. Cambridge: Harvard University Press, 2008.

———. "Reverse Mission: A Discourse in Search of Reality?" *PentecoStudies: An Interdisciplinary Journal for Research on the Pentecostal and Charismatic Movements* 9, no. 2 (2010): 153–74.

Freud, Sigmund. *The Future of an Illusion*. 1927. Eastford: Martino Fine Books, 2010.

Freyre, Gilberto. *The Masters and the Slaves (Casa-Grande e Senzala): A Study in the Development of Brazilian Civilization*. 1933. Translated by Samuel Putnam. Berkeley: University of California Press, 1987.

Fumanti, Mattia. "Virtuous Citizenship: Ethnicity and Encapsulation among Akan-Speaking Ghanaian Methodists in London." *African Diaspora* 3, no. 1 (2010): 12–41.

Garcia, Angela. *The Pastoral Clinic: Addiction and Dispossession along the Rio Grande*. Berkeley: University of California Press, 2010.

Geertz, Clifford. *The Interpretation of Cultures*. 1973. New York: Basic Books, 2017.

———. "Religion as a Cultural System." In *The Interpretation of Cultures*, 93–135. New York: Basic Books, 2017.

Gilroy, Paul. *Postcolonial Melancholia*. New York: Columbia University Press, 2006.

Goza, Franklin. "Brazilian Immigration to North America." *International Migration Review* 28, no. 1 (1994): 136–52.

Green, James N. *We Cannot Remain Silent: Opposition to the Brazilian Military Dictatorship in the United States.* Durham: Duke University Press, 2010.

Greenleaf, Floyd. *A Land of Hope: The Growth of the Seventh-Day Adventist Church in South America.* Tatuí: Casa Publicadora Brasileira, 2011.

Gulbas, L. E., L. H. Zayas, H. Yoon, H. Szlyk, S. Aguilar-Gaxiola, and G. Natera. "Deportation Experiences and Depression among U.S. Citizen-Children with Undocumented Mexican Parents." *Child: Care, Health and Development* 42, no. 2 (2016): 220–30.

Guyer, Jane. "Prophecy and the Near Future: Thoughts on Macroeconomic, Evangelical, and Punctuated Time." *American Ethnologist* 34, no. 3 (2007): 409–21.

Haeri, Niloofar. "The Private Performance of Salat Prayers: Repetition, Time and Meaning." *Anthropological Quarterly* 86, no. 1 (2013): 5–34.

———. *Say What Your Longing Heart Desires: Women, Prayer, and Poetry in Iran.* Palo Alto: Stanford University Press, 2020.

Hanchard, Michael George. *Orpheus and Power: The Movimento Negro of Rio de Janeiro and São Paulo, Brazil, 1945–1988.* Princeton: Princeton University Press, 1994.

Hann, Chris. "The Heart of the Matter: Christianity, Materiality, and Modernity." *Current Anthropology* 55, no. S10 (2014): S182–92.

Harding, Susan Friend. *The Book of Jerry Falwell: Fundamentalist Language and Politics.* Princeton: Princeton University Press, 2000.

———. "Representing Fundamentalism: The Problem of the Repugnant Cultural Other." *Social Research* 58, no. 2 (1991): 373–93.

Helgen, Erika. *Religious Conflict in Brazil: Protestants, Catholics, and the Rise of Religious Pluralism in the Early Twentieth Century.* New Haven: Yale University Press, 2020.

Hess, David. "The Many Rooms of Spiritism in Brazil." *Luso-Brazilian Review* 24, no. 2 (1987): 15–34.

Hess, Sabine, and Annette Puckhaber. "'Big Sisters' Are Better Domestic Servants?! Comments on the Booming Au Pair Business." In "Labour Migrations: Women on the Move." Special issue, *Feminist Review* 77, no. 1 (2004): 65–78.

Hochschild, Arlie Russell. *The Managed Heart: Commercialization of Human Feeling.* Berkeley: University of California Press, 2012.

Humphrey, Caroline. "Schism, Event, and Revolution: The Old Believers of Trans-Baikalia." *Current Anthropology* 55, no. S10 (2014): S216–55.

Ikeuchi, Suma. "From Slaves to Agents: Pentecostal Ethic and Precarious Labor among Brazilian Migrants in Toyota, Japan." *Journal of the American Academy of Religion* 87, no. 3 (2019): 791–823.

———. *Jesus Loves Japan: Return Migration and Global Pentecostalism in a Brazilian Diaspora.* Palo Alto: Stanford University Press, 2019.

"Immigrants in the District of Columbia." American Immigration Council. August 1, 2015. https://www.americanimmigrationcouncil.org/research/immigrants-in-washington-dc.

Instituto Paracleto. "Entre os pentecostais, os batistas e adventistas cresceram no Brasil." *Blog Paracleto* (blog). April 27, 2013. https://institutoparacleto.org/2013/04/27/entre-os-pentecostais-os-batistas-e-adventistas-cresceram-no-brasil/.

Ireland, Rowan. *Kingdoms Come: Religion and Politics in Brazil.* Pittsburgh: University of Pittsburgh Press, 1992.

"It's Time to End the Pandemic Emergency at the Border." *New York Times*, November 13, 2021, sec. Opinion. https://www.nytimes.com/2021/11/13/opinion/immigration-trump-biden-covid.html.

Jackson, Michael D. *The Palm at the End of the Mind: Relatedness, Religiosity and the Real.* Durham: Duke University Press, 2009.

Jacobs, Andrew. "Brazil's Lower House of Congress Votes for Impeachment of Dilma Rousseff." *New York Times*, April 17, 2016. http://www.nytimes.com/2016/04/18/world/americas/brazil-dilma-rousseff-impeachment-vote.html?_r=0.

James, William. *The Varieties of Religious Experience: A Study in Human Nature.* 1902. New York: Penguin Classics, 1982.

Jesus, Josimar Gonçalves de, and Rodolfo Hoffman. "De norte a sul, de leste a oeste: Mudança na identificação racial no Brasil." *Revista Brasileira de Estudos de População* 37 (2020): 1–25.

Johnson, Paul C. *Secrets, Gossip and Gods: The Transformation of Brazilian Candomblé.* New York: Oxford University Press, 2002.

Jordan, Candace. "Bearing Witness to Testimonies of Antiblackness." *SSRC Immanent Frame*, January 21, 2021. https://tif.ssrc.org/2021/01/21/bearing-witness-to-testimonies-of-antiblackness/.

Jordan, Miriam. "Judge Rules DACA Is Unlawful and Suspends Applications." *New York Times*, July 16, 2021, updated September 27, 2021, sec. U.S. https://www.nytimes.com/2021/07/16/us/court-daca-dreamers.html July 16.

Joseph, Tiffany D. *Race on the Move: Brazilian Migrants and the Global Reconstruction of Race.* Palo Alto: Stanford University Press, 2015.

Kardec, Allan. *The Gospel According to Spiritism.* 1864. Miami Beach: Edicei of America, 2011.

———. *The Spirits' Book.* 1857. Miami Beach: Edicei of America, 2008.

Keane, Webb. *Christian Moderns: Freedom and Fetish in the Mission Encounter.* Berkeley: University of California Press, 2007.

———. "Sincerity, 'Modernity,' and the Protestants." *Cultural Anthropology* 17, no. 1 (2002): 65–92.

Keller, Eva. *The Road to Clarity: Seventh-Day Adventism in Madagascar.* New York: Palgrave MacMillan, 2005.

Kleinman, Arthur. *Patients and Healers in the Context of Culture: An Exploration of the Borderland between Anthropology, Medicine and Psychiatry.* Berkeley: University of California Press, 1980.

———. *What Really Matters: Living a Moral Life amidst Uncertainty and Danger.* New York: Oxford University Press, 2006.

Kleinman, Arthur, Veena Das, and Margaret Lock. "Introduction." In *Social Suffering*, edited by Arthur Kleinman, Veena Das, and Margaret Lock, ix–xxv. Berkeley: University of California Press, 1997.

Kleinman, Arthur, and Byron Good, eds. *Culture and Depression: Studies in the Anthropology and Cross-Cultural Psychiatry of Affect and Disorder.* Berkeley: University of California Press, 1985.

Kramer, Eric W. "Spectacle and the Staging of Power in Brazilian Neo-Pentecostalism." *Latin American Perspectives* 32, no. 1 (2005): 95–120.

Kramer, Fredrica D. "The Role for Public Funding of Faith-Based Organizations Delivering Behavioral Health Services: Guideposts for Monitoring and Evaluation." *American Journal of Community Psychology* 46, no. 3–4 (2010): 342–60.

Kymlicka, Will. *Multicultural Citizenship: A Liberal Theory of Minority Rights*. New York: Oxford University Press, 1995.

Landing, James E. *Black Judaism: Story of an American Movement*. Durham: Carolina Academic Press, 2002.

Lehmann, David. *Struggle for the Spirit: Religious Transformation and Populist Culture in Brazil and Latin America*. Cambridge, UK: Polity, 1996.

Leinaweaver, Jessaca B. *Adoptive Migration: Raising Latinos in Spain*. Durham: Duke University Press, 2013.

Lemons, J. Derrick, ed. *Theologically Engaged Anthropology*. Oxford: Oxford University Press, 2018.

Lesser, Jeff. *Immigration, Ethnicity and National Identity in Brazil, 1808 to the Present*. Cambridge: Cambridge University Press, 2013.

Lester, Rebecca J. *Jesus in Our Wombs: Embodying Modernity in a Mexican Convent*. Berkeley: University of California Press, 2005.

Lévi-Strauss, Claude. "The Effectiveness of Symbols." In *Structural Anthropology*, 185–208. New York: Basic Books, 1963.

Levitt, Peggy. *God Needs No Passport: Immigrants and the Changing Religious Landscape*. New York: The New Press, 2007.

Leys, Ruth. "The Turn to Affect: A Critique." *Critical Inquiry* 37, no. 3 (2011): 434–72.

Liptak, Adam, and Michael D. Shear. "Trump Can't Immediately End DACA, Supreme Court Rules." *New York Times*, June 18, 2020, sec. U.S. https://www.nytimes.com/2020/06/18/us/trump-daca-supreme-court.html.

Locke, John. *Two Treatises of Government*. 1689. Edited by Peter Laslett. New York: Cambridge University Press, 2004.

Londoño, Ernesto. "As Brazil Faces Record Covid-19 Deaths, a Variant-Fueled Surge, and Lagging Vaccinations, Bolsonaro Disparages Masks." *New York Times*, February 26, 2021, updated October 10, 2021. https://www.nytimes.com/2021/02/26/world/Bolsonaro-face-masks.html.

Londoño, Ernesto, and Letícia Casado. "Brazil under Bolsonaro Has Message for Teenagers: Save Sex for Marriage." *New York Times*, January 26, 2020, sec. World. https://www.nytimes.com/2020/01/26/world/americas/brazil-teen-pregnancy-Bolsonaro.html.

———. "Will an Ex-Missionary Shield Brazil's Tribes from Outsiders?" *New York Times*, February 5, 2020, sec. World. https://www.nytimes.com/2020/02/05/world/americas/Brazil-indigenous-missionary.html.

———. "With a Second President in Jail, Brazil's Carwash Probe Lives On." *New York Times*, March 22, 2019, sec. World. https://www.nytimes.com/2019/03/22/world/americas/brazil-car-wash-corruption-temer.html.

Londoño, Ernesto, and Flávia Milhorance. "Brazil Vaccine Scandal Imperils Bolsonaro as Protests Spread." *New York Times*, July 3, 2021, updated September 21, 2021, sec. World. https://www.nytimes.com/2021/07/03/world/americas/brazil-bolsonaro-vaccine-scandal.html.

Luhrmann, T. M. *How God Becomes Real: Kindling the Presence of Invisible Others*. Princeton: Princeton University Press, 2020.

———. "Metakinesis: How God Becomes Intimate in Contemporary U.S. Christianity." *American Anthropologist* 106, no. 3 (2004): 518–28.

———. "Subjectivity." *Anthropological Theory* 6, no. 3 (2006): 345–61.

———. "What We Believe about Prophecies." *New York Times*, May 20, 2021, sec. Opinion. https://www.nytimes.com/2021/05/20/special-series/t-m-luhrmann-what-we-believe -about-prophecies.html.

———. *When God Talks Back: Understanding the American Evangelical Relationship with God*. New York: Knopf, 2012.

Lutz, Catherine. *Unnatural Emotions: Everyday Sentiments on a Micronesian Atoll and Their Challenge to Western Theory*. Chicago: University of Chicago Press, 1988.

Lutz, Catherine, and Geoffrey M. White. "The Anthropology of Emotions." *Annual Review of Anthropology* 15, no. 1 (1986): 405–36.

Mafra, Clara. "Santidade e sinceridade na formação da pessoa cristã." *Religião & Sociedade* 34 (June 2014): 173–92.

Mahmood, Saba. "Feminist Theory and the Egyptian Islamic Revival." *Cultural Anthropology* 16, no. 2 (2001): 202–36.

———. *Politics of Piety: The Islamic Revival and the Feminist Subject*. Princeton: Princeton University Press, 2005.

Malkki, Liisa H. *The Need to Help: The Domestic Arts of International Humanitarianism*. Durham: Duke University Press, 2015.

Marcus, Alan P. "Brazilian Immigration to the U.S. and the Geographical Imagination." *Geographical Review*, no. 99 (2009): 481–98.

———. "Convenient Liaisons: Brazilian Immigration/Emigration and the Spatial-Relationships of Religious Networks." *Espace Populations Sociétés* 2–3 (2014): 1–13.

Margolis, Maxine L. *Goodbye, Brazil: Émigrés from the Land of Soccer and Samba*. Madison: University of Wisconsin Press, 2013.

———. *An Invisible Minority: Brazilians in New York City*. Gainesville: University Press of Florida, 2009.

———. *Little Brazil: An Ethnography of Brazilian Immigrants in New York City*. Princeton: Princeton University Press, 1994.

Mariz, Cecília Loreto. *Coping with Poverty: Pentecostals and Christian Base Communities in Brazil*. Philadelphia: Temple University Press, 1994.

———. "Missão religiosa e migração: 'Novas comunidades' e igrejas pentecostais brasileiras no exterior." *Análise Social* 44, no. 190 (2009): 161–87.

Markowitz, Fran. "Leaving Babylon to Come Home to Israel: Closing the Circle of the Black Diaspora." In *Homecomings: Unsettling Paths of Return*, edited by Fran Markowitz and Anders H. Stefansson, 183–98. New York: Lexington Books, 2004.

Marsden, George M. *Fundamentalism and American Culture*. New York: Oxford University Press, 2006.

Martes, Ana Cristina. "Neither Hispanic, nor Black: We're Brazilian." In *The Other Latinos: Central and South Americans in the United States*, edited by José Luis Falconi and José Antonio Mazzotti, 231–56. David Rockefeller Center Series on Latin American Studies. Cambridge: Harvard University Press, 2008.

———. *New Immigrants, New Land: A Study of Brazilians in Massachusetts*. Gainesville: University Press of Florida, 2011.

Martin, David. *Pentecostalism: The World Their Parish*. Malden: Blackwell, 2002.

Marx, Karl. *Critique of Hegel's "Philosophy of Right."* Edited by Joseph O'Malley. Translated by Annette Jolin. New York: Cambridge University Press, 1977.

Massumi, Brian. "The Autonomy of Affect." *Cultural Critique*, no. 31 (1995): 83–109.

Mattingly, Cheryl. *Healing Dramas and Clinical Plots: The Narrative Structure of Experience.* New York: Cambridge University Press, 1998.

———. *The Paradox of Hope: Journeys through a Clinical Borderland.* Berkeley: University of California Press, 2010.

Mazzarella, William. "Affect: What Is It Good For?" In *Enchantments of Modernity: Empire, Nation, Globalization,* edited by Saurabh Dube, 291–309. New York: Routledge, 2009.

McCann, Bryan. *The Throes of Democracy: Brazil since 1989.* London: Zed, 2008.

Mead, Margaret. *Growing Up in New Guinea.* 1930. New York: Harper Perennial Modern Classics, 2001.

Meyer, Birgit. "'Make a Complete Break with the Past': Memory and Post-Colonial Modernity in Ghanaian Pentecostalist Discourse. *Journal of Religion in Africa* 28, no. 3 (1998): 316–49.

———. *Translating the Devil: Religion and Modernity among the Ewe in Ghana.* Edinburgh: Edinburgh University Press, 1999.

Meyer, Joyce. *The Battlefield of the Mind: Winning the Battle in Your Mind.* Brentwood: Warner Faith, 2002.

Migration Policy Institute. "State Demographics Data–D.C." Accessed February 24, 2021. https://www.migrationpolicy.org/data/state-profiles/state/demographics/DC.

Mill, John Stuart. *On Liberty (1859).* Edited by David Bromwich and George Kateb. New Haven: Yale University Press, 2003.

Miller, Donald E. *Reinventing American Protestantism: Christianity in the New Millennium.* Berkeley: University of California Press, 1997.

Muehlebach, Andrea. *The Moral Neoliberal: Welfare and Citizenship in Italy.* Chicago: University of Chicago Press, 2012.

Nicas, Jack. "Brazilian Leader Accused of Crimes against Humanity in Pandemic Response." *New York Times,* October 19, 2021, sec. World. https://www.nytimes.com/2021/10/19/world/americas/bolsonaro-covid-19-brazil.html.

Obeyesekere, Gananath. *The Awakened Ones: Phenomenology of Visionary Experience.* New York: Columbia University Press, 2012.

———. *Medusa's Hair: An Essay on Personal Symbols and Religious Experience.* Chicago: University of Chicago Press, 1984.

———. *The Work of Culture: Symbolic Transformation in Psychoanalysis and Anthropology.* Chicago: University of Chicago Press, 1990.

Olupona, Jacob K., and Regina Gemignani, eds. *African Immigrant Religions in America.* New York: New York University Press, 2007.

O'Neill, Bruce. "Cast Aside: Boredom, Downward Mobility, and Homelessness in Post-Communist Bucharest." *Cultural Anthropology* 29, no. 1 (2014): 8–31.

———. *The Space of Boredom: Homelessness in the Slowing Global Order.* Durham: Duke University Press, 2017.

O'Neill, Kevin L. "Beyond Broken: Affective Spaces and the Study of American Religion." *Journal of the American Academy of Religion* 81, no. 4 (2013): 1093–116.

———. *City of God: Christian Citizenship in Postwar Guatemala.* Berkeley: University of California Press, 2010.

———. *Secure the Soul: Christian Piety and Gang Prevention in Guatemala.* Oakland: University of California Press, 2015.

Oosterbaan, Martijn. "Spiritual Attunement: Pentecostal Radio in the Soundscape of a Favela in Rio de Janeiro." *Social Text* 26, no. 3 (2008): 123–45.

Oosterbaan, Martijn, Linda van de Kamp, and Joana Bahia, eds. *Global Trajectories of Brazilian Religion: Lusospheres.* New York: Bloomsbury, 2019.

Oro, Ari Pedro, André Corten, and Jean-Pierre Dozon, eds. *Igreja Universal do Reino de Deus—Os novos conquistadores da fé.* São Paulo: Paulinas, 2003.

Oro, Ari Pedro, and Pablo Semán. "Pentecostalism in the Southern Cone Countries: Overview and Perspectives." *International Sociology* 15, no. 4 (2000): 605–27.

Park, Kyeyoung. "'Born Again': What Does It Mean to Korean-Americans in New York City?" *Journal of Ritual Studies* 3, no. 2 (1989): 287–301.

Park, Robert E., and Ernest W. Burgess. *The City.* 1925. Chicago: University of Chicago Press, 2019.

Pattillo-McCoy, Mary. "Church Culture as a Strategy of Action in the Black Community." *American Sociological Review* 63, no. 6 (1998): 767–84.

Pew Research Center. "America's Changing Religious Landscape." *Pew Research Center's Religion and Public Life Project* (blog). May 12, 2015. https://www.pewforum.org/2015/05/12/americas-changing-religious-landscape/.

———. "Brazil's Changing Religious Landscape." *Pew Research Center's Religion and Public Life Project* (blog). July 18, 2013. https://www.pewforum.org/2013/07/18/brazils-changing-religious-landscape/.

———. "In U.S., Decline of Christianity Continues at Rapid Pace." *Pew Research Center's Religion and Public Life Project* (blog). October 17, 2019. https://www.pewforum.org/2019/10/17/in-u-s-decline-of-christianity-continues-at-rapid-pace/.

———. "A Nation of Immigrants." *Pew Research Center's Hispanic Trends Project.* January 29, 2013. https://www.pewresearch.org/hispanic/2013/01/29/a-nation-of-immigrants/.

———. "Religion in America: U.S. Religious Data, Demographics, and Statistics." *Pew Research Center's Religion and Public Life Project* (blog). 2014. https://www.pewforum.org/religious-landscape-study/.

———. "Religion in Latin America." *Pew Research Center's Religion and Public Life Project* (blog). November 13, 2014. https://www.pewforum.org/2014/11/13/religion-in-latin-america/.

———. "The Religious Affiliation of U.S. Immigrants: Majority Christian, Rising Share of Other Faiths." *Pew Research Center's Religion and Public Life Project* (blog). May 17, 2013. https://www.pewforum.org/2013/05/17/the-religious-affiliation-of-us-immigrants/#overview.

———. "U.S. Religious Landscape Survey: Religious Affiliation." *Pew Research Center's Religion and Public Life Project* (blog). February 1, 2008. https://www.pewforum.org/2008/02/01/u-s-religious-landscape-survey-religious-affiliation/.

Phillips, Dom. "Brazil's Former President Lula Walks Free from Prison after Supreme Court Ruling." *Guardian,* November 8, 2019. https://www.theguardian.com/world/2019/nov/08/lula-brazil-released-prison-supreme-court-ruling.

Phillips, Tom. "A Nurse's Journey from Treating Covid in Brazil to Death in the US Desert." *Guardian,* October 18, 2021. https://www.theguardian.com/world/2021/oct/18/brazil-migrant-death-us-border-desert-dream.

Plascencia, Imelda, Alma Leyva, Mayra Yoana Jaimes Pena, and Saba Waheed. "Undocumented and Uninsured Part 3: Pol[Ice] in My Head." UCLA Labor Center. 2015. https://www.labor.ucla.edu/publication/undocumented-and-uninsured-part-3-police-in-my-head/.

Polimédio, Chayenne. "The Rise of the Brazilian Evangelicals." *Atlantic,* January 24, 2018. https://www.theatlantic.com/international/archive/2018/01/the-evangelical-takeover-of-brazilian-politics/551423/.

Poloma, Margaret M., and Ralph W. Hood Jr. *Blood and Fire: Godly Love in a Pentecostal Emerging Church.* New York: New York University Press, 2008.

Potochnick, Stephanie R., and Krista M. Perreira. "Depression and Anxiety among First-Generation Immigrant Latino Youth: Key Correlates and Implications for Future Research." *Journal of Nervous and Mental Disease* 198, no. 7 (2010): 470–77.

Povinelli, Elizabeth A. *Economies of Abandonment: Social Belonging and Endurance in Late Liberalism.* Durham: Duke University Press, 2011.

———. *The Empire of Love: Toward a Theory of Intimacy, Genealogy, and Carnality.* Durham: Duke University Press, 2006.

"Presidential Approval Ratings—Donald Trump." *Gallup Polls.* Accessed May 4, 2021. https://news.gallup.com/poll/203198/presidential-approval-ratings-donald-trump.aspx.

Putnam, Robert D. *Bowling Alone: The Collapse and Revival of American Community.* New York: Simon & Schuster, 2001.

Rambo, Lewis R. *Understanding Religious Conversion.* New Haven: Yale University Press, 1993.

Rawls, John. *Political Liberalism.* New York: Columbia University Press, 1993.

Reinhardt, Bruno. "Soaking in Tapes: The Haptic Voice of Global Pentecostal Pedagogy in Ghana." *Journal of the Royal Anthropological Institute* 20, no. 2 (2014): 315–36.

Repak, Terry. *Waiting on Washington: Central American Workers in the Nation's Capital.* Philadelphia: Temple University Press, 1995.

Reuters. "Brazil to Investigate Evangelical Church's Funds." *New York Times,* December 26, 1995, sec. World. https://www.nytimes.com/1995/12/26/world/brazil-to-investigate-evangelical-church-s-funds.html.

Richlin, Johanna Bard. "The Affective Therapeutics of Migrant Faith: Evangelical Christianity among Brazilians in Greater Washington, DC." *Current Anthropology* 60, no. 3 (2019): 369–90.

Robbins, Joel. "Anthropology and Theology: An Awkward Relationship?" *Anthropological Quarterly* 79, no. 2 (2006): 285–94.

———. "The Anthropology of Christianity: Unity, Diversity, New Directions: An Introduction to Supplement 10." *Current Anthropology* 55, no. S10 (2014): S157–71.

———. *Becoming Sinners: Christianity and Moral Torment in a Papua New Guinea Society.* Berkeley: University of California Press, 2004.

———. "Beyond the Suffering Subject: Toward an Anthropology of the Good." *Journal of the Royal Anthropological Institute* 19, no. 3 (2013): 447–62.

———. "The Globalization of Pentecostal and Charismatic Christianity." *Annual Review of Anthropology* 33, no. 1 (2004): 117–43.

———. *Theology and the Anthropology of Christian Life.* New York: Oxford University Press, 2020.

Roberts, Nathaniel. *To Be Cared For: The Power of Conversion and Foreignness of Belonging in an Indian Slum.* Oakland: University of California Press, 2016.

Rocha, Cristina. "'God Is in Control': Middle-Class Pentecostalism and International Student Migration." *Journal of Contemporary Religion* 34, no. 1 (2019): 21–37.

———. *John of God: The Globalization of Brazilian Faith Healing.* New York: Oxford University Press, 2017.

———. "Two Faces of God: Religion and Social Class in the Brazilian Diaspora in Sydney." In *Religious Pluralism in the Diaspora,* edited by P. P. Kumar, 147–60. Boston: Brill, 2006.

Rocha, Cristina, and Manuel A. Vásquez, eds. *The Diaspora of Brazilian Religions.* Boston: Brill, 2013.

Rodrigues, Donizete. *Jesus in Sacred Gotham: Brazilian Immigrants and Pentecostalism in New York City.* Lexington, KY: CreateSpace Independent Publishing Platform, 2014.

Rodríguez, Encarnación Gutiérrez. "The 'Hidden Side' of the New Economy: On Transnational Migration, Domestic Work, and Unprecedented Intimacy." *Frontiers: A Journal of Women Studies* 28, no. 3 (2007): 60–83.

Rogozen-Soltar, Mikaela H. *Spain Unmoored: Migration, Conversion, and the Politics of Islam.* Bloomington: Indiana University Press, 2017.

Rohter, Larry. "Brazilian Pentecostal Leaders Caught in a Scandal." *New York Times,* March 19, 2007, sec. World. https://www.nytimes.com/2007/03/19/world/americas/19iht-brazil.4955931.html.

Romero, Mary. *Maid in the U.S.A.* 10th anniversary ed. New York: Routledge, 2002.

Romero, Mary, Valerie Preston, and Wenona Giles, eds. *When Care Work Goes Global: Locating the Social Relations of Domestic Work.* New York: Routledge, 2014.

Romero, Simon. "Brazil on Edge as World Cup Exposes Rift." *New York Times,* June 9, 2014. http://www.nytimes.com/2014/06/10/world/americas/apprehension-and-apathy-compete-with-excitement-in-world-cup-host-brazil.html.

Romero, Simon, and Vinod Sreeharsha. "Dilma Rousseff Targeted in Brazil by Lawmakers Facing Scandals of Their Own." *New York Times,* April 14, 2016. http://www.nytimes.com/2016/04/15/world/americas/dilma-rousseff-targeted-in-brazil-by-lawmakers-facing-graft-cases-of-their-own.html.

Rosaldo, Renato. "Grief and a Headhunter's Rage: On the Cultural Force of Emotions." In *Text, Play and Story: The Construction and Reconstruction of Self and Society,* edited by Stuart Plattner and Edward M. Bruner, 178–95. Washington, DC: American Ethnology Society, 1984.

Rose, Nikolas S. *Governing the Soul: The Shaping of the Private Self.* 2nd ed. New York: Free Association Books, 1999.

Runions, Erin. "Immobile Theologies, Carceral Affects: Interest and Debt in Faith-Based Prison Programs." In *Religion, Emotion, Sensation: Affect Theories and Theologies,* edited by Karen Bray and Stephen D. More, 55–84. Fordham: Fordham University Press, 2019.

Said, Edward W. *Orientalism.* New York: Vintage Books, 1979.

Sales, Teresa. *Brazilians Away from Home.* New York: Center for Migration Studies, 2003.

Sarat, Leah. *Fire in the Canyon: Religion, Migration and the Mexican Dream.* New York: New York University Press, 2013.

Sassen, Saskia. *Globalization and Its Discontents*. New York: The New Press, 1998.

———. *The Mobility of Labor and Capital: A Study in International Investment and Labor Flow*. New York: Cambridge University Press, 1988.

Scalabrinians. "Scalabrinians: Missionaries of St. Charles." Accessed March 24, 2016. http://www.scalabrinians.org/website.

Schaefer, Donovan O. *Religious Affects: Animality, Evolution, and Power*. Durham: Duke University Press, 2015.

Scheper-Hughes, Nancy. *Death without Weeping: The Violence of Everyday Life in Brazil*. Berkeley: University of California Press, 1993.

Schieffelin, Bambi B. "Christianizing Language and the Dis-Placement of Culture in Bosavi, Papua New Guinea." *Current Anthropology* 55, no. S10 (2014): S226–37.

Schreiber, Evelyn Jaffe. "Repressed Memory, Testimony, and Agency in Toni Morrison's *Home*." *Modern Fiction Studies* 66, no. 4 (2020): 724–54.

Schueths, April, and Jodie Lawston, eds. *Living Together, Living Apart: Mixed Status Families and U.S. Immigration Policy*. Seattle: University of Washington Press, 2015.

Seligman, Rebecca. *Possessing Spirits and Healing Selves: Embodiment and Transformation in an Afro-Brazilian Religion*. New York: Palgrave Macmillan, 2014.

———. "The Unmaking and Making of Self: Embodied Suffering and Mind-Body Healing in Brazilian Candomblé." *Ethos* 38, no. 3 (2010): 297–320.

Shear, Michael D. "Biden's Immigration Plan Would Offer Path to Citizenship for Millions." *New York Times*, February 18, 2021, updated May 18, 2021. https://www.nytimes.com/2021/02/18/us/congressional-democrats-roll-out-bidens-immigration-plan-offering-an-eight-year-path-to-citizenship.html.

———. "Obama, Daring Congress, Acts to Overhaul Immigration." *New York Times*, November 21, 2014. https://www.nytimes.com/2014/11/21/us/obama-immigration-speech.html.

Shear, Michael, and Julie Preston. "Dealt Setback, Obama Puts Off Immigrant Plan." *New York Times*, February 17, 2015. https://www.nytimes.com/2015/02/18/us/obama-immigration-policy-halted-by-federal-judge-in-texas.html.

Sheringham, Olivia. *Transnational Religious Spaces: Faith and the Brazilian Migration Experience*. New York: Palgrave Macmillan, 2013.

Singer, Audrey. "Metropolitan Washington: A New Immigrant Gateway." In *Hispanic Migration and Urban Development: Studies from Washington, DC*, 3–24. Research in Race and Ethnic Relations 17. Washington, DC: Emerald, 2012.

Siqueira, Sueli. "Emigrants from the Micro-Region of Governador Valadares in the USA: Projects of Return and Investment." In *Becoming Brazuca: Brazilian Immigration to the United States*, edited by Clémence Jouët-Pastré and Leticia J. Braga, 175–93. David Rockefeller Center Series on Latin American Studies. Cambridge: Harvard University Press, 2008.

———. *Sonhos, sucesso e frustrações na emigração de retorno*. Belo Horizonte: Argumentum, 2009.

Skidmore, Thomas. *Brazil: Five Centuries of Change*. 2nd ed. New York: Oxford University Press, 2010.

Slominski, Kristy. "How Religion Made Modern Sex Ed." *The Immanent Frame: Secularism, Religion and the Public Square*, August 21, 2020. https://tif.ssrc.org/2020/08/21/how-religion-made-modern-sex-ed/.

Smilde, David. *Reason to Believe: Cultural Agency in Latin American Evangelicalism*. Berkeley: University of California Press, 2007.

Smith, Anthony D. *Chosen People: Sacred Sources of National Identity*. New York: Oxford University Press, 2003.

Sniderman, Paul M., and Louk Hagendoorn. *When Ways of Life Collide: Multiculturalism and Its Discontents in the Netherlands*. Princeton: Princeton University Press, 2009.

Sotomayor, Marianna. "Biden Will Pledge to Tackle Immigration Overhaul in Address to Congress." *Washington Post*, April 28, 2021. https://www.washingtonpost.com/politics/biden-will -pledge-to-tackle-immigration-in-address-to-congress-while-signaling-openness-to-more -targeted-deal/2021/04/27/f00324d6-a795-11eb-8c1a-56f0cb4ff3b5_story.html.

Stephen, Lynn. *We Are the Face of Oaxaca: Testimony and Social Movements*. Durham: Duke University Press, 2013.

Stewart, David. "The Hermeneutics of Suspicion." *Journal of Literature and Theology* 3, no. 3 (1989): 296–307.

Stewart, Kathleen. *Ordinary Affects*. Durham: Duke University Press, 2007.

Stillman, Sarah. "The Race to Dismantle Trump's Immigration Policies." *New Yorker*, February 1, 2021. https://www.newyorker.com/magazine/2021/02/08/the-race-to-dismantle-trumps -immigration-policies.

Stoll, David. *Is Latin America Turning Protestant? The Politics of Evangelical Growth*. Berkeley: University of California Press, 1991.

Streensland, Brian, and Philip Goff, eds. *The New Evangelical Social Engagement*. New York: Oxford University Press, 2013.

Stromberg, Peter G. *Language and Self-Transformation: A Study of the Christian Conversion Narrative*. New York: Cambridge University Press, 1993.

Suárez-Orozco, Carola. "Identities under Siege: Immigration Stress and Social Mirroring among the Children of Immigrants." In *The New Immigration: An Interdisciplinary Reader*, edited by Marcelo M. Suárez-Orozco, Carola Suárez-Orozco, and Desirée Qin-Hilliard, 149–70. New York: Routledge, 2004.

Suárez-Orozco, Carola, Hee Jin Bang, and Ha Yeon Kim. "I Felt Like My Heart Was Staying Behind: Psychological Implications of Family Separations & Reunifications for Immigrant Youth." *Journal of Adolescent Research* 26, no. 2 (2011): 222–57.

Suh, Sharon A. *Being Buddhist in a Christian World: Gender and Community in a Korean American Temple*. Seattle: University of Washington Press, 2004.

Sullivan, Eileen, and Miriam Jordan. "Illegal Border Crossings, Driven by Pandemic and Natural Disasters, Soar to Record High." *New York Times*, October 22, 2021, sec. U.S. https://www .nytimes.com/2021/10/22/us/politics/border-crossings-immigration-record-high.html.

Tambiah, Stanley Jeyaraja. "A Performative Approach to Ritual." In *Culture, Thought and Social Action: An Anthropological Perspective*, 123–66. Cambridge: Harvard University Press, 1985.

Tatian, Peter A., Sara McTarnaghan, Olivia Arena, and Yipeng Su. "State of Immigrants in the District of Columbia." Urban Institute. December 18, 2018. https://www.urban.org/research /publication/state-immigrants-district-columbia.

Tavernise, Sabrina, and Richard Gebeloff. "How Voters Turned Virginia from Deep Red to Solid Blue." *New York Times*, November 9, 2019. https://www.nytimes.com/2019/11/09/us /virginia-elections-democrats-republicans.html.

Taylor, Charles. "The Politics of Recognition." In *Multiculturalism*, edited by Amy Gutman, 25–74. Princeton: Princeton University Press, 1994.

Toulis, Nicole Rodriguez. *Believing Identity: Pentecostalism and the Mediation of Jamaican Ethnicity and Gender in England.* New York: Routledge, 1997.

Tremura, Lucília V. "Transnational Migrant Brazilian Women in 'Pink Collar Jobs' in the Greater Washington D.C. Area." PhD diss., American University, 2011.

Turner, Victor. *The Ritual Process: Structure and Anti-Structure.* 1969. New York: Routledge, 1995.

Tylor, E. B. "Animism." 1871. In *Primitive Culture: Researches into the Development of Mythology, Philosophy, Religion, Language, Art, and Custom,* 1:377–453. Cambridge Library Series. New York: Cambridge University Press, 2010.

U.S. Immigration and Customs Enforcement. "U.S. Immigration and Customs Enforcement Fiscal Year 2019 Enforcement and Removal Operations Report." https://www.ice.gov/sites/default/files/documents/Document/2019/eroReportFY2019.pdf.

Van de Port, Mattijs. *Ecstatic Encounters: Bahian Candomblé and the Quest for the Really Real.* Amsterdam: Amsterdam University Press, 2011.

Vásquez, Manuel A. "Beyond *Homo Anomicus*: Interpersonal Networks, Space and Religion among Brazilians in Broward County." In *A Place to Be: Brazilian, Guatemalan, and Mexican Immigrants in Florida's New Destinations,* edited by Philip J. Williams, Timothy J. Steigenga, and Manuel A. Vásquez, 33–35. New Brunswick: Rutgers University Press, 2009.

———. "Pentecostalism, Collective Identity, and Transnationalism among Salvadorans and Peruvians in the U.S." *Journal of the American Academy of Religion* 67, no. 3 (1999): 617–36.

Warnock, Raphael. *The Divided Mind of the Black Church: Theology, Piety and Public Witness.* New York: New York University Press, 2013.

Warren Jr., Donald. "Spiritism in Brazil." *Journal of Inter-American Studies* 10, no. 3 (1968): 393–405.

Watt, Alan J. *Farm Workers and the Churches: The Movement in California and Texas.* College Station: Texas A&M University Press, 2010.

Weaver, Blanche Henry Clark. "Confederate Immigrants and Evangelical Churches in Brazil." *Journal of Southern History* 18, no. 4 (1952): 446–68.

Weber, Max. *The Protestant Work Ethic and the Spirit of Capitalism.* 1930. New York: Penguin Classics, 2002.

Williams, Philip J., Timothy J. Steigenga, and Manuel A. Vásquez, eds. *A Place to Be: Brazilian, Guatemalan, and Mexican Immigrants in Florida's New Destinations.* New Brunswick: Rutgers University Press, 2009.

Williams, Raymond. "Structures of Feeling." In *Marxism and Literature*, 128–35. New York: Oxford University Press, 1977.

World Bank. Data: Brazil. Accessed May 6, 2016. http://data.worldbank.org/country/brazil.

Yarris, Kristin E. *Care across Generations: Solidarity and Sacrifice in Transnational Families.* Palo Alto: Stanford University Press, 2017.

INDEX

acculturation, Spiritist approach to, 153, 154–55

AcheiUSA, 57

Adam, as walking with God, 93

Adams, Vincanne, 194, 203n19

adversity, Spiritist viewpoint regarding, 177–78

affect, 7–9, 11, 74, 204n26, 205n38

affective experience, 4–5, 60–67

affective therapeutics: accomplishments through, 107; being God's vessel as, 89–90; benefits of, 132; defined, 74; of evangelical churches, 5, 182; evangelical efficacy of, 131–32; results of, 192–95

affect *versus* emotion, 7–9

Africa, 221n41

African migrants, faith of, 10

Afro-Brazilians, 143, 228n6

Ahmed, Sara, 69, 81

alcohol abuse, 64

Alex, story of, 123–24

Alícia, story of, 65

Allison, Anne, 203n22

altruism, 150

ambassadors, Christians as, 128–32

American Christianity, 75–77. *See also* Christianity; evangelical Christianity

americanização, 19

amor e dor, 77–81

Anderson, story of, 48–49, 58, 188

Andersson, Ruben, 204n22

Angela, story of, 45, 47, 97–98

anthropology: of affect and emotion, 9, 11, 204n26, 205n38; of Christianity, 11–12,

205–6n44, 222–23n1; of migration, 144; of religion, 106–7; subjectivity within, 132

anxiety, 39, 61, 63–67, 152

Appletree Condominiums, 37, 225n26

Arlington, Virginia, 32, 59, 138, 139, 140–44, 169

Assembly of God, 214n52

atonement, migration as, 153, 156–58, 160

Baltimore, Maryland, 230n21

baptism, 134

Baptists, 31, 197–200, 224n17

Battlefield of the Mind (Meyer), 84–85, 185

Beatriz, story of, 45–47, 62

belonging, compensatory model of, 128–32

Bernardo, Father, 145–47, 170

Bible, recipe for living within, 88

Biden, Joseph, 42, 189, 221n35, 233n2

bitterness, 65–67

Black Americans, testimony of, 119

blessings, viewpoint regarding, 189

bodily betrayal, 61–63

Bolivar, Simón, 207n6

Bolsonaro, Jair, 15, 187, 217n18, 232n1

boredom, 203–4n22

Boston, Massachusetts, 26, 58, 212n36, 213n47, 228n2

Boyer, Pascal, 90

Brazil: Catholicism within, 21, 24, 136; corruption within, 22–23; crime within, 54–55; economy of, 15, 187, 203n14, 207n3, 207n5, 217–18n23; ethnic diversity within, 208n14; evangelical Christianity within, 21–22, 130–31, 210n27; immigration to, 208n14;

A NOTE ON THE TYPE

This book has been composed in Arno, an Old-style serif typeface in the classic Venetian tradition, designed by Robert Slimbach at Adobe.